Japanese and American
Horror

Japanese and American Horror

A Comparative Study of Film, Fiction, Graphic Novels and Video Games

KATARZYNA MARAK

McFarland & Company, Inc., Publishers
Jefferson, North Carolina

LIBRARY OF CONGRESS CATALOGUING-IN-PUBLICATION DATA

Marak, Katarzyna, 1984–
    Japanese and American horror : a comparative study of film, fiction, graphic novels and video games / Katarzyna Marak.
        p.   cm.
    Includes bibliographical references and index.

    ISBN 978-0-7864-9666-2 (softcover : acid free paper) ∞
    ISBN 978-1-4766-1792-3 (ebook)

    1. Horror tales, American—History and criticism. 2. Horror tales, Japanese—History and criticism. 3. Horror films—United States—History and criticism. 4. Horror films—Japan—History and criticism. 5. Horror comic books, strips, etc.—History and criticism. 6. Horror in mass media.   I. Title.
    PS374.H67M37 2014
    813'.0873809—dc23   2014040124

BRITISH LIBRARY CATALOGUING DATA ARE AVAILABLE

© 2015 Katarzyna Marak. All rights reserved

No part of this book may be reproduced or transmitted in any form or by any means, electronic or mechanical, including photocopying or recording, or by any information storage and retrieval system, without permission in writing from the publisher.

On the cover: David Dorfman from the 2005 film *The Ring Two*, directed by Hideo Nakata (Dreamworks/Photofest)

Printed in the United States of America

McFarland & Company, Inc., Publishers
  Box 611, Jefferson, North Carolina 28640
    www.mcfarlandpub.com

Table of Contents

Preface

1

Introduction

5

1. Ghosts

17

2. Monsters and Monstrosities

83

3. The Divine and the Unholy

158

Conclusion: Different Shades of the Universal

197

Notes

207

Bibliography

212

Index

221

Preface

Horror narratives can take many forms and shapes, constituting variations upon variations; on the one hand, tales of horror told in one culture will be different from those enjoyed in another, and on the other hand, there are certain semi-universal, recurring motifs and elements that can be easily recognized. But can they be as easily understood? In this book I highlight and juxtapose such elements and motifs in horror narratives originating from two very distinct cultures—American and Japanese.

The choice of works discussed is based primarily on popularity and availability in a broad sense of both terms. I opted for narratives that belong beyond doubt to the horror genre and decided to leave out narratives that merely feature terrifying elements. Additional criterion was the extent to which the narratives present the given horror element in an interesting manner. By choosing titles commonly considered mainstream and juxtaposing them with secondary representatives, which are either less known or unorthodox, I hoped to sketch a possibly broad but consistent picture of "what is scary" and "how it is scary" in American and Japanese horror fiction. A number of the most important or most noticeable aspects of American and Japanese horror fiction are touched upon in this book; I use a variety of titles as the starting point for further discussion and refer to numerous other literary works, films, graphic novels and video game scenarios. The primary goal of this book is to examine those aspects, together with the elements necessary for horror comprehension, and to highlight the differences and similarities between them, as well as to explain their cultural context as comprehensibly as possible.

I wanted to approach the horror texts not as texts belonging to specific media or conventions, but simply as stories. Therefore I have settled on the term "narratives" rather than "works of literature and cinema" or "games" or "comics" because it encompasses a wider variety of stories. That which qualifies a story as a narrative is, for the purpose of this book, a fixed, identifiable narrative structure. I did not aspire to lay down clean, firm borders of what does or does not belong to the horror genre—this has been discussed repeatedly by many scholars, and creating yet another definition just for this book would serve no purpose. Instead, I decided to focus on the specific sort of narratives that exist within what is referred to as the horror genre or horror fiction. Throughout the book, I refer to them as horror narratives and define them as follows: narratives dealing with fear evoked by invasion of the supernatural unfamiliar onto or into the everyday familiar, which reflect fears otherwise difficult to concretize. Such an approach excludes folklore and any kind of hypertext, at the same time allowing video game storylines[1] and handling even several versions of film adaptations or film remakes as autonomous narratives. It also provides an opportunity to analyze the horror stories wherever they blossom: in the form of literature (e.g., works of Stephen King and Kōji Suzuki), graphic novels (such as Junji Itō's *Tomie* or Steve Niles and Ben Templesmiths's *30 Days of Night*), TV series (for example, *Supernatural* created by Eric Kripke or *100 Tales of Horror* produced by Kumiko Nakashima, Hiroyuki Goto and Minoru Sakai), through video games (such as *Silent Hill*, published by Konami or *Alone in the Dark*, published by Infogrames) to films. All those have in common one important feature: establishing an atmosphere of fear, woven around some sort of a narrative structure. I wanted to use this variety of cultural texts and forms as an opportunity to paint a more accurate image of the genre and create a selection as representative as possible of American and Japanese horror fiction. The selected texts display a number of motives and themes characteristic to both their own cultural background and their native concept of what constitutes horror fiction. My intention was to show how certain cultural elements, such as folklore influence, social influence, religious influence and aesthetic influence, manifest themselves in certain, for want of a better word, exemplary narratives of both cultures (although not all of those narratives may necessarily be representative of national literature, cinema or other medium of the genre).

The selection of the works discussed in this book, however wide, concerns only those Japanese titles that are available to an American audience—that is, an audience that presumably cannot understand the Japanese language. The opportunity to access works available in the audience's native language is the starting point for discussion; the main focus of the comparative approach presented here is the point of contact of the two cultures in question, the point that has been emerging for some time now due to the technological progress and the significant changes in information handling and distribution. Since some of the literary works have been adapted for cinema and some of the films have been remade more than once, for the sake of clarity I used the original titles (even if the book or a film was distributed in the United States with an English title).

Lastly, all the titles belong to the same genre, supernatural horror, and concern storylines dealing with the intrusion of the supernatural element into an otherwise natural environment or situation. The term "horror" naturally covers a much wider variety of sub-genres, such as psychological thrillers (such as Hitchcock's *Psycho* [1960], or the *Saw* series [2004—]), slashers (*The Sleepaway Camp* [1983], directed by Hiltzik, or Craven's *Scream* [1994]) or any films with supernatural themes (Weitz's *Cirque du Freak: The Vampire's Assistant* [2009], or *Twilight* [2008], directed by Hardwicke). This work deals with supernatural horror and the monsters dwelling within it.

Completing this book without anyone's help would not have been an impossible task. It simply would not be a good book, though. Therefore, I would like to thank Tadeusz Rachwał, who was my mentor—a very patient and supportive one—throughout my graduate studies at Nicolaus Copernicus University in Toruń, for all the guidance and encouragement he provided me. I also owe a great debt of gratitude to Elżbieta Kostowska-Watanabe, who selflessly offered her time, knowledge and sources to an inexperienced graduate student, and Dariusz Brzostek, whose insight and suggestions greatly benefited this project. I would also like to express my deepest gratitude to my parents, my sister and my husband for their unfailing support.

Introduction

Cultural values and values constructed within cultures are not absolute. Almost all aspects of art and culture are relative, although the claim itself is nowhere near objective; deeply embedded in Western view of the world, it assumes two or more opposite points of view from which some premise or concept actually *can* be relative. From within the Western—or Euroamerican—point of view, it is only natural to cut the world into comprehensible units that qualify either as "us" or "our," or as "them" or "their." From those units, or rather from the world composed of such units, relativity emerges. The concept of right and wrong is relative, the premises such as affection, bravery or common sense are relative, and, naturally, so is the concept of fear and horror.

Left-Hand and Right-Hand Traffic

In their book *Ghosts and the Japanese* Michiko Iwasaka and Barre Toelken present a great analogy for experiencing an alien culture by analyzing the seemingly trivial matter of traffic organization. When using a public stairway in Japan, e.g., a subway stairway, an American or European will tend to automatically position himself on the side of the stairway or pavement that feels natural to them—i.e., the right-hand side. He will either be forced to evade the oncoming crowd or, during rush hours, be rendered unable to move—or even pushed back down by the mass of commuters. The Japanese, on the other hand, will ignore the foreigner's odd behavior or maybe be baffled or even irritated with his inability to grasp the obvious and common rules and customs—that is, obvious and common for the Japanese. A Japanese person moving forward will normally position himself on the left-hand side of the stairway or pavement. Such is the group dynamic of pedestrian traffic in Japan (Iwasaka and Toelken 1994: 4). Exceptions can take place, naturally—larger groups may exert a right-of-way over individual members of the crowd. To a confused foreigner, this might seem even more puzzling or, at times, hazardous. Neither the Japanese nor American movement pattern is more arrogant, obstinate or counter-intuitive than the other. Both patterns are consistent and based on subconscious assumptions integrated into cultural values, customs and everyday actions (Iwasaka and Toelken 1994: 4). Within every culture there are values and norms so obvious and natural to the members of that culture, so basic to their sense of normality, that they are sometimes brought to attention only when someone does not conform to them; "[e]very culture which remains alive is well supplied with these codes of everyday behavior and value, along with attendant emotions, regardless of how many other philosophies it may have borrowed and how literate and sophisticated its members may be"—and both America and Japan have a plethora of such "customs of cultural and social communication" (Iwasaka and Toelken 1994: 4–5). Those codes and customs are assimilated by the members of a given culture involuntarily, through stories told by others, through jokes and anecdotes, and through actions of other community members. Based on all those, a person existing within a certain cultural frame acquires understanding of values and ideas that constitute normality, values and ideas that are not articulated or questioned (Iwasaka and Toelken 1994: 4–5). Realizing that such a complex, dynamic level of communication exists puts a whole new perspective on our experience with culture—both one's own and foreign. What might have been confusing or unclear before can now be put in context and will therefore make sense (Iwasaka and Toelken 1994: 5). The familiar is only familiar because it is familiar to us. "Figuratively speaking," Iwasaka and Toelken insist, "we should be willing to experience both sides of the stairway"—we should be ready to "become aware of the familiar (as obvious and simple as that may sound) in such a way that cultural practices different from our own will register as adventures in the kaleidoscope of human meaning rather than confirmation that other peoples are crude or backward" (Iwasaka and Toelken 1994: 5).

That which is "obvious" to the members of any given culture remains invisible to the conscious eye. For this reason, it is by no means redundant to re-state some basics about our own cultural conditions and notions, but it is only necessary in order to juxtapose what we take for granted with what we lack knowledge of. In other words, in order to understand left-hand traffic, we must first acknowledge the significance and cultural consequences of being in right-hand traffic.

The Performance of Horror Narratives

As Roland Kelts states, "[t]hanks to the Internet, nonstop flights, and restless new generations, Japan is a lot closer to America than ever before" (Kelts 2006: 8); translation of works of literature and graphic novels, distribution of consumer DVD releases of films (often subtitled) and, first and foremost, the Internet allow easy access to books, graphic novels, films and music for the American audience interested in the artifacts of Japanese popular culture and vice versa. In such circumstances it is not perhaps very surprising that Japanese horror fiction is tremendously popular with the American audience. And yet this audience, however interested, is more often than not culturally unprepared for what they encounter, for to understand any genre of fiction that originates within a different cultural frame the knowledge of building blocks of that culture is necessary. Horror, just like other literary or cinematic devices, is defined by and constructed within a certain cultural frame. For the horror element to successfully fulfill its role, it must be embedded in its native cultural environment, and the cultural environment itself must be understood by the audience.[1]

Any work of horror fiction expresses the range and limitations of its genre—i.e., it operates within a set of "conventionalized parameters" (Grixti 1989: 5). A genre—any genre—is a fixed cultural pattern. Whether or not a melodrama is moving or a comedy is amusing depends solely on the fixed parameters those genres allow for. Just as cultural premises and values are relative, so are the genres existing within them. Horror fiction can fulfill its role only if its symbolic nature is fully comprehensible to the audience. To put it in simpler terms, a ghost is scary because the audience shares an already existing comprehension of what a ghost is and all the cultural conceptual attachments connected with the figure of the ghost. Without that comprehension, a ghost would still be scary, but folklore, history and culture allow the audience to become apprehensive even before the ghost appears, simply owing to the presence of the signs that prepare them for the real fear. In a similar way, it is impossible for the Euroamerican audience to approach vampire narratives without taking into account the underlying European folklore, or even Bram Stoker's story of Dracula. When the audience encounter a pale character who avoids sunlight and has no reflection in the mirror, they know they should be afraid even before it bares its teeth and starts drinking blood. Although not addressed explicitly, this underlying knowledge and comprehension will always be there, establishing a reality for the audience to experience, setting a narrative in a particular point of time, and making it more believable.

Approaches to Horror in Japanese and American Cultures

Horror, similar to comedy and other genres dependent specifically on the emotional response of the audience, requires a whole spectrum of factors to perform its function optimally. The reason for this lies in the complex nature of the relationship between people and the culture they belong to. Cultural norms, values and beliefs influence not only outlook and behavior, but also human emotions (Turner and Stets 2005: 3). Human beings are capable of experiencing emotions, including fear, not only when they are confronted with real, immediate danger, but also over cultural symbols and arbitrary concepts (Turner and Stets 2005: 23). The natural fear we feel when we encounter a tiger is just as real, even if different, as the arbitrary fear brought out by the thoughts of war, darkness or a vampire.

The task of horror is to render its audience terrified; this is its distinguishing feature. Horror is, "irrespective of its medium or transition, a type of narrative which deals in messages about fear and experiences associated with fear" (Grixti 1989: xii). Like any genre that relies on evoking emotions, horror must rely on that arbitrary, conditional fear contingent upon its cultural environment. It needs cues and hints, auguries and heralds. A Euroamerican audience not familiar with a Thai legend of Lady Nak will not fully appreciate either *Nang Nak* (1999) or *The Ghost of Mae Nak* (2005), which draw inspiration from the story of Lady Nak's ghost, as horror productions (See Knee 2005). A work of horror can genuinely frighten its audience only when the audience understands clearly what it is that they should be afraid of.

Contemporary horror encompasses a wide variety of media, sub-genres and influences. It is, in a way, a result of what is considered to be terrifying within the cultural frame to which the target audience belongs, of the successive literary styles and genres existent in that culture, of new creative ideas, and of foreign influences. In its form and purpose, horror fiction must maintain a subtle balance of all those factors. This balance between the known and the new is crucial to the genre, which must draw from familiar cultural elements and remain relevant to cultural reality and simultaneously introduce unfamiliar elements to captivate its audience, as Philips points out:

> To be horrific, to fulfill their primary narrative function, horror films must not simply offer us something novel, they must shock us. In the truly groundbreaking horror films of American history this level of shock is caused not merely by the introduction of some new monster but through an almost systematic violation of the rules of the game [Philips 2005: 7].

According to Philips, familiarity is devastating to the horror genre; it generates not only boredom but, what is worse, derision. Many a horror figure, once formidable and shocking, gradually lost their potential to horrify, and sometimes even ended up evoking an effect contrary to the desired one. "As a general rule of thumb," Philips sums up, "monsters that are too familiar become the objects of ridicule" (Philips 2005: 7).

While the task and mechanism of horror fiction seem straightforward and easy to define, there is no one definition of the genre. Numerous definitions of horror have been formed over the years. Many of them overlap, more often than not agreeing as far as the major premises are concerned. The one matter upon which all definitions concur is that the horror fiction is fiction whose dominant—and distinguishing—function is to scare the audience. And yet, the same scholars who agree as to what horror is and what it is not tend to argue over what can be classified as belonging to the horror genre. It would seem that the common agreement is to count such films as *Night of the Living Dead* (1968), *The Exorcist* (1973), *A Nightmare on Elm Street* (1984), *Jacob's Ladder* (1990) and *Silent Hill* (2006) as proud representatives of the horror genre; productions such as *Alien* (1979), *The Fly* (1986) or *Cloverfield* (2008), on the other hand, tend to slip that collection, blending into other genres, whereas *Psycho* (1960), *Jaws* (1975) or *Silence of the Lambs* (1991) encounter even more problems, sometimes being excluded from the genre altogether, instead labeled as thrillers, suspense or action films. On the other hand, works belonging to other genres might sometimes be mislabeled as horror fiction solely on the basis of employing a supernatural element usually (although not necessarily) associated with horror: a vampire (*Interview with a Vampire* by Anne Rice or *Vampire Hunter D* by Hideyuki Kikuchi), killing machines (*Second Variety,* Philip K. Dick) or terrifying transformation (*The Standing Woman,* Yasutaka Tsutsui). Apart from a multitude of sub-genres and media, horror spans also a number of target audiences; it is directed at varied groups of age and maturity, ranging from mature material for adults, through young adult novels, manga and video games, to stylized horror for younger recipients.[2]

Kiyoshi Kurosawa, an accomplished Japanese director, on the other hand, proposed a loose definition of what is scary, based on the Japanese understanding of the world and the supernatural:

> For example, giant monsters flying down from another planet and rampaging through the streets is unarguably scary.... I assuredly do not want to be in that situation. But it isn't horror. The reason being, this scariness is something that can be conquered. Sure enough, a brilliant scientist will locate the weakness of the

giant monsters, and when the survivors join forces, the disaster will pass and at last peace will return. The situation is the same for monstrous mass murderers. When the criminal is apprehended or shot dead, life returns to normal.... On the other hand, the scariness we're talking about when we say that horror movies are scary is of a completely different type. For example: On the other side of the fence stands the darkened figure of a human being. When you look carefully, it looks like a friend who has died. You gasp in surprise. In the next instant, the figure disappears. So, how do you overcome this fear? To put it bluntly, there is no way of escaping this fear as long as you live. Your life will undergo a great change from that moment on [Kurosawa 1993].

In other words, the fear characteristic of the horror genre would be the fear of what cannot be avoided, controlled or conquered in any fashion. Following this simple and clear-cut (not to mention culturally justified) assumption, Kurosawa proceeds to present a quite revolutionary point of view on what sort of films he considers to be horror and what sort should not be labeled so:

Alien [dir. Ridley Scott, 1979] is not a horror film because, however frightening it may be, it is possible to overcome an alien invasion, theoretically speaking. In the same way, films such as *Psycho* [dir. Alfred Hitchcock, 1960] or *The Night of the Hunter* [dir. Charles Laughton, 1955] or *Silence of the Lambs* [dir. Jonathan Demme, 1991] are not horror.... To take it one step further, the zombie films of George A. Romero are not horror. David Cronenberg's works are also not horror. Yet another separate genre of "action films" exists for that group of movies whose climactic battles are decided by firearms [Kurosawa 1993].

This list—somewhat astonishing to the Euroamerican horror audience—contains other works considered by some to be milestones (or at least fine representatives) of horror: *Frankenstein* [1931], *The Fly* [1958 and 1986] *Mill of the Stone Woman* [1960] and *Eyes Without a Face* [1959].

The point of view presented by Kurosawa serves here not so much as an illustration of the supposedly impassable cultural barrier between the American and Japanese concept of horror, but rather as a suggestion of the considerable number of disparate connotations and qualities underlying the presented horror elements. The sheer fact that both American and Japanese audiences react strongly to a ghost as a frightening figure does not necessarily mean that the response is triggered by the same processes and impulses. Furthermore, the origins of a given monster or horror trope affect greatly its representation in fiction produced in the given culture. Virtually all popular-culture horror monsters originate from folk beliefs; in some cases their heritage may be difficult to trace, but in some cases it is very clear. Alan Dundes comments on the explicit folk origins of a very well known horror character, the vampire, in the following way:

One thing we do know, however, is that the original source of both literary and popular cultural representations of the vampire came from folklore, not the other way round. Bram Stoker's *Dracula* of 1897 may well have influenced the literary works and films which appeared after that date, but Bram Stoker, an Irishman by birth, did not invent the Transylvanian vampire. That figure existed long before Stoker wrote his famous novel (...) [Dundes 1998: 17].

What is more, the vampire is not, as Dundes insists, universal by any means; there is not even "one single myth, legend, or folktale which is universal in the sense of being known by all human populations, past and present" (Dundes 2008: 18). This last statement is very significant in the context of this work, especially when juxtaposed with Hideyuki Kikuchi's post-script to the English edition of the fifth volume of the *Vampire Hunter D* series, *The Stuff of Dreams*:

Japan, the land of my birth, has developed a culture quite different from that of the English-speaking world.... [E]ven when I use something like the European vampire theme in my work, it differs fundamentally from what might be created in your world. Perhaps that's what makes the Vampire Hunter D series so enjoyable [Kikuchi 2006: 173].

Naturally, Kikuchi refers here to the image of the vampire commonly depicted in popular culture products, not to its folkloric form, which is even more diverse and culture-specific. Both Kikuchi's and Dundes' remarks, seemingly simplistic and casual, convey in fact a very basic and tremendously important truth about horror fantasies (but not about all fantasies in general). No horror fantasy is universal in terms of shape and form, despite the fact that they are expressions of a universal emotion that is fear. Therefore, the character of the vampire, despite being immediately recognizable as a "vampire," will differ from culture to culture—as will all monsters inhabiting the horror genre.

The American Abject and Japanese Pluralism

Two important concepts that need to be addressed if horror fiction is to be discussed are the concepts of Self/Other distinction and the exclusion/inclusion of the supernatural in American and Japanese horror narratives. Both are firmly rooted in the cultural realities of those countries, and both are immensely important in the context of the horror genre.

The concept of the Self, the Other and that which comes in between is inherent to the American conceptual frame of horror fiction, and to Julia Kristeva's concept of the abject. Euroamerican horror narratives portray the Other in a plethora of ways, and they tend to do so by means of abject mechanisms, where the characters—and the audience—can distance themselves and reject the Other, banish it to the periphery of consciousness in an attempt to "keep it at arm's length, and, what is important, to attain a sense of *self-with-borders* or boundaries" (Olivier 2009: 451, my emphasis). It is exactly that periphery of consciousness where the abject Other takes its concrete form of the autonomous monster of the horror fiction: a misshapen monster, a vampire or a rotting zombie. This autonomy is also what stresses the most important aspect of the relation between the subject and the unwanted: "the attempt to ... attain a sense of *self-with-borders* or boundaries." Outside the boundaries of the clearly defined, single and unique self of the Western subject, lies the disgusting, border-defying *le visquex,* the slimy abject of the unwanted fear (Baumann 2000: 53). Western abject relies very much on the sensation of repulsion. The repulsion concerns many aspects of the abject, the most immediate being the way the abject form looks: its appearance, its smell and shape. In American cinema the same tendency can be observed; horror films tend to rely on the same disgusting abjectness as horror literature. The cinema is literally crawling with bugs, insects, maggots, decaying corpses or disfigured, mutilated entities, anything that reminds the audience of or usually accompanies the corpse or decay. The terrifying is repulsive, unbearable; the installation of the horror factor within the abject realm is the first important aspect of the American concept of horror.

To interpret the logic of fear in Japanese fiction in the context of the Self/Other opposition—as well as the way it works—it is necessary to mention the subject-object opposition. A Japanese subject exists, of course, but it does not possess (or strive to establish) firm boundaries that would sever it from the reality and others. Takie Sugiyama Lebra describes the Japanese cultural logic as contingent, in contrast to the Western oppositional one (Lebra 2004: 2). According to oppositional cultural logic, if something is white, it cannot be black. If I am me, then I cannot be you, nor can you be me, or, for that matter, anyone else. The West functions within dichotomies and binary oppositions—a unified, prominent Self entails the necessary existence of the Other. To the Japanese audience the relation "subject—rest of the world" blurs within a non-oppositional, contingent world view (Lebra 2004: 2). If the West prefers dichotomies and opposition, Japan leans towards pluralism (Moeran in Ben-Ari et al. 1994: 6).

The second key concept related to the horror genre concerns the exclusion/inclusion of the supernatural in the cultural reality—as well as the actual nature and status of the supernatural—to which a horror narrative belongs. In the Euroamerican cultural reality the supernatural is always the strange, the alien, the impossible. The real and the supernatural interact, but not only are they two separate "worlds," but also they invoke a set of binary oppositions such as "the real"/"the rational" as opposed to "not-real (supernatural)"/"the irrational." This is related directly to the fact that the American concept of a scary tale naturally stems from the European understanding of a scary tale, which underwent a significant transformation in the Enlightenment. It was during the Enlightenment when the priority of reason was demystifying the world, labeling all that was supernatural as irrational and not real. Consequently, this world of "precise causality brought about by the Age of Enlightenment," as Dariusz Brzostek points out, has in turn brought about the "literature of pure horror" (Brzostek 2009: 26). Accordingly, the second crucial characteristic of the Euroamerican (and, therefore, American) horror fiction is the element of impossibility and shock. The characters confronted with the supernatural danger are not equipped with any kind of knowledge or logic that would allow them to process and deal with the (usually) imminent peril. Despite having perceived or experienced the supernatural, the characters provided with an Euroamerican world-view dismiss the obvious as impossible.

In the Japanese horror fiction—or any fiction, for that matter—entities such as ghosts, demons or shapeshifters are not unnatural—neither are they technically *super*natural. As Chambers notes in his discussion of Akinari Ueda's *Tales of Moonlight and Rain* (*Ugetsu monogatari*), the notion of "supernatural" is in and of itself relative, and while "strange" and "mysterious" are commonly attributed to Japanese scary tales, "supernatural" is probably "an inappropriate word, since what is considered to be supernatural in one culture is regarded as merely strange—but natural—in another" (Chambers in Ueda 2008: 16). Similarly, the term "fantastic" as it is defined by Tzvetan Todorov is not accurate either, since the fantastic relies on the ambiguity as to whether or not an event is supernatural—and there is no such ambiguity in the world presented in *Tales of Moonlight and Rain;* this stems from the fact that belief in apparitions, spirit possessions, and other phenomena that the Euroamerican culture regards as "supernatural" was widespread in eighteenth-century Japan (Chambers in Ueda 2008: 16). Instead, terms such as "strange" and "anomalous" are more useful when discussing *Tales of Moonlight and Rain* (Chambers in Ueda 2008: 16), as well as other ghost narratives, shape-shifter narratives or demon narratives that belong to the *kaidan*, literally "tales of the strange." The Japanese pluralistic world-view even today assumes the existence of interaction with the spirit realm (Kasulis 2004: 78). This which is described as "supernatural" in Japanese horror fiction is "supernatural" only from the Western point of view.[3]

Since in the Japanese cultural frame the presence of ghosts and other otherworldly beings of entities, considered to be supernatural in Western eyes, is regarded merely in the context of strangeness, not their actual existence or lack thereof, such a presence produces entirely different problems and reactions in the eyes of the Japanese. The matter does not, therefore, concern the ontological status of the otherworldly visitor, but ethics. The question is not "Is it possible that what I see is a ghost/demon/*yōkai?*" but "Why do I see a ghost/demon/*yōkai?*" In the greater part of Japanese horror narratives this matter ("Why do I see this entity?") is related to the matter of karma. As Ian Reader explains, karma (*innen*) is "the notion that all events and actions have repercussions, often referred to in Buddhist terms as the law of cause and effect, may be immediate and direct, returning to the person most intimately associated with the actions that set the whole process in motion" (Reader 1991: 47). More importantly, because people do not live in isolation, but in communities, they are closely bound with each other through various, interconnected relationships and ties and defined by them (more than they are defined as individual), and therefore karma may be transmitted and shared (Reader 1991: 47). Japanese horror narratives, even if they do not explicitly address the concept of karmic causality, tend to be karmic in their overall tone; they more often than not emphasize the horrible consequences of actions such as committing a forbidden act or hurting someone. In case of ghost narratives, e.g., hurting someone or allowing them to die a bad death, brings about the *urami* (rancor created by someone's deliberate or unjust lack of empathy; see Lebra 1976: 43) of the one who was hurt. Therefore, the appearance of the ghost in a ghost narrative automatically signifies a violation of moral order.

It would not be unreasonable to risk at this point a statement that within the Euroamerican—and consequently, American—cultural frame the nature of horror narrative relies on epistemological conflict; it is concerned with what and how, whereas within the Japanese cultural frame the conflict underlying the horror narratives tends to be ethical in its nature, striving to find out why and what for. For the Japanese, the mere presence of a ghost or other supernatural being is not a problem in itself as much as it is a signal that something is wrong in the world surrounding them, that somewhere, something happened that should not have occurred—or, on the contrary, that something that was supposed to take place never did. Japanese horror narratives are more often than not concerned with ethically problematic scenarios concentrating on punishment for breaking the rules, innocent people being wronged or victims exacting revenge or cursing their tormentors. The issues of justice or virtue and vice tend to intertwine and collide with the relative matters of morality and good and evil, testing the protagonist's strength of heart (*kokoro*) and involving them in the complex ethical dilemma. The American storylines, on the other hand, conventionally resort to portraying a strong opposition between the attacking and the attacked, with the motives or intentions of the attacker remaining of secondary importance. The primary concern of the protagonist is the sheer fact that the attacker exists; it is a fact that must be dealt with, skeptically challenged, before being eventually accepted. Once the protagonist ascertains the nature of the force or creature invading the familiar reality, they immediately proceed to establish any and all feasible ways of opposing (and preferably defeating) the attacker. In this sense, Japanese horror narratives pose the horror element as something that needs to be explained, whereas American horror presents it as an obstacle to be acknowledged and overcome.

Chris Pruett suggests that "[i]n attempting to define what "Japanese horror" is, we must also define "Western horror" in order to draw distinctions between the two" (Pruett 2010: 11). It has probably become clear by now that even the loose main assumption made here, i.e., the invasion of the supernatural abnormal onto the normal, although feasible as a criterion, does necessarily refer to the same quality of fear in American horror and Japanese horror and will not necessarily follow the same patterns plot-wise. Naturally there will be similarities at times, just as at other times significant differences will arise. It is the aim of this book to present a possibly broad, diverse outline of the shape of the horrible in Japanese and American horror narratives.

It is also important to note that due to the highly commercial nature of Hollywood productions, the majority of American horror films are directed at younger audiences, with the preferable rating being PG-13, i.e., with some of the content possibly "Inappropriate for Children Under 13" (http://www.mpaa.org/). The PG-13 rating allows the producers to avoid narrowing the prospective audience to people above the age of seventeen, or perhaps even eighteen (compare the ratings R and NC-17), which, considering the young age of an average American movie-goer, would be marketing suicide (see CAC Nielsen Cinema Audience Report, years 2003–2009). The same could be said about horror video games, which are distributed with an ESRB analogous to PG-13, i.e., T (http://www.esrb.org/). Therefore, although the horror genre in America, as in any other cultural environment, reflects the anxieties of the society, the profit oriented disposition of the film and gaming industry results in some of the mature, sexual, violent or disturbing content being filtered out, therefore influencing the nature of the narrative itself.

1

Ghosts

The ghost is a creature of the most logical and simultaneously most extraordinary nature among the army of monstrosities inhabiting horror fiction. On the one hand, its presence is completely logical because the fear of death is one of the most prevalent fears in all cultures. The veil separating those who died from those who live is impenetrable, and for ages people have been wondering about the afterlife; the idea that the spirits of the dead might be subject to the same passions and attachments as the living is not absurd. And yet, on the other hand, the presence of a ghost in horror fiction is also extraordinary, for it brings the horrific, abjectful Other (death, in this case) closer than any other horror monster, closer even than the zombie. The monster is not unlike the protagonist—on the contrary, it is identical to the protagonist (and, consequently, the audience), only dead. And because death is inevitable, it is not unimaginable that everyone may become a monster at some point.

In *Icons of Horror and the Supernatural: An Encyclopedia of Our Worst Fears* Melissa Hall insists that

> [t]he haunting allure of the ghost creates a seductive mystique and a very marketable icon that appeals to all ages. The apparition of a dead person or animal—the disembodied spirit that can be manifested as sound, touch, smell, or vision, and possess or manipulate objects or do any number of frightening or inspiring things—is without a doubt one of the most enduring staples of horror and the supernatural. The ghost's popularity might wax and wane, wavering in and out of sight, but it never truly vanishes [Hall in Joshi 2007: 215–216].

Despite its prevalence (or maybe because of it) the ghost is not always portrayed in the same manner. For the sake of discussion, let us define the ghost as a manifestation of the consciousness of a person who has died (usually human beings become ghosts, although animal ghosts are not unheard of in horror fiction). It is not corporeal, but often times it can affect both living beings and the material world. The details may turn out to be dissimilar from story to story, sometimes even contradictory, but the heart of any ghost story remains the same: It concerns some sort of penetration of the world of the living by the consciousness of a deceased person or persons. This temporary incursion of the dead into the world of the living, together with the reason for it being some unfinished business which, once over, no longer holds the spirit in the land of the living, are mentioned by Colin Davis as the two primary characteristic elements of a ghost story (Davis in Blanco and Peeren 2010: 67–68).

Another immensely important characteristic that all ghost stories share is brought up in this fragment: the ghost's motivation. Regardless of whether the ghost is tormenting the living or pleading with them for their help, the motivation of the ghost remains an indispensable element of any ghost narrative. In other words, the nature of the "unfinished business" must be clearly specified and introduced to the audience.

As Mary Snodgrass notes in *Encyclopedia of Gothic Literature,* the ghost story—i.e., stories about ghosts and their interaction the world of the living— is an exceptionally old and widespread form of narrative:

> Based on fears of the dark and about death, the ghost story is a pervasive folk genre in world culture from earliest times, for example, Japanese oral *kaidan* tales of horror and revenge.... Gothic trappings color suspenseful tales of supernatural beings that return from death to wreak vengeance, expose a crime, or enlighten or harry victims, particularly former lovers and the sin-laden.... [Snodgrass 2006: 140–141].

The Japanese ghost story mentioned by Snodgrass, *kaidan,* is a particular sort of ghost story. *Kaidan* are tales of the strange (literally: "mysterious tales"), which enjoyed tremendous popularity during the Edo period. They were associated with gatherings known as *hyakumonogatari kaidankai* ("gatherings of one hundred *kaidan* tales"), which consisted of people taking turns to tell a total of one hundred stories in order to induce a supernatural phenomenon. Such gatherings were common among all classes of people; *kaidan,* whether told or printed, were a favorite leisure activity for people living in Edo Japan (Reider 2000:281). Noriko Reider believes that one of the reasons for the *kaidan*'s popularity was that the tales were relevant to the reality of the people living in Edo period; they presented "explanations for the inexplicable events in daily life, exoticism, and/or mild criticism of social and political institutions" (Reider 2000:281). A plethora of Japanese modern ghost stories derive from the *kaidan* tradition, and retain many important characteristics of *kaidan.* Modern ghost stories in the United States, in turn, do not differ greatly from the rest of American folklore, i.e., they are a complex combination of the folklore imported into the fledgling American culture by the first settlers, elements loaned from Native American culture and the normal evolution that the fiction of any country undergoes. Popular among both children and adults, ghost stories abound in print and in the mass media in United States, as well as in oral tradition (Tucker 1998: 693–694).

The American cultural frame exists within the Euroamerican frame of culture; therefore, it naturally shares the heritage of the Age of Enlightenment. American people may find entertainment in ghost stories, but they "do not accept ghosts as everyday reality, nor do they 'know' that ghosts exist; [the ghosts] occupy a dimension that is separate from daily reality, and they exist, above all, in human faith" (Ward in Brunvand 1998: 448). In Japan, on the other hand, as Iwasaka and Toelken explain in *Ghosts and the Japanese,* the world of the dead lies "not far from the world of the living, and the souls of departed ... remain among the survivors, or at least close enough to visit the family during Obon season" (Iwasaka and Toelken 1994: 8). The spirits reside in a realm or their own, adjacent to our world, called *takai* (otherworld), in which space and time differ from those of the world of the living, and which they can relatively freely leave at any time, crossing the borders for limited periods of time; a ghost cannot, however, change its nature and stay in the human world (Tatarczuk 2011: 29–30).

Despite the difference in attitude towards the departed, in both cultures the dead may return to interact with the living, and in both cultures such a return is a reason for concern. Similarly, in both cultures the presence of a ghost might be centered around a place or a person—a haunting, or it may realize the ghost's personal affair of some sort, predominantly retribution. Although the two tend to overlap in the majority of ghost stories, the subtle difference between a haunting and a retribution is that hauntings present themselves indiscriminately to anyone who comes within range. They may be centered around a person or a group of people, or even an object, but there is no ultimate aim to them. Retribution, meanwhile, has a specific purpose, a goal to be reached; more importantly, it is directed at specific people and encompasses only those who get in the way.

A technical matter that needs to be addressed at this point is the matter of dimensions and layers. Layers and dimensions are two concepts useful in analyzing narratives with more intricate, composite structures. In the context of this book, the layers of a narrative are event horizons of the storyline; they replace one another once the audience gathers more information about the characters and events of the given narrative. Usually narratives that make use of misdirection and twist endings contain numerous layers, making the transition from rational into irrational gradual. In comparison, non-layered narratives[1] feature a rapid transition from skepticism to acceptance of the supernatural. The dimensions of a narrative, on the other hand, are different aspects of horror generated by the story. They may overlap but will not replace each other; their effect is additive. Ghost narratives tend to employ layers for better horror effect.

Haunting and Regret

In *Icons of Horror* S. T. Joshi points out that Sigmund Freud's concept of the uncanny could not, as Freud himself noted in his famous essay, exist without the concept of home, as the German word for "uncanny" (*unheimlich*) is the opposite of the word for "homely" (*heimlich*) (Joshi 2007: 268). Among other definitions of *heimlich,* Freud offers "belonging to the house; not strange; familiar; intimate; friendly" (Joshi 2007: 268). Naturally, that which is strange and not intimate must evoke anxiety and unease. One's home is one's shelter; it ensures safety and constitutes a stronghold against all sort of danger, both real and metaphorical:

> A house provides a sense of containment, of enclosure, warmth, protection from the elements, a sense of intimacy and nurture.... Home is the center of one's existence and one's security.... Given that we have such a significant investment in the physical and emotional aspects of our house, it is not surprising that the notion of it being violated by something threatening—worse, something unnatural—feels so fearful [Mariconda in Joshi 2007: 268].

It is no wonder that with such a broad range of association, home is a powerful instrument in the hands of horror fiction authors. In traditional haunted house narratives, the protagonists experience the reversal of those values: the place of safety becomes an insidious place of threat. In every haunted house we can observe and recognize "a unique, discrete space which belongs to darkness" (Aguirre 1990: 148). The nature of the darkness may be manifold: a curse, ghosts, bizarre supernatural phenomena. Tony Magistrale notes that "[i]n most horror films and Gothic novels, the haunted house/castle serves as a vehicle for mirroring the inner psychology of its inhabitants" (Magistrale 2005: 90). Whether containing a threat of internal nature (the darkness dwelling in the protagonist) or external nature (some other consciousness or phenomena), the haunted house is by definition a "not-home," as Aquirre puts it—"an unheimlich centre" (Aguirre 1990: 92).

Hauntings, however, are not restricted to buildings, nor even to places. Next to the motif of the haunted house, Gothic fiction introduced a complementary concept—the figure of the haunted individual (Aguirre 1990: 116). As Aguirre points out, "[w]e tend to think of the haunted house as a building, but it can equally well be a lineage, a title, a family" (Aguirre 1990: 95) or even a single person. The most important characteristic of a haunting is the connection between the spirit and the object of its haunting. The exact nature of the connection is irrelevant. Anger, love, sorrow or loyalty may equally well be the basis of the ghost's attachment.

Shirley Jackson's *The Haunting of the Hill House* is a remarkable haunted house story—in fact, it may very well be the most famous American haunted house story. The Hill House is a cursed place, haunted in many ways: by its past, by its former inhabitants, even, in a sense, by the guests staying there during the duration of the story, invited there to observe paranormal phenomena. Strange things occur in the house, sounds are heard, cold drafts chill the characters to the bone, and yet there is no singular ghost in the Hill House, but a plethora of different voices and different manifestations. It is not a spirit of one person but the Hill House itself that is the pivotal point of *The Haunting of the Hill House*. Juxtaposed with the old, colossal mansion is the protagonist of the novel—Eleanor Vance; her vivid imagination and emotionally unstable state of mind render her a perfect conductor for the horror which is to be conveyed to the readers of the story.

The Haunting of the Hill House opens with a memorable passage that Stephen King describes in *Danse Macabre* as one of the finest descriptive passages in the English language (King 1982: 267):

> No live organism can continue for long to exist sanely under conditions of absolute reality; even larks and katydids are supposed, by some, to dream. Hill House, not sane, stood by itself against its hills, holding darkness within; it had stood so for eighty years and might stand for eighty more. Within, walls continued upright, bricks met neatly, floors were firm, and doors were sensibly shut; silence lay steadily against the wood and stone of Hill House, and whatever walked there, walked alone [Jackson 1999: 3].

This short passage introduces all the information necessary to begin a haunted house tale. The readers learn that the Hill House is a house with quite a long history and that it resembles, if not actually is, a living organism, i.e., something with a consciousness. The fragment emphasizes how deceptively normal and inconspicuous Hill House looks at first glance ("walls continued upright, bricks met neatly, floors were firm"). Most importantly, the reader is told openly that there is certainly something that walks the corridors and rooms of Hill House, and it is beyond doubt not human ("*whatever* walked there").

Eleanor comes to the house because of Doctor Montague's invitation. Having never left her home before in her life, she is full of enthusiasm and the sense of adventure. Therefore her reaction to Hill House is all the more significant; despite arriving in high spirits, hopeful and expectant, Eleanor does not take kindly to Hill House when she lays her eyes on it for the first time—she believes it is "vile" and "diseased" (Jackson 1999: 32–33). Eleanor's initial impression of the house again constructs Hill House in terms of something animate and sentient. This pattern of discourse permeates the novel, portraying Hill House as a building that is majestic, overwhelming and dominating, but most of all alive:

> No human eye can isolate the unhappy coincidence of line and place which suggests evil in the face of a house, and yet somehow a maniac juxtaposition, a badly turned angle, some chance meeting of roof and sky, turned Hill House into a place of despair, more frightening because the face of Hill House seemed awake…. This house, which seemed somehow to have formed itself, flying together into its own powerful pattern under the hands of its builders, fitting itself into its own construction of lines and angles, reared its great head back against the sky without concession to humanity. It was a house without kindness, never meant to be lived in, not a fit place for people or for love or for hope. Exorcism cannot alter the countenance of a house; Hill House would stay as it was until it was destroyed [Jackson 1999: 34–35].

Interestingly enough, in contrast to its majestic, imposing exterior, Hill House is surprisingly unsightly and bleak inside. It welcomes its guests with a combination of disquieting shapes and unpleasant colors that create an inhospitable, uncomfortable environment. As Eleanor enters the room designated for her bedroom, she is repulsed by it: "it was not nice at all, and only barely tolerable; it held enclosed the same clashing disharmony that marked Hill House throughout" (Jackson 1999: 246).

Hill House overwhelms Eleanor. Intimidated and apprehensive, she perceives the house as a threat, which reflects the way she thinks about it. Again the discourse of animation and consciousness surfaces in the narrative as Eleanor thinks: "I am like a small creature swallowed whole by a monster, … and the monster feels my tiny little movements inside" (Jackson 1999: 42). Eleanor seems to be, however, the only person who regards the house in terms of sentient life. Neither Theo's nor Luke's comments or remarks concerning Hill House at any point suggest that either of them feels threatened by their environment. As for Doctor Montague, he approaches the matter in a manner typical of a scientist. His attitude and observations provide sharp contrast to Eleanor's emotional, at times highly erratic, point of view. When he explains to his guests the focus of his research, he readily admits that Hill House may be dangerous, yet still retains a detached, methodical position. He does not shy away from referring to Hill House as a haunted house or otherwise depict is as an atrocious place, even if he uses mild words to convey that message. His open approach and choice of words apparently put his guests at ease regarding the phenomena occurring in Hill House—which might explain the moderate, almost nonchalant nature of their subsequent reactions to the supernatural incidents they witness. When Eleanor and Theo are confronted with the strange presence attempting to enter the room, they are petrified with fear; moments later, however, when the terrifying experience is over, they laugh wholeheartedly, showing a baffling disregard towards the supernatural phenomenon they have just witnessed.

Throughout the narrative the readers are made to understand that Hill House is a bad place—not only in the sense of being unfortunately located or of bad things having happened on its premises, but also in the sense of being evil. A variety of words is used to convey that idea: "vile," "diseased" (Jackson 1999: 33), "disturbed," "leprous" or "sick" (Jackson 1999: 70). The opening passage suggests that the house is, in fact, insane; although all the occurrences taking place in Hill House belong to the typical haunted house range of phenomena—cold spots, sounds, illusions and inexplicable phenomena—they are all characterized by a certain demented quality.

For Theo, Luke and Doctor Montague (as much as for the readers) the cold spot is the first element that broadens the atmosphere of horror that previously encompassed only Eleanor. The cold spot decidedly belongs to the assortment of a haunted house, and at this point Hill House consolidates its reputation as an eerie, haunted place. Again a balance is established between Eleanor's intuitive, sensual impression of the occurrence and Doctor Montague's sensible, rational reaction. Eleanor experiences "with incredulity" what to her is "piercing cold." She perceives the phenomenon in terms of sensations and images, concentrating on what she can feel and believe—e.g.,, she perceives the cold in terms of how it affects her ("piercing"), and in her mind she manufactures an image of "passing through a wall of ice." Like any ordinary person, Eleanor is trying to make sense of what is happening; she strains to "translate" the uncanny into an image or idea composed of familiar elements that would make sense. Doctor Montague, on the other hand, relies on observation and facts. Examining the cold spot near the nursery, he notices objectively—and enthusiastically—that "[t]he cold spot in Borley Rectory only dropped eleven degrees," in comparison to the one in Hill House, which is "considerably colder" (Jackson 1999: 119). His interest lies more in names of places, dates and values than in the meaning or impact of the phenomenon at hand. In this way *The Haunting of the Hill House* introduces a balance for Eleanor's increasingly unstable emotional and susceptible perception of Hill House and all that is happening around her.

At first the guests experience only vague, unspecified unease. The ghastly, unnerving atmosphere of Hill House, cold spots and the bizarre interior of the house fills the haphazard group with anxiety manifesting itself only in casual, undirected remarks. It is not long, however, before the occurrences taking place in Hill House begin to escalate. The first genuine moment of terror that cannot be attributed to imagination comes at night, when Eleanor awakens to what she initially believes to be her mother calling her name: "*Eleanor,* she heard, *Eleanor....* Then she thought, with a crashing shock which brought her awake, cold and shivering, out of bed and awake: *I am in Hill House"* (Jackson 1999: 127). Eleanor realizes that it was Theo calling her and joins her in her bedroom, and it is then that both women share their first experience in Hill House that is clearly supernatural in origin: the mysterious sound outside in the corridor. The passage introduces the phenomenon as something minor at first, even innocuous. "It is only a noise," Eleanor thinks to herself, and so does Theo. Steadily, the pounding on the door becomes louder and more menacing, more fervent. It moves away from Theo's room only to return moments later, louder. The occurrence witnessed by the women is tremendously interesting for at least two reasons. For one, the phenomenon is limited to the sound. Whatever is making the noise remains unseen, hidden from Eleanor's and Theo's sight. Furthermore, the source of the mysterious pounding keeps outside throughout the whole occurrence. Eleanor and Theodora have no way of knowing what it is that is seeking them; they only hear the sound and feel the piercing cold. The thing that is trying to get in is right behind the door, but dissociated, uninvited. The sound is threatening, but no intrusion takes place, although whatever is outside the door tries again and again:

> It started again, as though it had been listening, waiting to hear their voices and what they said, to identify them, to know how well prepared they were against it, waiting to hear if they were afraid. So suddenly that Eleanor leaped back against the bed and Theodora gasped and cried out, the iron crash came against their door, and both of them lifted their eyes in horror, because the hammering was against the upper edge of the door, higher than either of them could reach, higher than Luke or the doctor could reach, and the sickening, degrading cold came in waves from whatever was outside the door [Jackson 1999: 130].

Jackson manages to create a truly unforgettable, intense horror moment in this fragment. The threat is right outside, and Eleanor and Theo are separated from it only by the thin wood of the door. They do not know what it is that is trying to get in, and they seem to be unable to even imagine what it might be. The sound itself is deep and has an iron quality to it; it resonates on a height unattainable for any current resident of Hill House. More importantly, the source of the sound is apparently also the source of the paralyzing cold filling the room. The most important feature of the presence outside is the consciousness the women attribute to it ("as though it had been listening, waiting"). The narrative decidedly supports this notion; a variety of words and phrases indicating awareness and purposefulness is used, constructing the threat as not only capable of thought, but also vicious. In reaction to Eleanor's refusal to open the door, the presence reacts with determination and clear intent ("it was going to make its own way in," Jackson 1999: 131). The attributed intelligence becomes a certainty when the presence, carrying out its intent, stops demanding to be let in and instead begins to look for a way inside, "feeling the edges of the door," making "seeking sounds" (Jackson 1999: 131). Then, as it is unable to force its way in, the thing outside displays a disturbing emotional outburst—driven to fury, it begins to hammer at the door again. Eventually, it lets out a giggle that turns into a mad, gloating laughter. The presence is intelligent, relentless, sly and ominous, but it is also apparently insane, which makes it even more terrifying.

One of the strong points of Jackson's novel is the enigmatic character of the haunting that takes place in Hill House. The precise nature of the darkness filling Hill House is never really specified. It is alluded to and characterized, but it is not explained. It is unclear what it is that dwells in the house, and whether it is just one presence or more. The guests experience many diverse phenomena that seem to be unconnected; occurring in different parts of Hill House, with no particular order or timing to them (sometimes they even occur simultaneously), the happenings give no definite indications regarding the nature of the threat hidden in the house. One of the following nights, Eleanor once more bears witness to a supernatural incident. Once more she hears sounds, but this time the sound is a human voice. Initially just one, it is joined by others after some time, until Eleanor can discern three individual sounds, alternately mumbling, laughing and crying:

> From the room next door, the room which until that morning had been Theodora's, came the steady low sound of a voice babbling, too low to for words to be understood, too steady for disbelief. Holding hands so hard that each of them could feel the other's bones, Eleanor and Theodora listened, and the low, steady sound went on and on, the voice lifting sometimes for an emphasis on a mumbled word, falling sometimes to a breath, going on and on. Then, without

warning, there was a little laugh, the small gurgling laugh that broke through the babbling, and rose as it laughed, on up and up the scale, and then broke off suddenly in a little painful gasp, and the voice went on.... Then the little gurgling laugh came again, and the rising mad sound of it drowned out the voice, and then suddenly absolute silence. Eleanor took a breath, wondering if she could speak now, and then she heard a little soft cry which broke her heart, a little infinitely sad cry, a little sweet moan of wild sadness. It is a child, she thought with disbelief, a child is crying somewhere, and then, upon that thought, came the wild shrieking voice she had never heard before and yet knew she had heard always in her nightmares. "Go away!" it screamed. "Go away, go away, don't hurt me," and, after, sobbing, "Please don't hurt me. Please let me go home," and then the little sad crying again [Jackson 1999: 162].

The complex composition of this phenomenon poses a number of questions. Firstly, it is unknown whether Hill House is haunted by actual entities, or simply by the past echoes of what had taken place in it. It is known that it was Hugh Crain who built Hill House for his family, a wife and two daughters, who spent their days alone in the house after Mrs. Crain died tragically before ever setting foot in Hill House. What happened to the girls during the long years after their mother's death or what their relationship with their father was like is never revealed to the reader. It is, however, disclosed that Hugh Crain married two more times, and neither wife lived very long. Whatever might have taken place in Hill House during that time is never brought to light in the narrative. Secondly, if the house does harbor a presence (or multiple presences), it is difficult to estimate the exact number of them—whether it is just one consciousness or several distinct ghost entities, or perhaps even one collective entity comprised of an assembly of such entities. Many souls could possibly be tied to Hill House—those of Crain's daughters, Crain's wives, even the spirit of Crain himself. Thirdly, there is a practical possibility that Hill House is an individuality of its own, and superior to whatever it may be holding inside. In other words, Hill House does not simply provide a field for the ghosts or supernatural phenomena that occur inside it, but encompasses those ghosts and phenomena, bringing them together and governing them into one united organism. In a way, it is not Hill House that is haunted, but it is Hill House that haunts its guests.

It also is important to note the influence Hill House has on the attitudes and minds of its inhabitants. Theo, Luke and Doctor Montague are not in a hurry to leave the house despite all the occurrences, and neither is Eleanor. On the contrary, it would appear that the strange happenings somehow put her troubled mind in sync with the house. After her initial apprehension, Eleanor undergoes a change of heart and does not feel threatened by Hill

House anymore; she is happy and full of energy (Jackson 1999: 136). Both in terms of plot and in terms of the horror factor, this moment is a turning point in *The Haunting of Hill House*. For Eleanor to properly perform her function as a horror narrative protagonist, there must exist a bridge of understanding between her and the readers. Eleanor is the protagonist with whom the readers should identify, and her complete lack of a self-preservation instinct potentially undermines her role. Instead of striving to keep Eleanor in the place of a conventional protagonist, the narrative of *The Haunting of Hill House* makes use of Eleanor's unstable mindset as a very effective horror conductor. It is questionable whether Eleanor is losing the touch with reality or whether she is becoming possessed by Hill House. It is certain, however, that the house does affect Eleanor in a way it does not (or cannot) affect anyone else. She understands that Hill House is slowly absorbing them. This makes Hill House a particularly ghastly case of a haunted house, because it represents a danger far more menacing than the simple physical peril one might expect to encounter in a haunted house. Hill House is a threat to the soul; it invades the mind. As we observe Eleanor throughout the course of the story, we can see how her sense of reality slowly dissolves as she is being pulled into the darkness of Hill House. In a manner of speaking, Hill House gradually sucks Eleanor out of the world of the living even before her death, depriving her of individuality. In this respect, Hill House transgresses a conventional haunted house. It is not only the place of haunting, but it encompasses the protagonists into its haunting. Whereas an ordinary haunted house is a hostile and dangerous environment to anyone and everyone who might chose to enter, Hill House represents a two-fold threat. Those not chosen by the house are in danger of physical harm. Eleanor, on the other hand, experiences the danger of being chosen by Hill House. For her, Hill House is insidiously inviting and alluring, offering her understanding and attachment. The haunted house transgresses its own nature by becoming a place of imagined shelter. Eleanor feels accepted and appreciated; she feels like she belongs at last, and in her bliss, she drifts further and further away from the reality of other guests of the house. On the other hand, those who are not being seduced by Hill House—Doctor Montague, Theo, Luke—witness what they perceive as Eleanor's descent into madness.

    Distressed and suspicious, Dr. Montague attempts to save Eleanor by sending her away from Hill House. Eleanor, however, does not wish to be torn away from it; the thought of leaving appears so confounding to her that she laughs out loud and declares that she wants stay in Hill House, "walled up alive" (Jackson 1999: 240). At this point of the story, Eleanor has either crossed the line between susceptibility and delusion or is simply possessed by the house. Regardless of the cause, she is no longer a suitable anchor of identification for the readers. Instead, the readers can now relate to the other guests of Hill House, who are fully aware of the danger Eleanor is in. Doctor Montague, Luke, and Theo try to help Eleanor, but Hill House has no intentions of letting go of its prey. The house closes its trap before Eleanor can leave the premises; she drives her car into a tree, at the last moment wondering: "*Why* am I doing this?" (Jackson 1999: 246, italics in original).

Hill House, apart from being one of the most famous haunted houses, is also one of the scariest examples of that motif. It does not simply conceal a horde of hostile entities within its walls, but instead it itself constitutes a menacing entity. It actually *does* eat Eleanor alive, just like Theo said, and very much like the monster Eleanor initially imagined it to be. It is difficult to ascertain what exactly pulled Eleanor into the darkness of the house, but it in the end Eleanor cannot escape Hill House and is absorbed by it. The novel ends with a disquieting passage whose structure mirrors accurately the structure of the opening paragraph of *The Haunting of Hill House*. This resemblance only emphasizes nature of Hill House—a timeless, powerful presence that blends and fuses together with the ghostly entities inhabiting it, pulling in more souls, sharing its insanity:

> Hill House itself, not sane, stood against its hills, holding darkness within; it had stood so for eighty years and might stand for eighty more. Within, its walls continued upright, bricks met neatly, floors were firm, and doors were sensibly shut; silence lay steadily against the wood and stone of Hill House, and whatever walked there, walked alone [Jackson 1999: 38].

Now Eleanor walks alone in Hill House—the readers never really find out, however, whether it indeed is what she wanted. *The Haunting of Hill House* is a horror narrative that instead of perceptible, material danger[2] relies on the concepts of loneliness, oblivion, ceasing to exist. Hill House resembles a labyrinth in which not only the bodies, but also the minds of its inhabitants wander and lose their way. It dissolves and consumes everything and everyone into itself, always awake and forever insane.

Another title that takes up the theme of haunting is *Julia*, a 1975 novel by Peter Straub. The novel centers around a bereaved, emotionally disturbed woman, Julia Lofting, who has recently lost her only daughter. Julia tries to start a new life by separating from her husband and buying a house to live in all by herself. There is, however, something else that dwells in the house, a fact that Julia learns even before she sets foot inside as a proper owner. In contrast to many ghost narratives, which tend to present the first encounter with the ghost in an uncanny, hair-rising incident that takes place after dark, *Julia* introduces its ghost in a casual, concise fashion—and in broad daylight, without even indicating that there might be anything supernatural about the little girl who resembles Julia's deceased daughter. It is only when Julia keeps running into the strange girl in various places—on the street, in the park—that the readers may begin to suspect that the child is not all that she seems. Nearly at the same time strange things begin to take place in Julia's new home. The happenings, however, are very subtle, almost dismissible, and can at first be attributed to Julia's troubled emotions state—she has strange dreams, she hears rustling and hushed noises, and she feels a presence in the house. The strange occurrences bothering Julia are very moderate for a haunted house narrative—so moderate, in fact, that initially the protagonist does not interpret them as supernatural phenomena (and neither do the readers, in all probability). Instead, Julia suspects that it is her husband, Magnus, breaking into her house to stalk her. Unbeknownst to Julia, Magnus has indeed been coming to her house, only to experience the same disturbing sensation of a presence watching him:

> What was it that had frightened him that first night he had come in from the garden? He had been slightly more sober that night: he'd half wanted to pound sense into Julia's fuzzy mind, half simply to sit in her house and relish her atmosphere. He had lifted the vase of flowers to smell them. The house was a particularly taut web of noises, none of which he could identify. But he'd thought he could hear Julia moving about upstairs, talking to herself. Then, at first quietly, almost modestly, a feeling had grown in him that he was being watched, as if by some little animal. A feeling of eyes on him. Irrationally, this had grown: the mouse had become a tiger, something baleful and immense and savage. He had never felt such sudden terror. And it was as much despair as fear—an utter and complete hopelessness. Gripping the vase, he'd been afraid to turn around, knowing that something loathsome crouched behind him. Kate's death. That very second seemed to hang behind him, about to engulf him. His head had hurt intolerably. Something rushed toward him, and he threw down the vase, making an awful clatter, and raced outside into the little garden without looking around [Straub 1975: 124].

An interesting aspect of Straub's story is the fact Julia has just left a psychiatric hospital, where she had been recovering from her mental breakdown following the death of her daughter, Kate. The inexplicable, uncanny similarity between Kate and the phantom girl Julia keeps seeing obviously makes the audience wonder whether the haunting might not be happening entirely in Julia's troubled, broken mind. The readers find out only later in the story that not only Julia can see Olivia, but so can Magnus and Lily, Magnus' sister (just as it is revealed at a later point that Magnus also sensed a presence in Julia's house). Her ghost is, however, so seamlessly interwoven into Julia's psychosis that the horror aspect of the narrative is initially extraordinarily subtle. Julia is immersed in her dark, guilty feelings, in her love for Kate and her despair after Kate's death, and she is convinced that the girl appearing before her is Kate's spirit, for some reason filled with hatred towards her. In this respect, *Julia,* similar to *The Haunting of Hill House,* portrays a relationship between the haunting of the building and the haunting of the protagonist; it is not only Julia's apartment that is haunted, as she is haunted as well.

After the gentle start, *Julia* intensifies the horror atmosphere. The inexplicable occurrences in the house grow in intensity. Tableware and household equipment break, furniture is overturned, heaters turn on by themselves all the time. And yet Julia's thoughts turn to haunting only after two events that occur in close succession one after another. The first event is the séance organized in Julia's house by Lily. Lily's friend, Mrs. Fludd, asks Julia about the house and warns her that there might be something with it. She adds that Julia would only be in danger if she were "very receptive" or if she were "dominated by some strong destructive emotion," such as hate or envy: "Then, if the spirit wished revenge, it might influence you. That's rare, but it does happen, if the spirit is particularly malefic. Or, if some coincidence links you to it" (Straub 1976: 68–69). This conversation foreshadows two important elements of the narrative. Firstly, it emphasizes the difficult state Julia is in. The destructive emotion that fills her is guilt, although at the time of this conversation she is not aware of that fact. It is only at the end of the story that Julia (and the readers) learns that she was in fact responsible for her daughter's death. Mrs. Fludd's vague remark paves the way for one of the focal points of the narrative—Julia's recollection and acceptance of what she had done. Secondly, Mrs. Fludd's innocuous suggestion that there might be a coincidence linking the ghosts to Julia also turns out to be true, since it is revealed at a later point that Olivia was Magnus' illegitimate child. Her resemblance to Kate is, therefore, by no means coincidental, but a matter of course.

The second event that prompts Julia to start regarding the happenings in her house as supernatural is her discovery of the history of the house. Julia finds out that a mother and daughter named Heather and Olivia Rudge lived in her house before, and that Olivia was stabbed to death by her mother. She goes to see Heather Rudge in the asylum in order to ask her about Olivia. Heather reacts aggressively, telling Julia that Olivia was evil: "She was an evil person. Evil isn't like ordinary people. It can't be got rid of. It gets revenge. Revenge is what it wants, and it gets it" (Straub 1975: 131). At this point another aspect of the link mentioned by Mrs. Fludd becomes clear—while

Julia lost a daughter she profoundly cared for, Olivia had no one to care for her. She was rejected by her mother and eventually killed by her. In this way, *Julia* brings together two very distinct figures that naturally imply a connection: a forlorn, avid mother and a forlorn, avid daughter. Much later, after learning all the facts, Lily too notices that connection, and guesses correctly that Olivia "needed Julia to free her. Both ... daughters were stabbed to death by their mothers. Julia was what she needed" (Straub 1975: 239).

Once Julia discovers Olivia's story, her perception of the phenomena occurring in her house shifts, and she readily accepts the presence of Olivia's spirit as the cause of all strange happenings. When Julia arrives home after her visit to Mrs. Rudge, she is not taken aback by the mayhem that welcomes her upon her return. On the contrary, she interprets the disorder as the manifestation of Olivia's impatience. She believes that the girl's spirit is angry and demands Julia's assistance. Intent on finding out everything about Olivia, she temporarily forgets her fear and concentrates on her investigation of Olivia's life. The information she uncovers fleshes out the seemingly innocent, mysterious girl. Julia is told that despite her angelic face, Olivia was a corrupted, cruel and cold hearted girl who enjoyed hurting others. This makes Olivia an extremely interesting ghost figure. For one, she is (or rather was) a child, not an adult person. It would seem that emotions of a little girl could not suffice to imprint her spirit upon the house she used to live in. Nonetheless, Olivia's feelings are strong and violent. Moreover, Olivia is a spirit of an evil child. In contrast to the stereotypical role performed by a child spirit in a ghost narrative, Olivia is not a spirit of a girl who was hurt or unjustly killed. Her death was tragic and awful, but she was not wronged, or at least not innocently. The plot of Straub's novel is not layered, as at no point does Julia realize that what she believed about Olivia's nature was false. However, Olivia's nature makes it decidedly dimensional: Olivia is terrifying not only as a ghost—a supernatural entity—but as an evil, corrupted character.

It is exactly this moment, when Julia learns about Olivia's deeds, that the horror curve in *Julia* becomes complete. The potential mother-daughter connection is severed, leaving Julia afraid and reluctant towards Olivia. Once more alone in her sorrow and guilt, Julia can no longer relate to the spirit of the child murderess. She is now aware that there is no redemption or salvation for Olivia, because Olivia does not want to be redeemed or saved. There is only darkness and fury in her heart. Scared and heartbroken, Julia retreats to her bedroom, where she hides from Olivia's wrath:

> From downstairs came the noise of a rampage—she could hear glass breaking, a series of popping, hollow explosions, and ripping noises, fabric being torn. The

noises had started in the kitchen and then moved into the dining room. It sounded now like chairs being thrown up against the wall. I wanted to set you free, Julia thought, meaning that I wanted to send you away in peace. But you don't want peace. You want control. You hate all of us, and you hate this house. I did set you free, but in the wrong way. Wood splintered somewhere in the house, and this sharp sound was immediately followed by another series of popping explosions. The cups in the dining room. Then the broader, flatter sound of the china plates being broken [Straub 1975: 234].

In the entire novel, this scene is the most conventional haunting scene in terms of a haunted house narrative. The enraged spirit of Olivia is wreaking havoc on the house, throwing objects, breaking glass and furniture. The exceptional quality of this situation lies not in the nature of the phenomenon in and of itself, but in its extremely violent, destructive character. From what Julia can tell, Olivia's rage is tearing the house apart, although the exact extent of her aggression is left to the imagination. There is nothing Julia can do to soothe this fiery hatred because Olivia does not want peace.

Eventually Julia is taken by Olivia, although everyone she knew believes her death to be a suicide. Similar to Eleanor, she dissolves into the house and becomes Olivia's property. *Julia* is an ominous, uncomfortable ghost story with decidedly dark undertones, which constructs its narrative in a progressive, interrupted manner. Every time Julia reaches a certain plateau of fear upon which she grows more or less accustomed to the darkness surrounding her, she learns something new and plunges further into terror. In this way, the horror quality is gradually intensified, keeping the audience in the necessary state of apprehension. Additionally, Straub's story makes use of one of the more potent figures at the disposal of the ghost narrative, i.e., a ghost of an evil person, especially an evil child. A similar scenario is used in Tim Burton's adaptation of *The Legend of Sleepy Hollow, Sleepy Hollow* [1999], and in a Japanese horror film *One Missed Call* [2003], directed by Takashi Miike. All those titles overlap with the motif of ghostly retribution, albeit a warped one.

Not only places can be haunted, however. Sometimes the spirit (or a number of spirits) may haunt a person or a group of people, for a variety of reasons. While the haunting of places is usually associated with violent, negative emotions or events, such as anger or terror, or tragic death, haunting of a person may be caused by an entirely different sort of emotion. Among those, love, sense of duty, and regret are the most prominent ones. A title that explores both the concept of a haunted individual and the concept of haunting brought on by regret is M. Night Shyalaman's *The Sixth Sense* [1999]—a film popular enough to rekindle the demand for the traditional format of the ghost story (Phillips 2005: 194). *The Sixth Sense* pays tribute to the conventional atmosphere of an old-fashioned ghost-story, embellished by an original plot twist (Hutchings 2008: xxxii). It is atmospheric and beautifully shot, and, as Charles Derry notes, "[u]nlike the typical American film, [it] moves at a slow, even ponderous pace—more like the art house film of classic Antonioni" (Derry 2009:229). In contrast to the two titles discussed before, *The Sixth Sense* is "unusually quiet" (Derry 2009:229), both in terms of the score and sound effects used throughout the film, as well as in terms of ghosts' activity (the ghosts do not move objects or cause any damage). On the emotional level, Shyalaman's film is less concerned with sudden, pure terror than with profound, obscure dread. As Derry notes, *The Sixth Sense* is "moving toward transcendence and epiphany, refusing to wallow in violence" (Derry 2009:229).

Shyalaman's production employs a conventional (up to a point) storyline of an adult man trying to save a scared child from a danger of supernatural origin. It does, however, introduce an audacious twist at the end—a trick maybe not extraordinarily original, but most certainly well executed and thoroughly convincing. The proper horror narrative within Shyalaman's story begins with an excellent conductor of horror, i.e., a child. Nine year old Cole, raised only by his mother, is Malcolm Crowe's next patient—or so the audience is lead to believe. Cole is quiet, withdrawn and pale, and evidently troubled by something, all of which makes him a superb pivotal character for the purpose of a ghost narrative. Malcolm approaches him like any other patient; he asks questions, he makes suppositions, and he tries to understand. It is, however, clear that there is a wall between Cole and the rest of the world that impedes communication of any kind.

Cole is cursed (or blessed, depending on the point of view) with a unique gift. He can see spirits of those who are already dead. The interesting aspect of Shyalaman's film is the isolating nature of Cole's ability. Although surrounded by people, Cole is alone in a world that no one besides him can see. Cole's greatest wish is "not to be scared anymore"; there is no solace for him in the company of his mother or adults, characters who are normally figures of safety for a child. The impossibility of sharing his anguish with anyone makes the ability to see ghosts a secret Cole does not want to reveal—not to his mother, not to Malcolm. When Malcolm attempts to reach Cole, the boy tells him "You're nice. But you can't help me."

The "irrational" nature of Cole's gift is contrasted with Malcolm's efforts to find a rational way to help Cole overcome his problems. Philips points out that the balance of rationality and irrationality is something that governs the majority of the plot of *The Sixth Sense*:

In a familiar theme, *The Sixth Sense* suggests the limits of human knowledge. Just as with *Dracula* and *The Exorcist*, scientific knowledge is confronted with the unknown and is found wanting.... As Dr. Crowe encounters Cole, he is still wrapped within his psychiatric knowledge and unable to reach the young boy. His struggle to understand the boy parallels the audience's efforts to understand the film. Interestingly, while we see Cole's reaction to his haunting experiences, it is only after he has confessed his secret to Dr. Crowe that we first see the ghosts through Cole's eyes [Phillips 2005: 190].

Malcolm's scientific knowledge and experience is useless against that which threatens Cole, just like Doctor Montague's knowledge could not save Eleanor in *The Haunting of Hill House*. Some clues about the precise character of Cole's difficulties are given to the audience even before Cole's confession, in the form of Cole's remark about free associate writing (the text is shown to contain words and content beyond Cole's maturity) and flares on photographs of Cole (usually associated with ghostly presence in horror narratives). Those hints allow the audience to suspect that there is something more happening around Cole than simply his difficulties with interacting with others. However, it is only after his open admission in the most famous scene in *The Sixth Sense* that the extent of the hauntings tormenting him is revealed:

> COLE: I wanna tell you my secret now.
> MALCOLM: Okay.
> COLE: I see dead people.
> MALCOLM: In your dreams? While you're awake? Dead people, like, in graves, in coffins?
> COLE: Walking around like regular people. They don't see each other. They only see what they wanna see. They don't know they're dead.
> MALCOLM: How often do you see them?
> COLE: All the time. They're everywhere.

As Cole delivers his confession in a trembling voice, the terror he has been living in until that moment becomes clear to the audience. Apart from the traditional function of his speech, i.e., conducting the horror factor from the little boy on the screen to the viewers on the other side of the screen, Cole's words also establish *The Sixth Sense* as an instance of one of the most interesting variations of the haunting narrative. As Cole explains to Malcolm that the ghosts he sees "walk around like regular people," unaware that they're dead, and that they are "everywhere," *The Sixth Sense* reverses the traditional framework of the ghost story, specifically the haunted house story. In Shyalaman's production, it is not one particular place that is haunted, but every place. For Cole, the whole world is a haunted house.

The ghosts that appear to Cole are spirits of random people who met tragic death. Just as Cole tells Malcolm, they are unaware of their situation, seemingly looped in accidental moments of their lives, sometimes capable of interaction, but mostly trapped in what they perceive as their reality. What makes them special in the light of this analysis is that their lack of any purposeful hostility; they are not there to "haunt" Cole in any conventional sense of that term. In fact, they represent a variety of ghost figures specific to American fiction (especially American cinema) that is comparatively rare in Japanese fiction: an "unaware" ghost.[3] The "unaware" ghost is a spirit deprived of the awareness of its own situation and, therefore, one that does not display any intentional behavior towards the beholder and does not consciously pursue resolution to its unfinished affair. The majority of the ghosts encountered by Cole are such stray spirits who seek no one and nothing in particular. Their ignorance does not, however, diminish their scariness.

Even when Cole finally shares his secret with Malcolm, Malcolm does not believe him until he listens to a therapy tape of his failed patient and hears the recorded voice of a spirit. His "conversion" from the rational attitude of disbelief to acceptance of the supernatural, and subsequent conversation with Cole, establish the second pivotal point of the film—Malcolm suggests to Cole that perhaps the ghosts only seek his help and might go away if Cole indeed tries to help them. This moment is particularly significant for *The Sixth Sense* as a horror narrative. The storyline deflects from the horror at this point and develops into a drama film, focusing on the relationship between Cole and his mother as well as Malcolm and his wife. Although the peculiar mix of horror and drama is one of the defining features of any ghost story, Shyalaman's production not so much blends the two as much as it shifts the balance from one to the other. The horror potential of *The Sixth Sense* automatically dissipates once we learn that some of the ghosts can and want to interact peacefully with the living in order to attend to their unfinished affairs (like the ghost of the poisoned girl, Kyra). This illustrates an immensely important principle of the Euroamerican ghost story; the ghosts are only scary as long as they remain in the realm of the strange and unfamiliar—in other words, as long as they assume the role of the Other. Once Cole learns how to speak with the dead, he assumes control over the relationship between him and the ghosts and is no longer afraid. The horror element fizzles out and gives way to the dramatic and psychological aspects of the plot. In combination with the final twist of the Shyalaman's story, namely the fact that Malcolm is also a spirit, having died at the beginning of the film, *The Sixth Sense* constructs the ghosts as uncanny but essentially harmless beings who simply need the help of the living. It is also worth noticing that once Cole accepts the dead as helpless beings instead of monsters, he tells his mother that he is "ready to communicate" with her, thus symbolically leaving the world of the dead. By integrating an unconventional approach to the classic ghost story and psychological aspect of the haunting as well as the haunted, *The Sixth Sense* offers one of the most consistent and fullest, both in detail and substance, portrayals of the ghost among the Euroamerican horror ghost narratives.

The Sixth Sense is naturally layered as a narrative, but since those layers are not employed to amplify the horror, they are not discussed in detail here. A film that is layered similarly and makes full use of that fact for the purpose of scaring the audience is the next title discussed here, the 2001 film *The Others,* directed by Alejandro Amenábar.[4] Although following the same premise of employing a ghost protagonist, Amenábar's production, in contrast to *The Sixth Sense,* constructs a more traditional setting and aesthetics, suitable for a conventional haunted house story. The film follows a mother, Grace, living with her two small children in a secluded country house in the British Crown Dependency of Jersey, just after World War II. Out of the blue, three strangers appear on her doorstep, asking to be hired as servants. About the same time, strange things begin to happen around the house. Grace's children, Anne and Nicholas, believe that their house is haunted, but Grace is not ready to accept that possibility. Like every protagonist mentioned so far, Grace is a troubled woman. Neurotic and irascible, forever torn between the concern for her children's safety and her harsh Catholic upbringing, Grace is not the most amiable main character, but she is certainly a perfect conductor for fear.

In terms of the horror quality, *The Others* is extremely cleverly set up. Grace's children suffer from a rare disease that makes daylight dangerous to their lives (the description of the children's disease is consistent with extreme cases of a disease that actually exists, *xeroderma pigmentosum*). The fog that permanently surrounds the house locks it in some indeterminate season that could be either spring or autumn just as much as a very mild winter or a very cold summer. Within the narrative concerning Anne and Nicholas, the house exists in a time of perpetual night, night that can never come to an end and from which there is no relief of dawn. When Grace or the servants interact with each other, on the other hand, they are subject to the normal passage of day and night. Thus the scenes that take place during the daytime take on a relatively hyper-real tinge, which simultaneously gives all the scenes in which the children appear a more profoundly ghostly quality. Therefore, whenever Grace or the servants are with the children, they are imprisoned in an unending ghost hour, a time of no time at all, where clocks are of no consequence. The subtle, melodious score with the prevalence of flute music only emphasizes the fantastic atmosphere of the film.

The house itself is an ideal environment for a haunted house story. It is huge and spacious, full of unexplored nooks and crannies, and places out of sight of both the protagonists and the audience. Constantly darkened by heavy curtains, menacing, the house seems to be always filled with shadows, out of which the protagonists float out into focus and into which they disappear again. Grace's house is a place of overwhelming and simultaneously confining space of locked rooms. The creaking of heavy wooden doors and the jingling of many keys mark out every transition from room to room. Once the strange happenings typical for a haunted house begin to take place, the image of a conventional haunted house is complete. Anne claims that she can see a strange boy in the house; a piano is heard from inside a locked room when no one is inside. Among unfamiliar sounds and loud noises, abrupt thuds and whispering voices, Grace begins to fear that she might be losing her mind.

Despite her frail frame of mind typical of a horror protagonist, Grace resembles Malcolm in her rigid, uncompromising refusal to accept a paranormal explanation of what is happening around her. Her resistance, however, does not originate from a rational, scientific attitude, as it was the case with Malcolm, but from her religious beliefs. Her mind is not incapable of comprehending the supernatural at all, as she is an ardent Catholic—on the contrary, it is her faith in a specific supernatural order that prevents her from considering alternatives with an open mind—which can be observed in the scene where Grace, having introduced the newly hired servant, Mrs. Mills, to her duties, adds that her son and daughter tend to express strange ideas that Mrs. Mills should unconditionally disregard.

With this introduction, Amenábar's film prepares the audience to regard Anne and Nicholas as peculiar barometers of the supernatural. As is usually the case with a multitude of horror narratives, the children are the characters who are the most susceptible to any supernatural influence. Grace's stubborn opposition of all supernatural explanations of the phenomena taking place in the house further implicates that her children are the ones who are capable (or, at least, more capable than Grace) of perceiving the truth. At this point the film also establishes the first layer of horror, structured as a "haunted house" scenario.

Just as the children are indicated as the characters sensitive to the supernatural, the servants hired by Grace at the beginning of the film are presented as untrustworthy, suspect figures. They are a strange group consisting of one elderly woman, one elderly man and one young woman, not related by blood.

They appear out of nowhere, and from the moment they enter the house, their behavior is secretive and questionable. Their enigmatic, vague conversations and bizarre, ominous actions such as concealing the graves in the garden naturally evoke distrust in the audience. Against silent, timid Lydia and cheerful Mr. Tuttle, it is Mrs. Mills who gives off an air of menacing presence. Her inviolate composure and incessant comments and remarks provide a contrast with rash, sharp-tempered Grace, to whom control and security are extremely important issues. Especially the house and the children are the two aspects of her life she wishes so hard to control and to derive a sense of security from that control. She controls the house by locking and unlocking the doors, ordering the servants around and demanding silence, claiming that it is something that is "prized very highly in the house," and she maintains control over her children by giving them abstract tasks and punishments, and forcing her religious beliefs upon them.

The religious aspect of her behavior is actually very significant. As already mentioned, Grace is a devoted Catholic; she dedicates much time and attention to her faith. One might argue that her search of consolation and peace of mind in the complicated dogmas (e.g., the complicated system of four hells she demands her children memorize) is actually a sign of her desperate need of control over her spiritual life (which is interesting in the context of the subversive ending of the film, which contradicts the strongly Christian tone of the film until that point). Her reliance on the rules is so absolute that even after the incident in the junk room, where she has just experienced the strange presence for herself, and the following events in the living room, Grace wavers but cannot completely reject what she had been taught. Fixed and frozen in her doctrine, she is torn between her experience and what she believes to be the god-given truth. Certain that her god would never allow the "aberration" of the dead interacting with the living, Grace refuses to even name the presence she felt in the living room. The word "ghost" never actually crosses her lips; instead she says that she felt something "diabolical" and "not human," or "not at rest," because the alternative is "an unacceptable representation of being dead" (Giral and Rosales in Hansen 2011: 282). To accept the possibility of her house being haunted would require Grace to reject or at the very least critically consider what she has regarded her whole life as the order of the universe. Grace, however, is not ready to relinquish her control over the house and over her life just like that. In a desperate attempt to fight the changing reality, she attempts to summon a priest to bless the house, but the fog does not allow her to pass and she wanders for some time, lost. The fog seems to apportion the borders of the spiritual realm in which she is trapped. Grace cannot get out, but instead she stumbles into her husband, Charles, who died in combat during the war. The two of them interact briefly, and after this intermission Grace once again chooses to dismiss the idea of ghosts haunting her house. Only after an immediate threat presents itself, as Grace wakes up one day to find all the curtains in the house gone, her resolution falters. Having chased the servants away from the house, she discovers that Mrs. Mills, Lydia and Mr. Tuttle were actually dead all along. Abandoning all pretense, Mrs. Mills attempts to reason with Grace, but to no avail:

> MRS. MILL: We've been trying to make you understand.
> GRACE: Understand what?
> MRS. MILL: About the house. About the new situation.
> GRACE: What situation?
> MRS. MILL: We must all learn to live together, the living and the dead.
> GRACE: If you're dead, leave us in peace! Leave us in peace! Leave us in peace!

With this revelation, the film enters the second layer of horror; it is now obvious that the servants are dead and Grace and her children have been interacting with their spirits. Still convinced that she is alive (as is the audience at this point), Grace does not want to hear Mrs. Mills' explanation; she assumes that the strange presence and the servants are one and the same, or at least that they belong to the same realm. Despite being confronted with the spirits face to face, Grace is unable to adjust her rigid attitude, and still denies that which is obvious to the all the other characters and the audience. For a protagonist of a horror narrative, Grace is rather extraordinary in this regard. In the majority of horror narratives, the protagonist's awareness of the supernatural threat advances concurrently with the audience's understanding of the nature of the depicted horror. Grace, however, resists the understanding long after the audience has become accustomed to the concept of ghosts. There is a very important reason for this, as the audience learns at the end of the film.

At this point, the film enters the last of its horror layers. The audience finds out that all the people seen living in house are in fact spirits of the dead. Furthermore, it turns out that Grace and her children coexist temporarily and spatially with the living. Significantly, whenever Mrs. Mills tried to warn Grace earlier about the living, she uses the word "the Others," where an unsuspecting viewer might expect "the dead" or "ghosts." The only clue given to the audience is Mrs. Mill's remark that "The world of the dead gets mixed up with the world of the living," which the audience would obviously automatically assume to refer to ghosts. The other hints scattered throughout the story are the allusions to the "day Grace went mad." Talking to Mrs. Mills for the first time, Anne insists after the servants left "mummy went mad." The appearance of the husband serves to allude to the day when Grace had apparently done something atrocious. This mystery is solved along with the main mystery of the uncanny intruders. The "Others" turn out be living people who moved into the house where Grace and her children used to live, and the old woman whom Anne kept seeing (and, as Anne said, "asked her things") was a medium hired by them. Searching for Anne and Nicholas, Grace walks into the middle of a séance held by the current owners of the house. Grace's dramatic reaction—she drops her rosary to the floor and shouts "We're not dead!"—is significant in many aspects as it points to her symbolic journey that has been taking place throughout the story, from rejection to acceptance and from blind faith to doubt and loss. It is not the spirits of the dead that Grace so stubbornly refuses to believe in, but her own death and the death of her children:

> With the benefit of hindsight, we learn that Grace is doing the haunting but she does not want to be aware of it and keeps on searching for the origin of the haunting. Symbolically, she is looking for herself [Giral and Rosales in Hansen 2011: 283].

Although Amenábar's film makes use of the same underlying concept as *The Sixth Sense*, *The Others* turns the conventional structure of a ghost story back to front. It is the dead who are haunted and threatened by the living, and not the living who are haunted by the spirits of the dead. Consequently, the manner in which the figure of the ghost is constructed is far more complex and comprehensive, with emphasis on the feelings and thoughts of the spirits. Accordingly, *The Others* functions as a horror narrative on two levels. The first layer of horror is a regular horror narrative, with the ghost posed as the Other, a threat of unknown and incomprehensible nature, an intrusion into the cohesive fabric of the world of the living. On a more profound layer, *The Others* paints a horrific image of a mundane and endless afterlife full of loneliness, where no questions are answered, no doubts are dispelled and no resolution can be given to any unsolved affairs. On its primary level, *The Others* works very well, successfully reinvigorating the all-too-familiar genre of a haunted house story due to its innovative execution of a well-known concept, building up the suspense and dark, atmospheric aesthetics. On its secondary level, Amenábar's production displays the Other at an extremely close range without diminishing its uncanny potential.

In comparison to the Euroamerican representation of the ghost, the Japanese ghost does not necessarily have to be the spirit of a dead person. A wandering spirit may be a spirit of a living person, where the spirit has "left a body momentarily but the body remains alive" (Iwasaka and Toelken 1994: 18). An example of a living spirit is Lady Rokujō from Murasaki Shikibu's *Genji Monogatari,* whose wandering soul tormented and killed other women out of insane jealousy. Usually, however, the ghosts depicted in ghost stories are those of "genuinely dead persons," *shiryō* (Iwasaka and Toelken 1994: 18), although a broader term, more known in the Euroamerican cultural frame—*yūrei*—is also used (Tatarczuk 2011: 21, 28). In such stories, just like in the Euroamerican imagination, the *shiryō* is the "soul of a deceased person who for some reason has not departed for the land of the dead" (Tatarczuk 2011: 27). A typical image of *yūrei* existent in legends, *ukiyo-e* (woodblock prints or paintings) and *kaidan,* is a human silhouette, often times hovering in the air, who lingers around without a sound. The appearance of *yūrei* as it is depicted in popular literature and cinema is commonly very characteristic, and it most commonly involves a white burial kimono and loose, disheveled hair—both of which derive from funeral rites in the Edo period (Cherry 2009: 196). Although not all *yūrei* presented in Japanese fiction are the same, in the majority of them a number of characteristic features can be observed, such as long, disheveled hair or a white burial gown, often with faded feet. Most of those characteristics can be traced back to Maruyama Ōkyo's famous painting "The Ghost of Oyuki." Those kinds of motionless, silent ghost figures are featured in many traditional stories and legends (e.g., Lafcadio Hearn's *A Dead Secret,* where the ghost of a young woman merely stares silently at a *tansu* in which an important letter was secretly stashed). In longer, modern narratives, however, the ghosts take on not only more personality, but also more freedom and more power. They are rarely bound to particular places—instead, they follow people or objects, since their sentiment at the moment of their death is more important than the place of their death. Bridget Cherry additionally notes that "[the *yūrei*] is also associated with summer and humidity or water and haunts the living in a desire for revenge (as in *Ju-On: The Grudge, Honogurai mizu no soko kara,* and others)" (Cherry 2009: 196).

One of the more outstanding examples of a Japanese haunted house (or haunted place) story is *A Quiet Obsession* (*Mayu kakushi no rei*), written by Izumi Kyōka. *A Quiet Obsession* is structured like a campfire (or rather, candle-lit room) ghost story. Despite a fair amount of detail, the somewhat repetitive framework and at times broken continuity, the shape of the narrative that includes a recounted story within a recounted story give *A Quiet Obsession* a feel of authenticity crucial to a ghost story. In contrast to some of the American haunting narratives, Kyōka's story is not layered.

Kyōka's narrative recounts the story of Sakai, a traveler and apparently the narrator's friend. During his journey, Sakai by chance decides to stay in a small inn in the Kiso mountains, which he discovers to be haunted by a ghost of a beautiful woman with a peculiar habit.

It rains on the night of Sakai's arrival, and some time after that it begins to snow. Both the rain and the snow, as Charles Inouye points out in his essay about *A Quiet Obsession,* augur strange events (Inouye 1998: 300). After a peaceful night, uninterrupted by any occurrences of supernatural origin, Sakai experiences the first of many bizarre occurrences in the inn. Planning to take a hot bath, he goes to the bathhouse, which he finds illuminated not by electric light, but by an elegant lantern. He enters, but before he can even undress, he hears sounds coming from the room he believes to be empty. Notably, Sakai never catches so much as a glimpse of the ghostly visitor. The presence of the ghost is suggested only by auditory clues (the sound of water splashing against Otsuya's "body") and incredibly vivid olfactory sensations (the scent of her perfume and powder). For Sakai, who simply assumes that there was another guest in the bathhouse (as does the audience), there is nothing unearthly about this incident, but when Sakai mentions this seemingly innocent incident to the maid, she reacts in an astonishingly vehement way; she makes "a strange face, as if she were about to cry" and virtually runs away, making racket as she goes (Kyōka 2005: 81).

Soon after that, Sakai encounters the ghost for the first time. As he is looking out of the window, the light in his room suddenly goes out, and he feels cold. Sakai turns back to the room and sees a figure of a woman, described with an abundance of detail, including the colors ("blueish-gray" kimono, "white-and-light-crimson" sash, "dark violet silk band that showed blue"), patterns ("fine striped pattern") and even the texture (the fabric "damply clinging" to the woman, the hair "hanging" like a "drop of dew") (Kyōka 2005: 88). The sudden leap from Sakai merely guessing the woman's presence to the detailed, clear image of the ghost may seem abrupt, but it is consistent with the nature of *kaidan.* Japanese folklore can account for a whole variety of mysterious occurrences, and none of them need to be ghost activity. Objects moving on their own and inexplicable rustles and noises would not usually be interpreted by the Japanese as signs of haunting, because the majority of such phenomena is associated with various *yōkai.* For example, the experience of being watched by someone or something would be attributed to *mokumokuren,* the watching walls (Foster 2009: 66), moving objects could be the *tsukumogami,* common household items that have obtained spirit and life of their own (Foster 2009: 7), and oil disappearing from the lamp would be the fault of *himamushi nyūdō,* an oil-drinking *yōkai* (Foster 2009: 67). Whereas conventional

Euroamerican ghost stories, such as *The Haunting of Hill House*, offer sounds and bizarre phenomena as a ghostly presence, *A Quiet Obsession* introduces the ghost instantly, devoting a tremendous amount of detail to the spirit's appearance:

> She suddenly turned fully towards Sakai. She looked at him with her melon-shaped face, her thick eyelids and straight nose. Her skin was frighteningly white. She covered both her eyebrows with the paper, and looked directly at him with her big eyes. "Does this become me?"
> She smiled and revealed blackened teeth [Kyōka 2005: 86–87].

The peculiar behavior of the ghost is also not unusual to the Japanese ghost stories, where the ghosts can be concerned with the most trivial or strange matters, such as a letter that should have been destroyed (Hearn's *A Dead Secret*), or the incorrect content of the books (Hearn's *Shiryō*). Otsuya, the woman whose ghost is haunting the inn in Kiso, was obsessed with her appearance and the pretense—and so is her spirit. Although Otsuya did not die in the inn *per se,* she haunts its premises, including the rooms and the bathhouse. After Sakai's encounter with her ghost at the bathhouse and the maid's bizarre behavior, Isaku, the cook at the inn, tells Sakai the story of the woman who came to the inn a year before. A "stunningly attractive" woman, as he tells Sakai, "beautiful beyond compare"—Otsuya—came to the inn the previous year, exactly the same time of the year (Kyōka 2005: 88). She became transfixed with the story of the mysterious creature seen on the shores of the Bellflower Lake, a beautiful woman with shaved eyebrows (shaved eyebrows, together with blackened teeth, suggest being married—Inouye in Kyōka 2005: 63). Various incidents occurred and eventually it came to pass that Otsuya, accompanied by Isaku, was on her way to the village when their lantern went out. Isaku goes back for more candles, and during that time Otsuya is shot by an intoxicated hunter who mistakes her for the Bellflower specter (due to Otsuya's remarkable beauty and her inexplicable presence in the middle of the night on the road). It would be, therefore, understandable if Otsuya's appearances were related to the place of her death (the road to the village) or to either of the people connected to her death—Isaku, who left her alone on the snowy road, or Ishimatsu, the hunter who shot her. Instead, Otsuya's spirit is concerned only with that which occupied her mind when she was alive—her (perceived) marital status. Otsuya was not only involved with a married man and, later, asked to resolve another married couple's problem, but also seemed to long to become a wife. Otsuya's spirit is obsessed with being perceived as the loveliest and as married (Inouye in Kyōka 2005: 61).

After Isaku finishes his tale, Sakai's story also ends suddenly, without any observable resolution or conclusion:

> Sakai clenched his teeth. "Isaku-san. Don't be afraid. She doesn't blame you for what happened."
> But then the electric bulb in Sakai's room became a swirling comma. It floated darkly in the air, and suddenly a paper lantern appeared above their *kotatsu*.
> "Does this become me?" the beautiful one asked. And suddenly, the room filled with water, and snow carpeted the tatami like bellflowers blooming whitely at the water's edge [Kyōka 2005: 86].

Instead of appearing at the place of her death, Otsuya's spirit summons some of the place of her death to the room where she appears.[5] The room fills with water and snow, and, most importantly, with flowers—the symbol of Otsuya's undying obsession. Even in her final appearance, she never lets go of her fixation. In fact, her obsession in the end virtually identifies her with the Bellflower specter, as she is not referred to as "Otsuya," but "the beautiful one."

The abrupt ending may seem slightly unusual for a ghost story and most certainly a touch surprising for a reader accustomed to the modern narrative that "consistently keeps the past out of the present" (Inouye in Kyoka 2005: 167). Inouye notes that Otsuya's appearance and her question, "Does this become me?" "narrow the time frame of [the] narrative to the simple present, a moment of reunion when the living meet the dead and those who think they are still alive see themselves as being already dead" (Inouye 1998: 301). Kyōka's story represents both conventional and unconventional elements of a ghost story. The layered structure of the narrative provides a counterbalance for the traditional, almost old-fashioned content of the tale. The subtle character of the manifestations of Otsuya's presence and her influence over Isaku and the maid establish the extent of haunting to a degree much wider than a simple appearance might do. The addition of an independent character in the form of Sakai, who experiences the haunting but in fact remains only a witness, only enhances the genuine quality of the narrative. *A Quiet Obsession* is furnished with enough details and distinct elements to be convincing and realistic and simultaneously universal enough to retain the alluring charm of an old fashioned ghost story.

A more recent title employing the motif of a haunted house is a horror video game *Project Zero* (*Rei ~zero~;* the Japanese title is a play on words, as the ideogram that here means "zero" is pronounced as *rei*—which is also the pronunciation of a visually similar ideogram which stands for "ghost," "spirit," or "departed soul"), published by Tecmo in 2001. As far as this particular medium is concerned, the *Fatal Frame* (*Project Zero*)[6] series is quite remarkable

1. Ghosts 45

among other Japanese survival horror games. Similar to *Siren*, it established a convincing Japanese environment for Japanese characters. Whereas the producers of *Siren*, however, decided to introduce American heroes in later installments, the *Fatal Frame* series "remains within the chosen cultural frame and provides a clearly Japanese perspective" (Nitsche in Perron 2009: 202).

Tecmo's title starts out with a rather simple premise. Miku, the main character, is looking for her brother, Mafuyu, who disappeared in the ominous Himuro Mansion. Miku follows her brother and finds the Himuro Masion a terrifying, haunted place.

The primary horror factor in the game is, naturally, the ghosts who haunt the Himuro mansion. This differentiates *Project Zero* from other horror video games popular in the United States, such as *Siren*, *Silent Hill*, *Resident Evil* or *Kuon* [2004], where the player's avatar is assaulted by various monsters who surpass the player in size, speed and strength. Michael Nitsche points out that the horror in the series revolves around the fundamental opposition between the corporeal and the spiritual: the majority of the horror is "not necessarily physical but spiritual and its presentation is accordingly less tangible" (Nitsche in Perron 2009: 210). Any clear differentiation between good and evil regarding the ghosts is also avoided (Nitsche in Perron 2009: 210).

At the beginning of the story, the motivation of the ghosts is not clear, and to the player they are simply threatening, hostile beings who happen to inhabit the Himuro Mansion. Visually, they resemble a mixture of the Euroamerican depiction of ghosts and the Japanese conventional imagery. Whenever seen clearly, they are semi transparent, dressed in the clothes they happened to be wearing when they died, but their legs fade out into nothingness, just as it is with *yūrei*. They move in an interrupted manner, at times fairly slow and then, suddenly, lightning fast. They are not silent, although they do not speak as such; they only moan and hiss. At other times they are merely shadows on the wall. The game mechanics permits the ghosts to float easily in the air and through the walls and floors, as well as appear and disappear instantaneously behind Miku's back, which creates an atmosphere of constant tension and danger. As Ekman and Lanoski point out:

> *Fatal Frame* also uses the breach of humanness, this time in terms of living and dead. The monsters here are the hostile dead spirits of the mansion. These spirits are visually connotative of corpses, which can trigger disgust reactions. Many spirits are also portrayed in unnatural and painful positions, activating body mimicry and invoking images of pain, or deformation. In general, however, *Fatal*

Frame is utilizing disgust not in a gustatory aspect, but rather the notion of mental contamination, fear of insanity and spiritual decay. The monsters mainly use human vocalizations: they sigh, moan or lament. The sounds are often overly simplified and repetitive, which can be interpreted as another sign of mental incapacity. Spirits in *Fatal Frame* are hostile dead agents, but the main threat is not death, but a death without spiritual release. Again, the ambivalent nature of the spirit-monsters opens the way for multiple emotions: the player is invited to feel fear for and pity with the trapped souls, followed by joy as the spirits are relieved of their torment [Ekman and Lankoski in Perron 2009: 192].

Indeed, the horror quality of the ghosts does not lie in their presence alone. Many of them materialize before Miku in positions Ekman and Lankoski refer to as "unnatural and painful"; for instance, the ghost of the female guest who jumped off of the Moon Observatory in order to escape the Calamity always appears with her head hanging inertly over her back, glaring at Miku upside down. Another example is the Blinded Maiden, whose spirit is still wearing the mask that was used to pierce her eyes and blind her. What is even more disturbing, apart from the central ghost, Kirie, the spirits either repeat their last words over and over (e.g., the Blinded Maiden moans: "My eyes!") or call to Miku for help (Ogata and Tomoe can be heard doing that). At some point Miku encounters one of the priests slain by the Family Master, who repeats "Nobody leaves here alive."

It is worthwhile to devote some attention at this point to the instrument Miku uses to defend herself against the enemy that is not corporeal. Because Miku is surrounded by entities who can float through walls and floor as if they were air and have no bodies that could be injured and killed, it is all the more crucial that she has some way of defending herself. Miku's only weapon is an old fashioned camera (referred to as Camera Obscura in following installments of the series) which serves as an operational weapon, a familiar every-day device, and an occult instrument (Nitsche in Perron 2009: 206). As a tool for horror in *Fatal Frame,* Camera Obscura "builds on this combination of familiarity and unfamiliarity," both locating and simultaneously blurring "the threshold from the virtual to the real" (Nitsche in Perron 2009: 206). At the end of the story it is revealed that the camera contained a shard of the Holy Mirror, a sacred artifact of crucial importance to the success of the Strangling Ritual. In this sense, Camera Obscura is a link between the familiar and the unfamiliar. Also, as Nitche points out, the moments when the camera is actually used (at which point Miku disappears from the screen and the point of view is changed to the camera's viewfinder) dissolve the boundary between the virtual (that which is experienced by the player's avatar, Miku) and the real (that which is experienced by the player). In addition, given the manner in which Camera Obscura works against the angry spirits, it is impossible to discard the connotations of the prevalent but hard to isolate the superstitious conviction that a camera can steal the soul of those who are having their picture taken.[7]

Apart from the primary horror element, constituted by the ghosts, a secondary, background atmosphere of tension is built by means of bits and pieces of information that Miku encounters on her way. Left by other people who had previously ventured into the Himuro Mansion, the tapes, notes, diaries and scrapbooks facilitate the construction of the mansion as a proper haunted house with a dark past. For instance, the tapes recorded by Koji Ogata (an editor on the folklorist Ryozo Munakata's team), which Miku finds in a tape recorder, reveal to the audience that the Himuro Mansion had been empty for several decades and that the local people warned the team not to go there. Another fragment mentions a "white shadowy figure of a woman" that Ogata saw in the hallway near the entrance.

Apart from the haunted reality of the present that Miku experiences, the records allow the audience to participate in the mansion's haunted reality of the past. As Miku moves through the mansion and comes across more media left behind by those who were there before her, the dark past of the mansion begins to unfold. Tapes recorded by Takamine, a novelist, mention an old photograph, which depicts children playing tag. In the corner of the photograph the visitors noticed "a faint image of a young girl in a white kimono," looking "as if she [was] making some silent accusation…" Another tape, made by Tomoe, Takamine's assistant, found by Miku in the Anteroom, reveals more disturbing details—as Tomoe explains that the name of the woman in white kimono is Kirie, a ghostly whisper "Save us …" can be heard in the background. It is worth pointing out that in contrast to other popular horror video games, the protagonist of *Fatal Frame* does not interact with any other characters. She is completely alone in the Himuro Mansion, and the only voices that can be heard inside the mansion are the voices of the past.

From the materials and the visions she is experiencing in the mansion, Miku gradually learns the truth. The ghosts came into being after an incident referred to as the Calamity, a horrible disaster. The Calamity was the direct result of the Hell Gate (*yomi no mon*, also translated in the game as "Gates of the Underworld") bursting open when the Strangling Ritual (supposed to seal the Gates) failed tragically. Miku discovers the meaning and importance of this ritual after she comes across the Munakata's research documents, which assemble the bits and pieces of information scattered all over the Himuro Mansion. From those documents the player finds out that the "supposed purpose of the Strangling Ritual is to close the 'gate' to some sort of other-world," a gate that links the world of the living to the land of the dead. A disaster called the Calamity would occur if that gate opened, and the key to sealing the gate and preventing the Calamity was the sacrifice of a maiden by the Strangling Ritual. However, the last Strangling Ritual failed, and so the Calamity occurred. The Hell Gate flung open and Malice (*shōki*), a hellish force that was supposed to be held back by the Gates of the Underworld, spilled into the world of the living and spread throughout the mansion, infecting the spirits of everyone who died at that time. Because of this, the souls of all those who die in Himuro Mansion continue to haunt Himuro Mansion. Visitors who came to the mansion became cursed themselves, slowly beginning to bear the rope marks the last maiden bore, and eventually they died.

The central figure of the plot of *Fatal Frame*, and the primary source of horror, is the angry ghost of the Himuro Mansion, the last sacrificed maiden, Kirie Himuro. As the players learn halfway through the story, right before the Ritual Kirie met a young man whom she became infatuated with. The Himuro family sensed the danger and disposed of the young visitor, but it was too late—Kirie did not really want to die. Torn between regret and a sense of guilt over her beloved's death, her spirit was not strong enough to hold the Gates back. The Malice engulfed Kirie, and the malevolent, bitter spirit haunting the mansion was born.

Aesthetically, Kirie's spirit bears a close resemblance to the traditional image of *yūrei*. She is wearing the white ceremonial kimono she was wearing during the Ritual, and her long black hair covers her face. Around her neck and wrists the remnants of the strangling ropes can be seen. Her feet never touch the ground as she moves through the air or hovers within the cloud of the Malice over her head. Kirie's spirit is saturated with Malice to such an extent that it forms a visible, twitching and quavering tangle above her head, resembling a throng of ghostly bodies congealed into one mass. Within the *Fatal Frame* universe, the Malice is a force that makes the spirits of the deceased hostile and even evil, and in some cases can also affect the living, driving them mad. If the structure of the plot of *Fatal Frame* were to be compared to the conventional *kaidan* stories, the Malice might be an imaginative guise for the familiar concepts of *urami* (grudge) and *onnen*, which, in simplest terms, is anger powerful enough to affect the world of the living. Kirie's character, in fact, resembles spirits motivated by *onnen*. The crucial difference is that she has not actually been wronged in the proper sense of that word—she had been preparing for her role of the Rope Maiden for over ten years, and she understood what her duty entailed. Consequently, her end is not caused by fulfillment of retribution (of which there is very little to begin with), but by fulfilling that which she failed in her death: her duty.

Apart from the vengeful *onryō* of Kirie, the Himuro Mansion is also haunted by the an echo of Kirie's past feelings, specifically her unwavering resolution and sense of duty (this echo is, significantly, a "younger" manifestation). While Kirie's vengeful spirit acts upon the regret and anger, fuelled by Malice, the past reflection of Kirie is a representation of responsibility. Throughout the story she appears to Miku to help her or give her clues; she is the one who hands Miku the camera. At the end, she appears to Kirie to remind her of her duty as a maiden. She is not really an independent spirit entity, but rather a ghost of the past.

As the players find out near the end of the story, Kirie had taken Mafuyu because of his strong resemblance to her former lover, a young man who visited the mansion. When Miku finally finds all the pieces of the shattered Holy Mirror and puts them together, Kirie's spirit is purified of Malice and she releases Mafuyu. She then returns to the Hell Gate in order to perform her duty and to keep it closed, this time forever. The perception of Kirie's character that the audience may hold changes dramatically at this point, when Miku calls to her brother to run away, and Mafuyu declines. He explains to his sister:

> Miku ... The whole time Kirie was guiding me, I could hear her screaming. Screaming for help. As the Rope Shrine Maiden, she was destined to seal the gate. Yet she also wanted to be with the one she loved, but she couldn't have both, and was being torn apart by those two feelings, which resulted in the Calamity. Her spirit was touched by the Malice, and she became a creature that wanted to make others suffer, as she had. Now free of the Malice, she is about to fulfil her duty as the Rope Shrine Maiden. Her soul must remain here. Keeping this gate sealed off for all eternity, all alone. Endless pain. As long as she is free of pain, as long as she is not left hopeless, I wish to be by her side.

Mafuyu's words flesh Kirie out from a simple menacing, angry presence to a tormented, frenzied spirit tortured by conflicting feelings and memories. More importantly, however, they also distinguish Kirie from a prevailing model of the vengeful ghost. There is no one in particular that Kirie wishes to attack, and there is no revenge for her to take. Significantly, she also does not achieve peace in the end, but must carry on with her duty. Despite the presence of the once central spirit character filled with anger, *Fatal Frame* establishes its horror qualities as a haunted house narrative, not a retribution narrative. Tecmo's game blends in an efficient and effective manner the structure of a haunted house story, as it is known and recognized in the Euroamerican environment, with the atmosphere and landmarks of conventional Japanese horror fiction, in a complex plot-line based on a number of paradigmatic Japanese values such as duty, responsibility, and respect for tradition and family bonds. All of those characteristics make *Fatal Frame* not only a successful horror narrative, but also a fine representative of Japanese horror fiction.

Due to the fact that the haunted house narratives tend to involve the motif of bad death, which causes the spirits to be restless and angry (Long 2005: 68; see also Bestor and Yamagata 2011), oftentimes a haunted house story would automatically involve some elements of the retribution theme. Takashi Shimizu's *Ju-on: The Grudge* (*Ju on*), released theatrically in 2001, is such a title, falling into both the category of a haunted house narrative as well as a retribution narrative. The house featured in the film is not exactly haunted by Euroamerican standards, but the story originates within its walls. Shimizu's production centers on a place cursed by powerful emotions: rage, hate, fury. *Ju-on: The Grudge* opens with the following opening lines:

> Ju On: A curse born of a grudge held by someone who dies in the grip of powerful anger. It gathers in the places frequented by that person in life, working its spell on those who come in contact with it and thus creating itself anew.

This description roughly fits into the concept of *onnen*, a common theme in Japanese ghost stories. The innovative approach to *onnen* adopted by Shimizu consists of focusing that powerful force not around a person, but around a place instead. What is more, the "curse" spreads like an infection, spreading onto anyone who comes into contact with the Saeki house. Despite those traits, emotion remains central to the concept presented in *Ju-on: The Grudge*. Bliss Cua Lim insists that those opening lines not only explain "the supernatural blight that destroys a string of hapless protagonists," but also they "link death to memory, emotion, and place, highlighting *Ju-on*'s reinvention of the conventional haunted house motif" (Lim 2009: 206). In ghost narratives, Lim argues, space remembers, and the haunted place is in fact "a space of recollection charged with affect: alternately fearsome, thrilling, or tragic" (Lim 2009: 206).

Indeed, the storyline of Shimizu's film is not delivered in one smooth stream, characteristic to narratives centered around animate characters, but in arbitrarily arranged segments, named after the characters they follow, e.g., "Rika," "Katsuya," or "Hitomi." With the plot jumping back and forth between the past, present and future with six segments following six different characters all together, there is no main protagonist (or protagonists) to speak of. Instead, the story of the film revolves around the house, its dark past and the horrifying incident that took place in it, etched into the memory of the house, as Lim suggests. Most importantly, however, Shimizu's film focuses on the influence the house exerts on those who come into contact with it in one way or other—or rather about the influence of the horrible event the house remembers.

The film opens with a gruesome, grainy sequence of a murder committed on a young woman by an insane-looking man. The screen fades to black and, after the opening lines, the first segment, "Rika," begins. A young welfare worker, Rika Nishina, is on her way to visit an old lady. Before entering, Rika momentarily freezes in fear when she sees the house for the first time. Her reaction clearly conveys to the Japanese audience that the house is a bad place.

The Saeki house is indeed cursed. Years before, a man named Takeo Saeki murdered his wife, Kayako Saeki, in a mad fit of jealousy. Their son, Toshio, was never found. The memory of the horrific murder, as well as Kayako's despair and hate, linger in the house, and everyone who goes inside or otherwise comes into contact with it becomes affected; all installments of the *Ju-on* series revolve around the fate of those who come under the influence of the house. *Ju-on: The Grudge* focuses mainly on the family who moved into the Saeki residence—Katsuya Tokunaga and his wife Kazumi, Katsuya's mother Sachie and his sister Hitomi—but also on everyone else who enters the house and experiences something there, like Toyama, the detective, his daughter Idzumi and Rika. The "haunted house" layer of the narrative concentrates on the Tokunagas and the occurrences they witness, while the "curse" layer centers around the other people affected by Kayako's wrath. On the narrative plane, this difference manifests itself in the disparate nature of the experiences of the characters. Kazumi, Katsuya and Rika, being inside the house, observe phenomena typical for a haunted house story, such as strange sounds, looped echoes of the past (visions of Kayako, Takeo and Toshio). Toyama and Idzumi, on the other hand, who merely visit the house and leave, share a more extraordinary sort of haunting, where their present, past and future entangle momentarily (Idzumi's present from Toyama's future intertwines with Toyama's present—which, from Idzumi's perspective, is Toyama's past.) Lim points to this extraordinary structure as an essential, if not defining, feature of Shimizu's production—*Ju-on* reworks the traumatic space of a haunted house "through the motif of transposable contagion" and the "temporal and spatial reach of the terrible place," which is, in comparison to conventional haunted house narratives, enormous (Lim 2009: 206–207). Whereas in other haunted house narratives the protagonists are endangered only on the house's premises, the curse of the Saeki house is "place-rooted but peripatetic, able to snuff out several lives that come only indirectly into its compass, its malevolence reaching victims who seem to have been spared, only to consume them many years later, in other locales" (Lim 2009: 206–207). The Saeki house is like a quicksand, reaching through time and space for those marked by its darkness, and there is absolutely no way to escape its curse. Ordinarily, ghost stories tend to offer "emergency exit" procedures to the characters—appeasing the vengeful ghost or leaving the house that is haunted might eradicate the danger or at least diminish it. In *Ju-on: The Grudge,* neither is possible. Despite Rika's effort to understand Kayako, she still falls victim to the ghost of Takeo. Hitomi, having escaped from her brother's house, runs home and hides in her own bed, but is claimed by Kayako anyway. The most prominent trait of Shimizu's story is the suffocating sense of impossibility of finding shelter and the futility of running:

> *Ju-on: The Grudge* is a film that disallows its characters and, by extension, its audience, access to those conventional 'safe spaces' to which people most commonly retreat when the tension escalates or becomes too much to take. Peering through the fingers covering one's face does not distance the imperiled characters from that which is frightening; rather, it forces immediate confrontation with the horrific. Likewise, pulling the covers up over one's head does not provide a buffer zone but, instead, reveals that the monster you most fear has been in the bed with you the whole time [McRoy 2008: 98].

"Safe spaces" do not exist in Shimizu's film because there is no "unsafe space" to which the curse belongs. Both Kayako and Toshio remain predominantly on the premises of the house, but they can also follow freely anyone who has come in contact with the Saeki residence. As haunted house narrative figures, Kayako and Toshio are therefore shifted, misplaced. Misplacement characterizes strongly the overall shape of the whole plot and construction of *Ju-on: The Grudge:* the misplaced mechanical sound coming from Kayako's mouth, the misplaced cat's cry that Toshio makes, the misplaced objects (Hitomi's bear ornament lost in the Saeki house, which later mysteriously reappears in her house), misplaced temporal layers (Idzumi and Toyama's timelines). Shimizu's film constructs an unsettling environment with the aid of small details and sounds that play tricks on the eye and ears.

Ju-on: The Grudge is a very specific narrative. It introduces an innovative modification to the haunted house sub-genre, with the fragmented delivery of the storyline and the very concept of the nature of the haunting, portrayed as a seething, raging hatred directed not at any particular person, but at anyone and everyone. The independence of the two central haunting figures, Kayako and Toshio, of the house itself makes *Ju-on: The Grudge* a peculiar haunted house narrative. The misplacement of the elements and their lack of synchronization allows Shimizu's production to generate an unsettling atmosphere that lingers, haunting the audience.

Haunted house stories are a specific kind of ghost story that construct their narrative around contemptuous history, where the ghosts are locked in the point in space associated with something wicked that happened to them, instead of contemptuous deeds, in which case the ghosts follow those who had done something wicked to them. The haunted house narratives focus on events instead of persons. The haunted house itself can have many faces in the horror narrative. It might be an intimidating, menacing building that seems almost alive (*The Haunting of Hill House*) or a place with a dark, corrupt past (*Julia*). It may be a place seemingly secure but insidious to its inhabitants (*The Others*), a place of secrets and despair (*Fatal Frame*) or a place of a terrible harm (*Ju-on: The Grudge*). It may not be a house as such (*A Quiet Obsession*) or it may not even be a specific place (*The Sixth Sense*). The one thing that all haunted house narratives have in common is the protagonist who experiences the horror of haunting. The interruption of the dead past into the living present is what evokes fear in the characters—and consequently, in the audience.

Retribution and Curse

Euroamerican horror fiction concerning ghosts does not feature the theme of retribution as often, although it does feature revenge (which is not the same). There are also narratives featuring ghostly curses—such as Jay Anson's *The Amityville Horror* and its adaptations and sequels, or *Candyman* [1992], directed by Bernard Rose—but their focus usually lies elsewhere (in *The Amityville Horror* the characters do not so much interact with the ghosts as re-enact the tragedy, and in *Candyman* the ghost is merely an embodiment of an urban legend and can be replaced by another ghost). No specific laws of the universe explain the appearance of a Euroamerican ghost, although the emotions keeping it in the world of the living seem to be the same as in Japanese ghost stories: anger, anguish, suffering. American ghosts tend to demand justice rather than exact it, and for that they rely on the help of society, i.e., the characters.

The usual convention of American retribution narratives is well represented by *A Stir of Echoes* by Richard Matheson. The novel constructs a model scenario of a living protagonist witnessing the revenge of a spirit; the ghost wants justice, but it needs assistance and support. The vengeful spirit portrayed in *A Stir of Echoes* is full of resentment and hate, but it is relatively powerless insofar that within the Euroamerican world view hatred alone cannot change the world, unlike Japanese *onnen* (a concept addressed later).

The protagonist of Matheson's novel is Tom Wallace, a husband and father who leads an ordinary life until one evening, at a party, he is hypnotized by his wife's brother. Unbeknownst to Tom, a post-hypnotic suggestion is planted during his trance, which awakens in him psychic abilities he never knew he possessed. After that, Tom begins to sense and experience bizarre phenomena, like acute intuition and minor cases of clairvoyance. Among those phenomena, there is one that begins to dominate others: the image of a mysterious black-haired woman in a dark dress and a pearl necklace, whom Tom later identifies as Helen Driscoll.

The interesting aspect of Helen as a ghost is that she does not really know who killed her. In a manner typical of American ghosts, she appears to Tom from time to time and later communicates with him in one form or another, but apart from that, she does little else. She points, she presses, she nags, but in fact she needs Tom to uncover the truth for her and even bring the murderer to her. She does not act directly, and she does not interact with those who are directly involved. She intervenes only after being able to face the person who killed her.

Despite being able to sense the continual, strong presence of Helen's spirit in the house, Tom sees her only twice. Since Helen appears in the place of her death, *A Stir of Echoes* can be regarded as both a retribution narrative as well as a haunting narrative. The haunting aspect of the story is mainly psychological, not spatial—Helen does not affect the furniture or home appliances, but Tom constantly feels the oppressive, chilling presence of her ghost, sweeping away his willpower and paralyzing him (Matheson 1999: 56). Mainly, however, her presence is not overtly pronounced; she keeps to the place and does not appear until Tom discovers that he seems to possess psychic abilities. Initially, it looks like Helen's spirit is merely taking advantage of Tom's new talent; in the end, however, it turns out that his skills disappear together with her. Even when Tom sees her, she is simply there, like an emotional imprint left on the house, an echo of her anger and despair. In keeping with the greater part of American ghost narratives, she makes contact with few people and is also seen by few.

Despite the fact that *A Stir of Echoes* is a retribution narrative, Helen's spirit is for most of the novel more an angry spirit than a vengeful one, although it is clearly stated that Helen is driven by hatred, "violent anger" and "resentment" (Matheson 1999: 168). Until she learns the identity of her murderer, she cannot really desire retribution, since retribution is personal and oriented towards a specific person or people—and Helen Driscoll does not know *who* killed her in the darkness of her bedroom. Therefore, the only thing she wants from Tom at first is justice. She exacts retribution on her killer only after she learns the truth—the truth she needs Tom to uncover. Only through his assistance can she reach peace.

Eventually, unnerved by the fact that Tom is getting ever closer to the truth, Helen's murderer loses her nerve and reveals herself. As Tom and the audience—and, most importantly, Helen—learn, the one to murder Helen was Elisabeth, the neighbor who hated Helen for her promiscuity and, most for all, for luring Elisabeth's husband away from her. Not remorseful in the least, close to madness, Elisabeth boastfully reveals the truth, and Helen can finally take revenge, making Elisabeth face her:

> Elizabeth came backing from the hallway, an expression of utter horror on her face.
> "No," she mumbled. "No. No."
> She stumbled and caught herself, her eyes following something. *Something that moved after her.* I couldn't see anything but suddenly I knew what it was. I heard Richard crying.
> "Get away," Elizabeth said, her voice a hollow, inhuman sound. "Get away..."
> Her heel twisted under her and she fell back. A scream tore apart her lips. "Get away!" she howled. She jerked up the pistol and fired at the air; the explosion rocking deafeningly through the room. Richard screamed. With a choking, gagging sound, Elizabeth scuttled back one-handedly across the rug, saliva threading across her shaking jaw.
> "No," she cried. Abruptly, she raised the Luger to her own head and pulled the trigger. There was a clicking sound as the hammer hit the empty chamber. She pulled the trigger again, again; in vain. Then, with a wail of absolute terror, her eyes rolled back and her head thudded heavily on the floor [Matheson 1999: 209].

In comparison to a Japanese vengeful spirit, Helen is weak and non-intrusive—her presence is more tangible than visible (Matheson 1999: 56). She is capable of appearing to people, and she can communicate through a variety of methods, such as psychography (also known as spirit writing) (Matheson 1999: 158) and, much later, by means of speaking through Tom's son in a "hideous, doll voice" (Matheson 1999: 162). She does not, on the other hand, have any special powers—she cannot give visions (like Oiwa in *Ghost Stories at Yotsuya*) or curse people (like Sadako in *Ring*) or even interact physically with the real world (like Kayako in *Ju-on*). Also her appearance and behavior are rather underwhelming, as she does not glow, hover in the air, wail or climb out of walls or appliances.

A Stir of Echoes is a good representation of American retribution narratives. It creates an intense atmosphere of a subtle but relentless haunting by an angry spirit. Its main effect is produced by the juxtaposition of terror induced by a ghostly presence with so-called "kitchen-table" setting and "kitchen-table" tragedy. Both the place and the *dramatis personae* are surprisingly trivial: Tom does not live in a castle or a strange old house but in a suburban house. Also, Helen dies not at the hands of an evil mastermind or a cruel psychopath, but a jealous housewife driven over the edge. Those aspects of the narrative serve to enhance the realism of the story. By balancing skillfully the horrifying and the mundane, Matheson created a coherent, effective retribution narrative.

A great part of American retribution narratives is based on scenarios similar to that presented in *A Stir of Echoes;* examples include *What Lies Beneath* [2000] by Robert Zemeckis, *Gothika* [2003] directed by Mathieu Kassovitz and many others. The American ghost seeking retribution tends be able to approach its killer, or break through the barrier between the worlds, only during the final confrontation—after the complete truth has been revealed, and no sooner. Before that time comes, it needs an enormous amount of assistance.

In the American horror genre, *The Fog* [1980], directed by John Carpenter, is one of better known ghostly revenge horror narratives. *The Fog*, an atmospheric ghost story in and of itself, is above all a retribution tale, very similar in structure to many Japanese retribution tales. Carpenter constructed the narrative of *The Fog* like a traditional, old-fashioned ghost story in which all the facts are presented openly and in advance and the plot simply plays itself out, in contrast to the majority of American ghost retribution narratives, where the plot tends to be driven by a living person slowly unraveling the past.

The Fog tells the story of Antonio Bay, a small town on the coast, about to celebrate its one hundredth anniversary, and its inhabitants. Right before the day of the celebration strange, ominous events begin to occur; right as midnight strikes and the actual day of the town's anniversary begins, Antonio Bay is swallowed by a strange, luminous fog that brings with it the vengeful spirits of lepers murdered one hundred years ago by the town's founders.

The Fog opens with a group of children sitting around the camp fire and listening to an elderly man, Mr. Machen, telling them ghost stories. As the scene begins, Machen starts to tell a story that serves as an atmospheric, deliberately paced prologue to the film and presents for the audience both the past for Antonio Bay, as well as the future that awaits the town:

MR. MACHEN

11:55, almost midnight. Enough time for one more story. One more story before 12:00, just to keep us warm. In five minutes, it will be the 21st of April. One hundred years ago on the 21st of April, out in the waters around Spivey Point, a small clipper ship drew toward land. Suddenly, out of the night, the fog rolled in. For a moment, they could see nothing, not a foot in front of them. Then, they saw a light. By God, it was a fire burning on the shore, strong enough to penetrate the swirling mist. They steered a course toward the light. But it was a campfire, like this one. The ship crashed against the rocks, the hull sheared in two, mars snapped like a twig. The wreckage sank, with all the men aboard. At the bottom of the sea, lay the Elizabeth Dane, with her crew, their lungs filled with salt water, their eyes open, staring to the darkness. And above, as suddenly as it had come, the fog lifted, receded back across the ocean and never came again. But it is told by the fishermen, and their fathers and grandfathers, that when the fog returns to Antonio Bay, the men at the bottom of the sea, out in the water by Spivey Point will rise up and search for the campfire that led them to their dark, icy death.

Machen's narration in the opening scene performs two important functions. Firstly, it provides the audience with information about the real fate of Elisabeth Dane, which was wrecked from the shore by the Antonio Bay settlers one hundred years earlier by means of deploying false lights. Secondly, it establishes the atmosphere of Carpenter's production. Machen's ghost story is delivered at night, by a camp fire, to a group of listeners, in a manner reminiscent of traditional oral storytelling. As such, it is a very cleverly constructed ghost story within the ghost story that is the film. What is more, it is true—as both the events described in Machen's tale as well as the warning that the drowned will return with the fog actually take place in the film's reality.

The film then shifts to less dreamy, down-to-earth imagery. Right after midnight of the day of the final preparations for the anniversary celebration, strange phenomena begin to occur. Animals are upset, phones ring all at once, electric appliances randomly turn on, bells toll and lights flicker everywhere in town. All of those seemingly unimportant and non threatening events occur simultaneously; their insignificance is contradicted by their uncanny concurrence, and they serve as omens. Most importantly, together with all those small incidents comes the fog. Unlike any ordinary fog, it glows and moves against the wind at an eerie speed. It brings with it a phantom clipper ship, and on it the ghosts of the lepers, who seek revenge for the settlers' betrayal. Symbolically, the fog is a harbinger of death; it represents the invasion of the otherworld/afterlife into the world of the living and represents the crime originally committed by the settlers. Practically, it visually marks the areas where the world of the dead penetrates the world of the living.

Right before the phantom clipper ship and its ghostly crew, shrouded within the fog, appear for the first time by the coast, the local priest, Father Malone, finds the journal of his grandfather, Patrick Malone. The contents of Patrick Malone's old diary complements the "ghost story" told by Mr. Machen at the beginning of the film. It reveals the uncomfortable truth about the tragic fate of Elisabeth Dane and the history of the town:

December 9

Met with Blake this evening for the first time. He stood in the shadows to prevent me from getting a clear look at his face. What a vile disease this is. He is a rich man with a cursed condition, but this does not prevent him from trying to better his situation and that of his comrades at the colony.

December 11

Blake's proposition is simple, He wants to move off Tanzier Island and relocate the entire colony just north of here. He has purchased a clipper ship called the Elizabeth Dane with part of his fortune and asks only for permission to settle here. I must balance my feelings of mercy and compassion for this poor man, with my revulsion at the thought of a leper colony only a mile distant.

April 20

The six of us met tonight. From midnight until one o'clock, we planned the death of Blake and his comrades. I tell myself that Blake's gold will allow the church to be built, and our small settlement to become a township, but it does not soothe the horror that I feel being an accomplice to murder.

April 21

The deed is done. Blake followed our false fire on shore and the ship broke apart on the rocks off Spivey Point. We were aided by an unearthly fog that rolled in, as if Heaven sent, although God had no part in our actions tonight. Blake's gold will be recovered tomorrow, but may the Lord forgive us for what we've done.

These entries explain the tragedy that took place and at the same time establish the ghosts as wronged victims seeking satisfaction, and not mere murderous monsters. Additionally, it is worth noting that the vengeful spirits appear among the living two nights in a row between midnight and one in the morning. This period of time belongs to the spirits as it was at that time when the murder was planned by six of the settlers—it is also the time at which Elisabeth Dane presumably crashed against the rocks of Spivey Point and the crew of lepers drowned. One hundred years later, the fog appears in the town, and the ghosts appear for the first time at exactly that time: between midnight and one in the morning.

The ghosts brought by the fog are seldom fully visible. They loom in the fog patches, materializing within them, their faces almost always obscured with only a devilish red glow to their eyes. Their appearance points to the way they died—their clothes and hair are dripping wet and the skin is clammy and partially decomposed. It is also noteworthy that in contrast to the ghosts in the majority retribution horror narratives (both American and Japanese), Carpenter's ghosts carry various weapons, ranging from fishing hooks and similar equipment to swords. These weapons are not merely accessories and are used to kill their victims. The ghosts do not speak, and they do not chase or torment their victims, but immediately proceed to the task at hand. Their motivation is, naturally, retribution. Since their murderers are long dead, their wrath is directed at the killers' descendants. The toll they demand is six descendants, one for each person who took part in planning and executing the killing; Danny, son of Stevie, the local radio DJ, brings home a piece of driftwood, which is in fact a piece of the wreck of Elisabeth Dane (it is worth noting that initially Danny sees it as a gold coin, which is significant since the lepers were killed for their gold). Later that day, as Stevie is watching, a message appears on the piece of wood, reading "6 MUST DIE." The ghosts in *The Fog* stand out among their counterparts depicted in the majority of American retribution narratives in that they do not seem to care about uncovering the truth concerning their demise. In fact, Father Malone's discovery of the journal is purely coincidental and serves the audience rather than the spirits themselves.

One of the characteristic features of the specific stylization in which *The Fog* is structured, reminiscent an old-fashioned ghost story, is that the ontological problem of whether the ghosts exist or not is not emphasized. The characters seem shocked but not skeptic towards the extraordinary phenomena and are willing to explore them. This is visible when Father Malone reads the journal and believes its content without question—as do Sandy and Mrs. Williams—and when Stevie, after seeing the message "6 MUST DIE" on the piece of Elisabeth Dane wreckage, immediately calls her son and forbids him to pick up anything else from the beach and tells him to stay inside that night.

The Fog is a considerably famous ghost narrative title, and a rather remarkable American retribution narrative as far as its structure is concerned. The retribution motif is executed in the form of dramatic story rather than mystery; the ghosts do not need help, nor do they care for the living in any way. They come to Antonio Bay to exact retribution and they cannot and will not be stopped. In this regard, Carpenter's story is a rather isolated title, as the greater part of American retribution narratives fall into the same pattern as the previous title discussed in this chapter, *The Stir of Echoes*. *The Fog* is an effective combination of a contemporary setting, which includes cars, the radio, and electricity—all of which can be manipulated by the ghosts—and an old-fashioned narrative structure bearing all the characteristics of a classic ghost story in which the puzzle is waived in favor of an orderly, coherent explanation of the events. Instead of the living characters solving the mystery and paving the way for the ghost's entry, *The Fog* follows a direct plot of ghostly revenge, where the characters are not merely witnesses who accidentally brushed against the past, but are actual "heroes" of the story and of history.

Among many other American retribution narratives, one more title worth mentioning, however briefly, is *The Loveliest Dead,* by Ray Garton. *The Loveliest Dead* is predominantly a haunting narrative, but it does feature a retribution element. In Garton's novel, a family moves into a house in which, unbeknownst to anyone, a pedophile murderer raped and killed young boys. Both the spirit of the killer and the spirits of his victims haunt the house, and the family experiences supernatural activity and ambiguous messages (such as "HELP PUP-PEEZ," which refers to the boys tormented by the murderer). The main idea behind the haunting and the retribution motifs in the novel is idea that both the victims and the oppressor are dead; the ghosts of the boys are not even aware of the fact that they are dead. They still fear their tormentor (although nothing stops them from punishing a pedophile priest who happens into the house), and it is only after they realize that they are only spirits that they exact their revenge on their murderer. *The Loveliest Dead* is an interesting ghost narrative title because the retribution motive is not constructed upon the dead/living opposition. The struggle concerns only the dead, and the living get involved merely by accident.

Another noteworthy scenario is in *The Crow* [1994], directed by Alex Proyas (an adaptation of James O'Barr's comic book series of the same title). The pivotal motif of the film is ghostly retribution. The story of *The Crow* centers around a young man named Eric, whose ghost[8] rises from the grave one year after he and his girlfriend were brutally murdered. One by one, Eric finds and executes every person involved in the murder. Despite not falling exclusively into the horror genre, *The Crow* is one of very few American ghost stories with the central character being a ghost (or a creature strongly resembling one) who is motivated by revenge after being wronged in a cruel, undeserved way. It is also interesting to note that from the murdered pair it is Eric who rises, not his lover—whereas in a similar scenario in a Japanese narrative it is safe to assume that it would be the woman who would come after the killers.

The retribution is a much more prominent theme in Japanese horror fiction, as there exists a plethora of titles to choose from—especially since recently ghostly retribution narratives in the most genuine form have enjoyed a rebirth (Schlegel in Browning and Picart 2009: 269). The set of beliefs and practices of Japan equivalent to Euroamerican religious systems places major stress on the power of human *kokoro* (soul or heart) and the emotions born within it that can affect both the person feeling them and the person (or persons) it may be turned towards (Lebra 2004: 216). The emotion, regardless of its nature—whether it is rage, love, hate or sadness—can create a bond that will not only keep the spirit near the living, but allow for other phenomena. For example, in the short story *Of a Mirror and a Bell*, written by Lafcadio Hearn, the regret of a woman who had donated her bronze mirror to the Mugenyama bell was so powerful, that the feeling alone was enough to keep the mirror from melting inside the furnace (Hearn, *Of a Mirror and a Bell*). The rage of the man convicted to death in another story made his head, which had just been cut off, roll on and bite a stone, just to prove his determination (Hearn, *Diplomacy*). There are many reasons and motivations that cause the spirits to remain or return—some form of regret or unfinished business that keeps them in the world of the living, or, in most narratives, retribution. Many of the Japanese ghost stories are actually moral tales, describing stories of those who had been unjust to someone and then suffered punishment from the ghostly hands of their deceased victims (*Ghost Stories at Yotsuya, Banchō Sarayashiki,* etc). Almost all Japanese ghost stories are characterized by an underlying theme of justice; the retribution on those who have wronged the victim or treated them cruelly is something that cannot be stopped or hindered even by religious means or other spiritual rituals. This right to retribution seems to justify—at least to some extent—both the presence of the ghost among the living in the retribution narrative, as well as the cruelties induced by it.

In the Japanese cultural outlook the spirits of people who died peacefully (i.e., without anything or anyone they would be attached to so much as to stay among the living) are remembered, usually by the family members, and given offerings, since without proper rituals the spirit of the deceased might become a terrifying ghost that would wander and bring misfortune to the family (Stone and Walter 2008: 348). Such a wandering spirit in itself is an object of terror in Japanese culture, and a vengeful spirit all the more so. The Japanese tend to be fearful of *urami* and vulnerable to it, regardless of whether the grudge should come from the living or the dead (Lebra 1976: 44), so a grudge felt by a spirit can serve as a powerful source of horror.

Vengeful spirits are spirits who have most often died a bad death and are filled with hatred, rage or pain. This ill will or grudge, *urami,* is what drives them to interaction with the living (Smith 1974: 44). Such spirits, instead of resting peacefully in a family shrine, carry their *urami* upon the living; they bear a deep grudge and make those who hurt them the objects of their revenge (Plutschow 1996: 74). Anyone who died a bad death can become a vengeful spirit and cause evil. Spirits of those who died in specific "unnatural" circumstances, such as experiencing strong emotions (jealousy or grudges of any type), dying away from home (travel or exile), being a victim of injustice or not receiving proper funeral, were believed to be unable to rest until they either exacted their revenge or were placated by the appeasing efforts made by the living (Plutschow 1990: 204).

The concept of the grudge and retribution formulated in this way can be observed in most of the Japanese ghost stories. They are usually retribution tales, revolving around the concept of *onnen,* i.e., the idea that some emotions are so strong that they can reach from beyond the grave and affect the human world. *Onnen* is the driving idea of virtually all Japanese ghostly retribution narratives; it concerns those who died while in the throes of intense emotion. Usually, *onnen* is a grudge or need for vengeance, a hatred of someone who has been wronged, which comes from the consciousness of being a victim (see Pruett 2010, Perron 2009 and Ericson 1997).

An interesting characteristic of the Japanese vengeful spirit is its capacity to exert harmful influence not only on those who directly or indirectly brought about their grudge, but also those who are not related to the spirit's plight at all (Plutschow 1996: 73). The spirit can harm the villain and an unrelated witness alike. However, as Iwasaka and Toelken point out, no person is truly unrelated to the spirits;

> in many cases, the witness is an innocent passerby who is simply assaulted by a ghost whose uncontrollable passion results from the way he died, or the fact that the proper rituals were not observed in her behalf. But from the Japanese perspective, the apparently innocent victim may not be entirely exempt from involvement, for he or she is a member of the living, that group of people whose *obligation* it is to celebrate the souls of the dead. In this dramatic sense, anyone alive is fair game for the approach of a ghost [Iwasaka and Toelken 1994: 18].

In this sense, a vengeful ghost driven by *urami* portrayed in a Japanese retribution tale may sometimes cause more evil and bad deaths, creating an ongoing chain of evil that began with the victim and now goes on through the spirit's rage, thus creating new, previously unrelated victims. The *urami* may spread like a disease, but the revenge belongs only to the vengeful spirit. This can be seen in Oiwa's bloody toll in *Ghost Stories at Yotsuya* or revenge of Oshiga in *Kaidan,* Nakata's 2007 film loosely based on San'yūtei Enchō's *Shinkei Kasanegafuchi,* or Asa's curse in *Snake Woman's Curse* [1968], but also in contemporary narratives such as *Tales of Terror: Haunted Apartment* [2005].

Notably, the Japanese ghost demands from society that its soul be celebrated, but at the same time it does not require from the society any help with its retribution. On the contrary, the Japanese ghost does not point to their killer or direct others to find out about their demise, as the American ghost tends to do.

Tsuruya Nanboku's *Ghost Stories at Yotsuya* (also known as *Yotsuya Ghost Stories*) is one of the most famous traditional Japanese ghost stories. Despite the fact that *Ghost Stories at Yotsuya* is not a contemporary narrative, it is included in this work due to its immense popularity and representative characteristics, as well as its continuing influence on Japanese contemporary horror

1. Ghosts

narratives. Nanboku's play is, according to Richard Hand, the most frequently adapted horror play (Hand in McRoy 2005: 22):

> Thomas and Yuko Mihara Weisser cite eleven different versions between 1928 and 1994, all of which recount the same tale but variously shift emphasis from the cerebral to the violent or the sexual to the farcical. The most celebrated adaptation is the 1959 version by Nakagawa Nubuo [sic] ('the Nippon Hitchcock'), often regarded as a masterpiece of the horror genre. The Weissers do not discuss the silent versions of the story, and since their book was published, there has been the video release of an updated stage version [Hand in McRoy 2005: 22].

The appeal of Nanboku's story is so great that numerous adaptations, film and otherwise, of *Ghost Stories at Yotsuya* exist. To mention just a few, those adaptations include a novel *Yotsuya Kwaidan, or, Oiwa Inari*, written by James Benneville, as well as the opening stories in the anime series *Ayakashi* (*Kai ayakashi*) by Toei Animation [2006], as well as the first story in the TV series *100 Tales of Horror* (*Kaidan Hyaku Monogatari*), 2002. Nanboku's play still continues to exert influence over the Japanese horror industry.

Ghost Stories at Yotsuya is arguably the most representative title among Japanese retribution narratives. It contains the traditional Japanese vengeful ghost story themes, such as the concepts of betrayal and vengeance, and according to the kabuki ghost play convention the vengeful spirit is saved once it can exact its revenge (Plutschow 1990: 250–251). In this respect, kabuki plays, naturally including *Ghost Stories at Yotsuya,* are more closely related to the horror genre than nō plays (in which the ghost can be put to rest even it had not successfully avenged itself); the ghost's unstoppable and uncontrollable need to retaliate against its offenders, a need that cannot be extinguished with prayer or ceremony, provides a more solid foundation for horror.

The story of *Ghost Stories at Yotsuya* is relatively uncomplicated. Tamiya Iemon desires a young woman named Oiwa. He kills her father, Yotsuya Samon, who opposed this marriage, and then lies to Oiwa, telling her that someone else killed her father and that if she marries Iemon, he will avenge the murder. Their life in poverty soon bores Iemon, and when a young rich girl, Itō Oume, falls in love with him, Iemon jumps at the occasion. Hoping that Iemon would leave Oiwa to marry Oume, Oume's grandfather sends a disfiguring poison to Oiwa. Oiwa unknowingly takes the poison and dies in a fit of rage and hatred, cursing both Iemon and the Itō family, and Iemon blames her death on the servant Kohei. Her vengeful spirit appears during Iemon and Oume's wedding night, causing Oume's death, and haunts him until his death at the hands of Oiwa's brother-in-law, Yomoshichi.

As the most crucial part of the story—i.e., the second act—begins, it is clear that Iemon is an evil character, having committed murder, deception and blackmail. He imprisons Oiwa in a miserable marriage that makes both of them unhappy. Iemon loses interest in her and becomes resentful, and he neglects his duties as a husband and father. Even before Oiwa's death the audience is made aware that Iemon is responsible for Oiwa's pain by means of her soliloquy, when she says: "Living in this house is constant torture, with little wounds that never heal," and stage directions, which contain lines such as "*she hugs herself to endure emotional pain*" (Oshima in Brazell 1998: 465). In this way, they form the perfect villain-victim constellation of the Japanese retribution narratives, with clear and unambiguous division of roles. This is immensely significant, because the tenacity of Oiwa's spirit and the extent of her power is determined by the fact that her retribution is a rightful retaliation, and does not simply originate from malice or viciousness.

Oiwa takes the "medicine" sent from the Itō house, which disfigures her terribly; her face swells grotesquely and her hair falls out. When the masseur Takuetsu explains to her that Iemon "has run out of love" for her and "plotted to get himself rid of" her (Oshima in Brazell 1998: 476), Oiwa realizes she has been betrayed. Abandoned, disfigured and consumed by hatred, Oiwa vows to repay both Iemon and the Itō family:

> OIWA
> Every moment is uncertain, as the end comes for Oiwa.
> But one thing is sure, the moment I die he will marry that girl.
> I can see the scene right before my eyes.
> Now I have nothing but hatred for you, Iemon,
> and hate for the house of Kihei, hatred for the Itō family.
> None of you shall ever escape to a life of peace.
> The more I think about it
> the more my heart is filled with bitter, bitter hatred
> [Oshima in Brazell 1998: 478].

This monologue emphasizes Oiwa's emotional state—her wrath and humiliation, and how profoundly she had been hurt. Those feelings are crucial conditions for a spirit of the deceased person to become a vengeful spirit— an *onryō*. Oiwa fixates on her anger and hatred, on Iemon and the Itō house and it is with such thoughts that she dies. In the sense, Oiwa may be regarded as an incarnation of *urami* and *onnen,* since she has been wronged in life and she dies a bad death. From that point on, Oiwa's vengeance is the driving force of the plot and the primary horror factor of *Ghost Stories at Yotsuya*.

Iemon blames Kohei for Oiwa's death and happily awaits the consummation of his marriage. Iemon's new bride, beautiful young Oume, arrives with her father. Previously, Oume confesses to her maid that she is afraid of Oiwa, which foreshadows the first appearance of Oiwa's vengeful spirit during the wedding night. Indeed, as soon as Iemon approaches his young wife and tries to embrace her, instead of her lovely face he sees the ghastly, disfigured features of Oiwa, who glares at Iemon with hatred and cackles like a witch (Oshima in Brazell 1998: 482). Shocked, Iemon draws his sword and cuts off her head— but it is Oume's head that falls to the ground. In this regard, Oiwa's presence is initially is rather subtle: she does not attempt to attack or hurt Iemon in any way, but the prelude to her revenge is cruel. By possessing Oume (Oume's kimono and the amulet on her neck give evidence to her identity) she causes Iemon to inadvertently murder the young woman he desired so much. It is significant that Iemon is neither afraid nor remorseful—on the contrary, upon seeing Oiwa's face, he swings his sword at her.

It is also worth noting that Oiwa is not the only spirit tormenting Iemon—he is also haunted by the ghost of the servant he accused of murdering Oiwa and killed, Kohei. In a manner similar to Oiwa, he tricks Iemon's eyes, making him believe that his father-in-law, Kihei, who is rocking the baby, is actually Kohei devouring it. Unaware of the deception, Iemon kills his new father-in-law, beheading him. As Kohei's head falls to the ground, a snake appears and coils around it. This detail is significant since Kohei was born in the year of snake (in some version of the play rats may surround the head, as it takes place in the version given in *Early Japanese Literature: An Anthology* (Shirane 2002: 872)); earlier in the play, a rat appears right after Oiwa's death and tugs at Oiwa's baby (Oshima in Brazell 1998: 479); Oiwa, in turn, was born in the year of the rat. Both the snake and the rat continue to appear in the narrative, constituting symbols of the constant presence of the vengeful ghosts near Iemon.

Having unintentionally murdered his wife and his father-in-law, Iemon must flee. He cannot, however, escape Oiwa's wrath. Iemon runs to Snake Mountain Hermitage, where he hopes to find shelter from Oiwa's *onryō*. Oiwa, however, cannot be stopped, fooled or left behind; she haunts Iemon incessantly, tormenting him even in his dreams. Her constant presence slowly drives Iemon to insanity, reflecting upon Iemon's appearance, i.e., his "pale and feverish" face, his "bushy, unkempt hair" implying "illness bordering on madness," and in his dirty clothes (Oshima in Leiter 2002: 155). Oiwa not only haunts Iemon both when he is awake and when he is asleep, but she does so in a spectacular manner, emerging from a burning paper lantern in bloodstained clothes, with the child in her arms, trailing blood in the snow (Leiter 2002: 58). Her ghost (described earlier in the play) is that which Iemon has last seen, with the "horrible swelling" (Oshima in Brazell 1998: 472) above her right eye, and her mouth "messily covered" with teeth blackener, which makes her mouth appear "monstrously wide" (Oshima in Brazell 1998: 477). Her hair, loose and disheveled, is half fallen out, exposing her grotesquely disfigured face (Oshima in Brazell 1998: 478), which is "twisted with fury" (Oshima in Brazell 1998: 478). Her pale gray underkimono (Oshima in Brazell 1998: 473) completes the famous image of a vengeful spirit that was to influence the Japanese horror genre so greatly. Oiwa's characteristic appearance, together with her renown, was cemented permanently with the *Ghost of Yotsuya* (*Yotsuya Kaidan*), directed by Nobuo Nakagawa in 1959, after which the majority of *onryō* depicted in film, literature and other media were always comparable to Oiwa in one manner or another (Picard in Perron 2009: 106).

Furthermore, now Oiwa's spirit does not refrain from a direct attack. She assaults Iemon's parents and kills them in a gruesome and simultaneously dramatic manner. As an *onryō,* Oiwa is ruthless, persistent and, most importantly, powerful enough to disregard any religious barriers and protections such as protective prayers or symbols (incidentally, this is a characteristic now shared by virtually all vengeful spirits in Japanese horror narratives). This is another characteristic of a Japanese vengeful spirit that renders it so effective a horror character; it cannot be repelled or appeased, and it will not stop until its vengeance is complete. Despite the efforts of the hermit and his followers, Oiwa kills Iemon's parents, strangling his father and setting rats on his mother and then ripping her throat out. It is worth noting that thanks to the ingenious inventions of the kabuki stage, Oiwa's vengeful spirit is capable of impressive and terrifying stunts, and her attacks are not only frightening, but also marvelous, as she is capable of descending from the ceiling headfirst, is remarkably strong and can affect her victims without touching them:

(*Oiwa seizes Okuma by the collar and sends her body into massive contortions. Loud* tsuke *beats. The prayer circle disintegrates and the followers fall back. Iemon waves his sword above his head in a futile gesture. Loud* tsuke *beats.*)
IEMON
　　　Come on! Pray! (*They all chant more loudly. Oiwa strikes a* mie *to continuous* tsuke *beats while she stares at Iemon. Then she resumes tormenting Okuma.*) I feel the eyes of the ghost again? (*Horrified, Iemon strikes a* mie *to triple* tsuke *beats.*) Pray! (*They chant repeatedly as Oiwa seizes Okuma and, to the accompaniment of a flute, rips out Okuma's throat with her teeth. Iemon watches his mother die with a gurgling sound. The chanters scream in terror and rush out the rear door*) [Leiter 2002: 161].

It may seem a touch surprising for the Western audience that Oiwa chooses to attack and murder Okuma and Chōbei, but this behavior is perfectly logical from the Japanese point of view. The Japanese concept of the family assumes that it is the family, not an individual, that constitutes the basic social unit. Therefore, if a member of the family commits an offense, the entire family shares the responsibility and suffers with that person (Iwasaka and Toelken 1994: 114). This, as Iwasaka and Toelken point out, implies that "a person's actions and responsibilities are inseparable from the interests and welfare of others" (Iwasaka and Toelken 1994: 114).

Eventually Iemon is forced to flee the hermitage and is slain by Yomoshichi, Oiwa's brother-in-law, who comes forth as her avenger. During their sword duel, in some versions (e.g., in the version translated by Kenelly), numerous rats appear on Iemon's sword and cause him to drop it, thus allowing Yomoshichi a clear strike. In this way Oiwa's ghostly retribution is finally complete.

Ghost Stories at Yotsuya is a tremendously significant title in the context of this chapter; Nanboku's story is in all probability the most recognized, the most popular and the most influential ghost story among Japanese ghost narratives. It follows a traditional pattern of a sympathetic victim, wronged by an evil person, who transforms into a wrathful demon-like spirit, an *onryō*. What is more, the image of *onryō* presented in Nanboku's play cemented what is now recognized as the conventional image of *onryō*. *Ghost Stories at Yotsuya* combines all the elements that are now important and easily recognizable in Japanese retribution narratives, such as death in the grip of anger, revenge upon the former tormentor and inexorability until the retribution is completed, into one lucid but gripping tale of betrayal and vengeance.

A different image of a ghostly avenger is presented in *Strangers* (*Ijintachi to no natsu*), a novel by Taichi Yamada. The plot of *Strangers* is reasonably straightforward as far as the story is concerned. The narrative is, however, layered in a manner similar to some modern ghost narratives, such as *The Sixth Sense*. The initial layer concerns the protagonist, Harada, meeting his long dead parents. Although they appear benevolent, further meetings with them seem to drain the life out of the protagonist. His neighbor, Kei, whom he had begun an affair with, acts concerned. As it turns out, the parents do not intend Harada any harm—the neighbor, however, is in fact a vengeful spirit who wants to drag Harada to the underworld. *Strangers* is not a conventional Japanese rightful retribution narrative, but it does feature the element of *urami*.

Yamada's novel sets up an atmosphere associated with the traditional experience of the ghost story. In Japan, telling (or listening to) ghost stories is especially popular during the summer months, as the chill of fear is expected to relieve some of the unbearable hotness (Mueller 2007: 99). The story takes place during the hottest months of summer, July and August, in a building that becomes "desolate" and "dark" at nights (Yamada 2003: 5). The protagonist, a TV script-writer, Harada, is visited by his neighbor, a lonely, dejected woman, who offers to share a bottle of champagne with him and talk. Harada gives her the cold shoulder. Later, he visits his hometown, Asakusa, on an impulse and sees what he believes to be his own father. He has dinner with both his parents, who look and act as if they were alive, and heads home. Regretting his earlier behavior, he calls the strange neighbor, but she is changed beyond recognition. She appears lively and high spirited, in sharp contrast to her previous gentle, shy but desperate behavior. Harada is immediately able to sense that there is something wrong about her, something "out of keeping with her ... good humour," but he is unable to specify what that might be (Yamada 2003: 60). He does not know that Kei, forlorn and disillusioned, has committed suicide that same evening Harada turned her away from his door. In this respect, Kei does not resemble the traditional, famous characters of vengeful Oiwa or wailing Okiku from *Banchō Sarayashiki* ("The Plate Mansion at Banchō"),[9] but yet another, equally famous ghost character—Otsuyu from *Botan Dōrō* ("Peony Lantern"). In *Peony Lantern*, a man is visited at nights by his lover, Otsuyu, unaware that she is a ghost.[10] Kei is, indeed, as patient as Otsuyu, but her motivation is completely different. She does not love Harada or want to be close to him; she wants to destroy him for hurting her. Interestingly enough, Kei actually does have sexual intercourse with Harada as a ghost, which is rare to virtually non-existent in Euroamerican fiction. Sexual innuendo is present in many American ghost narratives (Stanley Kubrick's *The Shining* [1980], *Return to House on the Haunted Hill* [2007] directed by Victor Garcia, or Steve Beck's *Ghost Ship* [2002], just to name a few), but in the Japanese ghost narrative, it rarely takes place. Harada and Kei have sex numerous times, but she never allows Harada to see her otherwise than from behind, claiming that she has an ugly burn on her chest. Kei insists that Harada promise he would not look:

> "No," she said. "You mustn't see."
> She refused to budge. I could tell from the steel in her voice that she would not come one step closer until I had made my pledge.
> "Well, if it means that much to you," I nodded in assent.
> "Promise?"
> "I promise."
> Still she did not move. "You might think I'm blowing things all out of proportion," she said, "but this is like those stories in the ancient myths. The woman tells the man he mustn't look, but he does anyway, and nothing can undo the damage it causes between them" [Yamada 2003: 66].

The myths Kei refers to are a specific genre of fairy tales characteristic to Japan, which Hayao Kawai calls the "non-human wives" genre (Hayao

1998: 105). In such myths, a woman who is not of the human world forbids her lover to look at her in certain circumstances (e.g., when she is in a locked room), and when the lover eventually breaks his promise, her non-human nature is revealed and she leaves (Hayao 1998: 108). In *Strangers,* Kei's words serve as a foreshadowing device; once Harada is to learn Kei's true nature (which would mean seeing the wound on her chest), Kei will be forced to leave.

As time passes, Harada begins to deteriorate physically, becoming weaker and emaciated to the point where he looks like an "old man" (Yamada 2003: 141). For a long time Harada is actually unable to see for himself the detrimental effect the ghost's presence has on him. Unaware of the fact that Kei does not belong to the world of the living, he naturally (and misguidedly) suspects that it is his contact with the ghosts of his parents that probably affects him in this way, since they "[belong] to the world of the dead" (Yamada 2003: 111).

Even before noticing his condition, Harada has been wondering about their nature, initially believing himself to be hallucinating, and later suspecting that his "father" and "mother" might be shape-shifting foxes *(kitsune)* or badgers *(tanuki)*. Despite that, he enjoys his visits to his parents house even at the point when he believes they may be unintentionally doing harm to him. While it remains unclear whether the parents' appearance that summer was simply a coincidence or whether it was in fact an ancestral intervention to protect their son on their part, meeting them has beyond doubt a profound emotional influence on Harada, who is able to find some closure.

Upon discovering Harada's debilitating condition, his mother and father leave peacefully, leaving the protagonist their words of love and support. Harada is grief-stricken, but believes his problems have come to an end. At this point the narrative crosses over into the second layer. The ghosts of the parents have departed and Harada is under an illusion that he is getting better, when in fact he is not. Kei is still by his side, and it is Kei who is draining the life-force out of him. As a vengeful ghost, Kei naturally has no intention of departing peacefully; motivated by resentment and anger, she is intent on dragging Harada to hell with her. Her plans, however, are thwarted by Mamiya, Harada's agent, who is concerned by Harada's ever deteriorating condition. Mamiya tells Harada the truth—that he had seen him with a woman bearing a remarkable resemblance to a neighbor of Harada's who had killed herself out of loneliness near the end of July, stabbing herself in the chest with a knife. At last, Harada learns Kei's true nature; this knowledge severs the bond between

Harada and the ghost and when Kei appears one more time, she does so as a vengeful spirit:

> Kei stood in front of the elevator, some ten meters away, gazing steadily in our direction. She wore the white, sleeveless housedress that came down nearly to her ankles.... Her eyes were as cold as death. I had been searching them for signs of life as she approached, but even now, even at close quarters, I could discern no ray of warmth in them. They remained fixed on me in a frigid, icy stare.
> Her unpainted lips moved, parting ever so slightly, as though preparing to speak. Then they began to form words:
> "I'm sure you remember."
> A deep voice. A voice filled with scorn.
> "Remember what?" The venom in her words made my voice quiver. "The night of the champagne."
> ... Now I knew. On that very night, Kei had stabbed herself in the chest, seven times.
> "I'll drag you down with me," she hissed, pressing one step closer.
> I reflexively fell back, but she immediately closed the gap again. Try as I might to hold my ground, I found myself pushed backward once more by the violent hatred emanating from her two eyes, glaring at me from only a few centimeters away [Yamada 2003: 192–194].

As in many other Japanese ghost stories, a religious factor is introduced that proves useless again a vengeful spirit: Mamiya tries praying and keeping Kei's spirit away with a rosary, but, as it is usually the case with a Japanese *onryō*, neither the rosary nor the sutra are effective against Kei's spirit (just as a whole group of chanting monks could not stop Oiwa in *Ghost Stories at Yotsuya*)[11] (Yamada 2003: 192). Kei advances, unstoppable, but since Harada has been told the truth by Mamiya, the illusion is shattered. Unable to follow through with her plan, she gives up and disappears into the other world; her true nature revealed, as a dark bloodstain spreads over her chest, she fades: "Moment by moment she grew more transparent, until suddenly I realized I was seeing only an afterimage. It lingered briefly like the shimmering of hot air, and then it too was gone" (Yamada 2003: 196). Kei's appearance, i.e., the white dress and the way she moves (she glides, which is a manner of movement impossible to achieve on feet), is a reference to the traditional *yūrei* figure. Incidentally, the room in which Harada visited Kei in her apartment is a *tatami*-mat room arranged in a traditional Japanese style (Yamada 2003: 176). In fact, Kei, despite being a modern rendition of the ghost, retains a plethora of traits characteristic to a traditional *onryō*. She is driven by anger and *urami*; she is relentless and methodical and yet alluring and deceptive. By deliberately staying near Harada, she slowly sucks out the life out of him instead of cursing him to die or attacking him violently. The reason for this may be the fact that Kei has no right to a rightful retribution towards Harada. Kei's grudge was directed against the society that excluded her; additionally, Harada was not the one who caused her demise. He lacked empathy (*omoiyari*) and he hurt her, but he had not wronged her in any way.

The story told in *Strangers* is simple and very traditional at the same time. A sad, lonely woman is let down by the society that failed her, but her revenge is against the protagonist, who was in direct contact with her. *Strangers* features a number of classic Japanese ghost story elements: The action takes place in the summer, the protagonist is haunted by a wronged woman whose visits drain life from him, and her full appearance as *onryō* is that of a white-clad woman glaring with hatred. Yamada's story represents also a different kind of ghost story than the more brutal narratives (such as Nakata's *Ring* or Miike's *One Missed Call*), replacing the pure terror of ghost's attack with a more slow-paced and reflective atmosphere created by the ghost's intentions. In this way, *Strangers* creates a lingering mixture of sadness and anxiety.

The next title is one of the best known retribution titles discussed in this work. It is also the only title discussed here where the film adaptation is used instead of the original novel. The title in question is *Ring* (*Ringu*), directed in 1998 by Hideo Nakata, and it is based on the novel *Ring* by Kōji Suzuki. The choice to consider the film instead of the novel is based on the national and international popularity of the former. The influence of Nakata's film proved to be much greater than that of Suzuki's book, spurring a number of continuations and adaptations of its own. Among those, it is worthwhile to mention manga adaptations, such as Hiroshi Takahashi and Misao Inagaki's *The Ring,* film sequels, such as Jōji Iida's *Rasen* [1998] and Hideo Nakata's *Ring 2* [1999], prequels, like *Ring 0: Birthday* [2000], directed by Norio Tsuruta, games, like *The Ring: Terror's Realm,* published by Infogrames in 2000, or remakes outside Japan, such as Korean Kim Dong-bin's *The Ring Virus*[12] [2000] and Gore Verbinski's *The Ring* [2002]. Such popularity of Nakata's story might partially result from the fact that, upon its release, *Ring* became the highest grossing film in the country (Lacefield 2010: 4).

Nakata's *Ringu* has become the most successful Japanese horror film ever made as well as one of the most well known Japanese films in the international market. The film also helped to ignite the slumbering Japanese horror industry and paved the way for the popularity of films in the J-Horror genre made by numerous Japanese, Korean, and Hong Kong directors [Lacefield 2010: 4].

Nakata's story differs significantly from Suzuki's story in terms of the key idea and a number of crucial details, such as the sex and marital status of the main character, or the sex of the ghost, to an extent that it cannot be considered a mere audience expanding device. In comparison, Polanski's *Rosemary's Baby* did not introduce any major changes to Levin's *Rosemary's Baby*, in the same way Friedkin's *The Exorcist* does not differ much from Blatty's. In both cases the film adaptation simply helped the original story reach a wider audience, whereas Nakata's *Ring* can be considered to be a distinct narrative, and is therefore a better choice for the purpose of this book.

Suzuki's original novel is a rather unorthodox ghost story, mainly due to the fact that it features no ghost as such. Instead, the story focuses on the curse left behind by the angry spirit. The narrative is structured more like a detective story than a ghost narrative, and it is not clear at the beginning that supernatural occurrences are taking place. It is only later that the characters laboriously find out the truth: a social outcast, Sadako Yamamura (a person whom they believed to be an ordinary woman, but who was in fact biologically a man suffering from male pseudohermaphroditism), possessed uncanny powers, was murdered and thrown into an old well. Her spirit, full of anger, produced a curse transmitted by a video tape in a mechanism similar to a virus. The novel mixes the traditional supernatural (ghostly curse) with science fiction elements (the tape is like a spreading virus which is supposed to eventually infect everyone). In comparison, Nakata's text is substantially "hollywoodised" (Xu in Hunt and Leung 2008: 195). Unconventional elements, such as Sadako's gender identity or the science-fiction elements, are removed from the plot, and, most importantly, Sadako's ghost makes an appearance on screen.

The film begins with an opening sub-narrative reminiscent of a ghost story (*kaidan*) or urban legend (*toshi densetsu*) that sets the mood for the rest of the film and serves as foreshadowing. It is late night, late autumn, and Tomoko—and the audience together with her—is about to hear a scary story:

MASAMI
A grade-school boy was on holiday down in Izu with his family. He wanted to go out and play, but there was a TV show he didn't want to miss. So he recorded it on the VCR in their room. But the channels down there are different from Tokyo. No station there uses that channel, so it should have been blank. But when he played it back at home, there was a woman on the screen. "You will die in one week," she said. The kid stopped the tape, and then the phone rang. "You saw it." And a week later, the kid died!

Ring is paced very slowly—it begins more like a detective narrative than a horror narrative. Despite the fact that in the first ten minutes the audience witnesses Masami's story, Tomoko's death and Reiko's interview regarding the cursed tape, the film avoids the overtly supernatural accents. The unsettling atmosphere is achieved with very subtle details—in the case of the first scene when Tomoko dies, those details include seemingly trivial elements, such as the phone ringing to no end, the TV turning itself on, as well as hard to define scraping sounds.

When four high school students die at the same time and in the same manner, the protagonist, Reiko, takes interest in the story. She finds and watches Sadako's tape, and realizes that she too is now cursed. Interestingly enough, it is not the supernatural nature of that curse that is the most important horror factor but the burden of its consequence—when Reiko tells Ryūji about the curse, Ryūji light-heartedly advises her to go to a shrine and get exorcised (which, interestingly, Reiko does not choose to do). What is more important than the supernatural aspect of Sadako's curse (especially that both Yōichi—Reiko and Ryūji's son—and Ryūji himself are portrayed as sensitive to the presence from the beyond) is the strength of her *urami* and the inevitable consequences for Reiko and everyone else who has seen the tape. Instead, the story merges the terror of inevitable death not with disbelief or panic but with a distinct tone of sadness. One of the important scenes takes place on the Oshima island, when Reiko is waiting in an empty room for a phone call that would give her any clue as to how she should proceed. She is curled up, visibly dejected, and glances at her watch, reminding the audience that her time is running out. In contrast to other scenes so far, this scene is accompanied by soft, sad music. The atmosphere of this moment finds expression in Reiko's forlorn, desperate plea to Ryūji to be with her when she dies.

Their search eventually brings them to Sadako. Sadako is the creator of the cursed taped in both the novel and the film, but in the novel her actual ghost is never encountered—all she leaves behind is the curse. In the film, Sadako's ghost does make an appearance, but not until the end of the film, where she reveals herself, in a very *yūrei*-like fashion, to Ryūji. Before that, it is not exactly clear whether she is even dead. Nonetheless, her presence is not really necessary, as Reiko's and Ryūji's awareness of her wrath and their impending death is enough to establish a satisfactory atmosphere of terror.

Although Reiko and Ryūji do not immediately grasp that fact (initially they believe that they are looking for someone who is still alive), eventually they begin to understand the true nature of Sadako's curse; they realize that they are dealing with the anger of a spirit—*onnen* (or *tatari,* Reader 1991: 48) and that the tape is "not from this world" but is an embodiment of Sadako's fury (literally "pure *onnen," onnen sono mono*). Once Reiko and Ryūji associate the curse with a spirit's *onnen,* their attitude changes. As the "members of the living," they work hard without a complaint to uncover the mystery behind Sadako's death and to find out what her spirit might want. Their actions and reasoning clearly demonstrate the obligation and responsibility they feel towards Sadako's ghost:

RYŪJI: Let's find Sadako's body.
REIKO: Will that lift the curse? Will that save Yōichi?
RYŪJI: It's all we can do.

As Yu points out, Reiko and Ryūji search for some substantiation of Sadako's resentment, "believing that retrieving her remains and a proper burial would lay the unhappy ghost to rest" (Yu in Hessel and Huppert 2010: 97). The fact that proper burial and acknowledging her pain are apparently of no interest to Sadako contradicts the "anthropomorphic understanding of evil" (Yu in Hessel and Huppert 2010: 97).

Ryūji fails to fulfill Sadako's expectations and Sadako exacts her revenge on him. In this respect, *Ring* is very traditional—those targeted by the spirit's anger must perform certain rituals (see Iwasaka and Toelken 1994)—in this case, copying the tape, and when Ryūji does not perform this ritual, Sadako comes for him in a scene that might very well be one of the most famous (in the same way Regan's spinning head in *The Exorcist* is one of the most famous scenes in the horror genre) scenes in the horror genre, as well as one of the most "visually stunning" ones (Yu in Hessel and Huppert 2010: 106). Showing herself for the first time, Sadako climbs out of the well on the screen (the TV displays the very last frame of the cursed tape) and walks within the frame, still moving "inside the video" at this point (Yu in Hessel and Huppert 2010: 106). She then emerges out of the frame, climbing out of the television set and into the room, transgressing from one ontological level of reality within the narrative into another (Yu in Hessel and Huppert 2010: 106). She crawls awkwardly onto the floor, then gets up slowly and moves towards Ryūji. Since in the film Sadako possesses a distinct, easily recognizable shape—white gown-like dress, long disheveled hair—the scene successfully juxtaposes the traditional (the dress and the hair, the *urami* motivating Sadako) with the modern,[13] as Sadako literally crawls out of the TV screen.

Although the character of Sadako Yamamura was created by Kōji Suzuki, it was Nakata who constructed the apparition associated with the *Ring* franchise. The Sadako created by Nakata represents a specific type of an *onnen*-bearing ghost in the sense that she bears a grudge not against one person, but against the whole society. This pattern is not uncommon in modern horror, and it is used in the majority of contemporary Japanese ghost narratives, including titles discussed in this work. Nakata's Sadako, however, is remarkable in at least one very important aspect. In contrast to the majority of ghostly

1. Ghosts

avengers, she is impersonal. This might be related to the fact that Sadako's spirit as such is absent in the original novel, which focuses on her curse only. She appears in person only at the very end of the story; additionally, throughout the whole film she does not utter a single word, cry or make any other sound. Her silence is significant because virtually all Japanese ghosts, both the haunting ones and the vengeful ones, are capable of speech, and in this way they utter accusations or other words pointing to the nature of their *urami*.[14] Not only does Sadako never speak, she also never shows her face. To the characters and the audience, she is just a long-haired apparition that comes to claim her victims when the week is up, a shadowy threat lurking in the background, with just enough back-story to keep the viewer both intrigued and scared. Sadako is disturbing precisely because so little is known about her.

Even more importantly, Sadako's unique abilities definitely set her apart from other vengeful spirits (although similar motifs will later be repeated in other narratives, such as *One Missed Call* or *Calling*). Even her curse is created in an outstanding manner—by preserving her *onnen* on a videotape. Once Sadako's victims watched the tape, they had seven days to copy it and show it to someone else.[15] If this condition was not met, her vengeful spirit would emerge from the TV set to claim her victim. Such nature of the curse carries significant implications on the nature of Sadako as a vengeful spirit. In contrast to other ghosts, she is not limited by space; she is a "local" entity (Yu in Hessel and Huppert 2010: 102) insofar as she is connected to the well in which she died; she always crawls out of that well, but she can emerge from any given screen on which that well is displayed, regardless of place. Her presence is, therefore, not singular, but decentered and dispersed (Yu in Hessel and Huppert 2010: 103). Additionally, while traditional ghosts confine themselves to simple tasks, such as moving objects or rattling surfaces, Sadako produces a videotape containing various images from her mind—"a psychic video"—and uses the late-twentieth century technology to reproduce both her curse and herself; she thus demonstrates capabilities far superior to those ascribed to conventional ghosts, such as mere "interfering with the normal functioning of electrical appliances" (Yu in Hessel and Huppert 2010: 103). Sadako is a modern ghost in more than one sense. She exists in a modern setting and effectively makes use of modern technology; she also does not rely on conventional, direct violence but instead depends on precise, almost emotionless elimination of her victims.

The retribution narrative in *Ring* (the film) may not be that extraordinary, but Nakata's *onryō* and the story surrounding it proved to be very attractive to the American audience. In 2002, Gore Verbinski directed a remake of

Nakata's story, titled *The Ring*. Similar to the original, *The Ring* employs a single mother with a child, Rachel, as the protagonist, and a cursed video tape as the source of horror. However, *The Ring* differs considerably from *Ring*, not only in details, but in terms of general atmosphere and overtone. The very beginning of *The Ring* sets an entirely different mood. Verbinski's interpretation of the story begins less like a *kaidan,* and more like common, everyday situation, passing smoothly from casual conversation to the unpleasant, scary reality of the narrative:

> BECCA: Have you heard about this videotape that kills you when you watch it?
> KATIE: What kind of tape?
> BECCA: A tape, a regular tape. People rent it, I don't know. You start to play it and it's like somebody's nightmare. Then suddenly, this woman comes on smiling at you, right? Seeing you through the screen. And as soon as it's over ... your phone rings. Someone knows you've watched it. And what they say is: "You will die in seven days." And exactly seven days later—
> KATIE: Who told you that?
> BECCA: Somebody from Revere.... What's your problem?
> KATIE: I've watched it.

Becca's story resembles an urban legend rather than actual ghost story (it bears the quality of "it could happen to anyone" while actually having never happened to anyone). Whereas Masami's story bore the characteristics of a fictional ghost story, the opening narrative in *The Ring* introduces a unit of information relevant to the reality depicted in the film.

The American version of the film constructs Sadako's counterpart, Samara, as younger, more disturbed and even more powerful than Sadako; in the film, she is capable of physically hurting the characters before their foretold time comes. Those changes, however, do not affect the purpose of her presence in the story in any way. Samara creates the cursed tape and the characters must meet her conditions in order to survive. In contrast to Sadako, however, Samara normally interacts with the characters, both when she is alive (the tape of her session) and when she is a ghost (after seeing the tape Rachel gets a phone call from Samara, who says: "Seven days."). The remake attempts to develop Samara into a more rounded character, and in doing so it takes away the uncanny aspect of the original Sadako, who lurked in the background like a waiting shadow. By reconstructing Samara as a little girl who uses words such as "mommy" and "daddy," *The Ring* creates a dissonance between Samara's vulnerable image and her supposedly evil nature. Samara's nature is quite different from Sadako's: she is related neither to her "mother" nor her "father," and is presented as a creature inherently evil. Whereas in *Ring* it was Sadako who was hurt by society, in the American remake, it is Samara who does damage to society.

Both titles, *Ring* and *The Ring*, rely on an atmosphere of psychological terror in order to create the fear factor. In *Ring*, this atmosphere is evoked by the inevitable, mysterious and apparently painful death, the inevitability being its most important feature. Forced to race against the clock and frustrated by their lack of knowledge, the characters battle the suffocating awareness of closing and inescapable death. *The Ring*, on the other hand, makes use of all the above elements, depicting Rachel and Noah's struggle in a similar way *Ring* presents Reiko and Ryūji's. It does, however, gravitate towards graphic depiction of unpleasant experiences and violent deaths. Notably, whereas *Ring* is characterized by fear mixed with sorrowfulness (not for the ghost, but for the characters), *The Ring* operates with pure fear. This is noticaeble not only on the level of the plot, but also in the characters' behavior, who in Nakata's film are characterized by a certain resignation to their fate (as clearly visible in Reiko's despair on the island as in Tomoko's facial expression in the beginning of the film), while the American characters put up an angry, indignant fight.

Nakata's *Ring* is an important retribution title, partly because of the innovative portrayal of the vengeful spirit, and partly because of its popularity, both national and international, which sparked the wave of Japanese horror-inspired films and remakes in the United States. *Ring* skillfully merges the attraction of the classic ghost story with a believable setting of contemporary reality. Neither one of those traits is unheard of, but *Ring* made it work on a global scale, proving both popular and influential, and, most importantly, successfully adjusting the character of the traditional Japanese vengeful spirit into modernity.

A different take on the ghost bearing a grudge against society is presented in Kiyoshi Kurosawa's *Retribution* (*Sakebi*—lit. "scream") [2006]. What makes *Retribution* stand out among other ghostly retribution narratives is its complex story and, most importantly, the Woman in Red—the vengeful spirit itself, whose identity is not clear and fixed but disconnected and multifarious in comparison to other well known *onryō* characters. The supernatural aspect of the story is not based on the relation between one person (the ghost) and another person—or people—but on the feelings of the ghost and the feelings of the people involved.

The main character, Detective Yoshioka, is involved in a case of a murder. He is trying to catch an assumed serial killer whose latest victim, a young woman in a bright red dress, dubbed by the police as F18, was recently found drowned in a puddle of sea water. Soon he begins to see an apparition of a woman he does not know, wearing a similar red dress. The ghost, however, addresses him as if they knew each other, asking him why he didn't stay with her and saying that the two of them were fated to meet again and that she is happy to see him again.

It is worth noting how the blurred, indistinct identity of the ghost functions in the narrative. Although the Woman in Red (*akai fuku no onna*) is in fact the spirit of a former patient of the now abandoned asylum, she also represents the murdered woman, F18 (who later turns out be a young woman named Reiko Shibata) and Yoshioka's lover, Harue, whom Yoshioka killed under the influence of the curse. Apart from being herself, the Woman in Red embodies also those who died because of her curse, in this way being a symbol of the origin and of the consequences of the curse. Initially Yoshioka believes he is being haunted by the spirit of the murdered woman. As the narrative moves on, however, he discovers the primary identity of the ghost: a woman who was abandoned in the old asylum. People passing on the ferry, including Yoshioka, could see the asylum and her silhouette in the window, but they kept going by indifferently.

> WOMAN IN RED: A long time ago.... You found me.... And I found you. And yet everyone abandoned me.
> YOSHIOKA: You're that woman?
> WOMAN IN RED: You saw it, you knew it.... There were things you could have done. Do you know what happened to me after that? ... I stayed there for years and years, waiting and waiting, forgotten by everyone.... Then I died.

A quite exceptional characteristic of the Woman in Red is that she did not die a bad death. She was not killed, might have even not killed herself over some wrongdoing she had experienced. The crux of the story and an essential element of her nature as a ghost is that she died lonely and forgotten. "It was a long darkness ..." she said; "I was stuck there forever ... and lonely for so long. Then all of my senses and memories and all my emotions disappeared, one after the other, leaving behind only despair."

The Woman in Red is an immensely interesting ghost character, both aesthetically and functionally. In a bold departure from the conventional *onryō* image, she is always wearing an elegant red dress instead of a white one, and her hair is rather short and rarely obscures her face. That face, however, usually bears an eerie, dispassionate, almost vacant expression; this, additionally emphasized by long close-up shots, renders the Woman in Red positively uncanny. Although like most Japanese ghosts, the Woman in Red seems corporeal—she touches Yoshioka, pushes him, slaps his hand away—her screaming, heard on more than one occasion, is incorporeal; the sound accompanies her, but she does not open her mouth to make it. She moves slowly but deliberately, and she exacts her retribution in the same manner, impassive and unhurried.

The *urami* of the Woman in Red is directed at the whole of society. Her curse is just as deadly as that of any other vengeful spirit, but at the same time, it is exceptionally indirect. She neither kills nor hurts those whom she cursed. She does not even influence them to do harm to themselves. Instead, her victims turn against those whom they love—Yoshioka turns against his lover, Doctor Sakuma turns against his son, and Miyuki turns against Onoda. The victims of the Woman in Red discover that their feelings suddenly seem empty and bitter, replaced with profound disappointment and alienation. When Yoshioka asks Miyuki about the ghost, she explains:

> YOSHIOKA: Did you also see the woman in red? ... I saw her, too. What did you do after you saw her? Remember.
> MIYUKI: She was in the mirror.... When I noticed her, it was like she noticed me, too.
> YOSHIOKA: And then what happened?
> MIYUKI: Her emotions poured into me ..."Nobody notices me." "The world's forgotten about me." "The people closest to me don't see me at all." Onoda was like that. All of his future plans were just for himself. I didn't exist for him. Suddenly, I wanted to wipe everything out.... That's why I killed him.

All the cursed people feel this and all of them act in the same manner, attacking and drowning those they care about. A symbolic aspect of the curse is that the drowning is always executed in saltwater, usually intentionally obtained beforehand, which reflects the woman's experiences in the asylum.

The most unsettling aspect of the Woman in Red is her motivation. Her goal is not retaliation, but peculiarly comprehended balance. She does not want to see the society who wronged her in pain or punished, but simply no longer alive. This is expressed in her request uttered at the end of the film: "I died, so everyone else should die, too." The polite manner in which this request is formulated (*watashi wa shinda dakara minna mo shinde kudasai*, lit. "I died, so would everyone else please die too?") only strengthens its menacing effect.

In the end, Woman in Red chooses to forgive one person—just one person, Yoshioka. It is, however, unclear what she means by this, since Yoshioka has already experienced her curse and killed his lover, Harue. Harue appears throughout the story only as a ghost (although the audience learns this only at the end of the film). Initially, she is represented by the Woman in Red, as the victim of the curse, and later she appears as herself once Yoshioka discovers the truth. Despite having all the reason in the world to bear a grudge against Yoshioka and hate him profoundly, she does not. In fact, her spirit seems more concerned for Yoshioka's well being than for his moral attitude; confronted, she tells him: "That doesn't matter anymore. What's the point in hating? You've got your future to consider. Just forget about me." Harue provides an intriguing contrast to the Woman in Red. She does not wish ill on Yoshioka, nor does she want him to die. On the contrary, she believes he should concentrate on his future and no longer dwell on his crime. In this respect, the ghost of Harue and the ghost of the woman in the red dress represent oppositional concepts—while the Woman in Red symbolizes emptiness and isolation, Harue's ghost symbolizes affection and attachment.

Retribution is an uncommon retribution narrative insofar that it does not focus on bloody vengeance and retaliation for pain, but on loneliness and abandonment. The story is structured around people leaving behind other people and about the sense of alienation. The Woman in Red, left behind and forgotten by the rest of society, seeks retribution on those who were indifferent to her situation. She does that not by attacking them, but by influencing them. Instead of venting her pain and despair onto them in violent assault, she allows her victims to experience and understand that pain. Kurosawa's film is beyond doubt a retribution narrative, but its take on that familiar motif is delivered in a very distinct, unique manner.

Ju-On: The Grudge is a notable retribution title, although it is not a conventional ghostly retribution narrative (in the same way it is not a conventional haunting story). Many retribution stories may be interpreted as haunting stories in the sense that the characters wander into the place where the ghost had died. Yet haunting narratives are entirely different for a number of reasons. Firstly, the haunting is focused around the protagonist of the narrative but occurs only in a specific place or near a specific object, or perhaps a person. Secondly, haunting does not move away from that place, object or person. Thirdly, at first the occurrences tend to be rather subtle, indirect and often initially harmless. The place or object that is haunted is associated with the haunting, but the primary emotional charge is always ascribed to the source of the haunting, i.e., the ghost (a notable example would be *The Haunting of Hill House*). In *Ju-On: The Grudge* the Saeki house, on the other hand, is a place of moral and emotional decay, but it does not constrain the ghosts who dwell there. Once entered, it infects the careless visitor with Kayako's curse, and from that moment on that person is subject to her fury.

Kayako, the vengeful spirit of *Ju-On: The Grudge* is visually different from most traditional *onryō* in terms of her appearance. She does bear the very basic characteristics—she wears a white dress (the modern ghost's garment), and her long black hair is disheveled, but her form is "twisted and bloody" (Harper 2008: 117) and limbs "broken and bent" (Balmain 2008: 147). Furthermore, she does not speak—she only croaks like a broken mechanical toy.

It is possible that she is unable to speak at all, and the croaking is in fact an attempt to speak.

Kayako has, as the opening of the film states, "died in a grip of strong anger." Having died unjustly, at someone else's hand (Balmain actually calls Kayako "the innocent victim of patriarchal oppression" [Balmain in Balmain and Drawmer 2009: 30]), in the grip of powerful emotions positions Kayako among traditional *urami*-bearing vengeful spirits. Kayako, however, just like Sadako, is not a typical *onryō*. Her hatred is directed not against one person or even society in general, but at just about anyone and everyone. Her spirit is hurt, tormented, and angry, but her murderer, Takeo, is long dead; Kayako's uncontrolled fury has no one to focus on. Consequently, her wrath affects anyone who comes in contact with her. Her *onnen* is strong enough for her curse to spread and follow those who came close to her. Nowhere is safe once they have entered the house. In this sense, Kayako is similar to Sadako—once someone comes in contact with her curse, time and space are overcome.

Despite the vivid similarities that Kayako bears to Sadako, as Kayako's ghostly self is also dispersed, de-localized and object-less (there is no one person to blame and no one person to attack), Kayako's curse varies significantly from Sadako's methodical approach (in the end, the tape had to be voluntarily watched and voluntarily passed on). The curse of Kayako is more violent; Kayako is powerful and vengeful but completely undiscriminating about her victims. Pained, she lashes out at anyone who comes near and does not let them go even if they try to run. There is also nothing that can be done to appease her.

Despite being considerably unorthodox, Kayako is tremendously effective as a vengeful ghost figure. Her effectiveness seems to stem from the joining of the traditional and the modern ghost characteristics. The elaborate ways in which the victims of her curse meet their ends bring to mind the violent, spectacular blood-thirst of ghosts such as Oiwa or the spirit of the deceased wife in *Of a Promise Broken*.[16] Simultaneously, Kayako exhibits the characteristic territorial freedom and replicable nature of the modern ghost, such as Sadako in *Ring*. Those traits, combined with the blind fury that motivates Kayako, make *Ju-on: The Grudge* a noteworthy title in regard to retribution ghost narratives.

It is also worth noting that a specific plot pattern recurring among the Japanese retribution narratives focuses on a comrade left behind by a group. This particular narrative pattern concerns a regular retaliation element, but with emphasis on the aspect of disloyalty from the group of those who enjoyed trust. A good example of this so-called sub-genre, is *Vanished* (*Oyayubi*

Sagashi) [2006], directed by Naoto Kumazawa. The plot follows a group of six elementary school students who decide to play a spirit game, but upon the game's completion they discover that one of their lot, a girl named Yumiko, is missing; scared, they run away. Eight years later, the remaining five meet again. Guilt-ridden over the past, they attempt to play the game one more time to find Yumiko. This time, they start to disappear one by one as Yumiko exacts her revenge for having been abandoned, until her remains are found. A similar motif driving the narrative is present in Takashi Shimizu's *Shock Labirynth* [2009] or *Kokkurisan: Gekijōban* [2011], directed by Nahae Jiro. This variety of retribution narratives is much less popular in American fiction, but titles of similar structure exist. *Forget Me Not* [2009], directed by Tyler Oliver, is an example of such a narrative. *Forget Me Not* follows a plot analogous to *Vanished*. Like the majority of these particular narratives, it begins with a group of children playing. The group plays a prank on a girl from their midst, Angela, who collapses and hits her head. The other children flee without making sure whether or not she is fine. Years later, the main character, Sandy, and her brother, who were part of the original group, arrange an eerie game of tag in the cemetery. They are unaware that they are joined by Angela's spirit. Once the game is finished, the friends begin to die, one after another. The significant but interesting difference between *Vanished* and *Forget Me Not* is the fact that Angela's revenge affects the whole group but is directed at Sandy, who was the last one to see her. As her friends die one by one, they seem to disappear from people's memories as well, and only Sandy fully comprehends what is happening. Titles belonging to this particular kind of retribution narrative explore not only the motif of revenge, but also concepts such as betrayal of trust, rejection by those one depended on—usually friends—and, often times, guilt.

In comparison to the American retribution ghost story, which tends to feature a ghost that calls to the living for justice, the Japanese ghost story places the ghost in a more powerful position, where it roams the world freely until its anger is appeased. The ghost's presence is also an indication of some wrongdoing, prior to the person's death, that had brought about the rightful retribution of the ghost. For this reason priests, monks and other people who perform religious ceremonies never win in the battle against the spirit (e.g., the failed exorcism in *One Missed Call* [2003] or the futile prayers in *Ju-On: Black Ghost* [2009]); the law of retribution is stronger. There is no such concept as "rightful retribution" in American ghost narratives; the ghosts often times appear by chance, and it is, in fact, actually imaginable that their call to the living could remain unanswered.

2

Monsters and Monstrosities

Socially and culturally, monsters fulfill important functions, providing, according to Gilmore, a "convenient pictorial metaphor" for human qualities that need to be "repudiated, externalized, and defeated" (Gilmore 2003: 4). In comparison to other creatures inhabiting the horror genre, monsters tend to bear more symbolism, and as Poole suggests, even more than our fears they also represent our hatreds (Poole 2011: 13). Therefore, whatever evokes disgust and repulsion of the audience, be it natural or supernatural, can be defined as a monster, for "the monster is the sickening Other" (Poole 2011: 13).

But what *is* a monster? Even if limited to the supernatural entities, the term "monster" is so broad it can denote everything from the spirit of a dead person to a giant, malformed man-eating creature living in the darkness. For example, in *The Philosophy of Horror, or Paradoxes of the Heart* Carroll uses the term referring to all supernatural and preternatural horrific entities furnishing the horror genre without discrimination: ghosts, vampires, werewolves, zombies and other creatures. He notes that all those creatures as "monsters" are characterized by a particular set of traits, which can be loosely described as ontological and symbolic impurity. Impurity is related to being categorically interstitial, categorically contradictory, incomplete or formless—and the monsters of the horror genre are, as Carroll notes, "beings or creatures that specialize in formlessness, incompleteness, categorical interstitiality, and categorical contradictoriness" (Carroll 1990: 32). However, for the purpose of this book, the term "monster" will denote only a handful of corporeal monsters: the vampire, the werewolf, the "proper monster," i.e., the shapeless, nameless creatures, and the undead.

The vampire and the werewolf are included in this chapter because they are physical (as opposed to spirits and religious fears and creatures related to religion) and related primarily to the fear of death or dying badly (similar to the undead). They also differ from other monsters significantly (apart from the zombie) in that they prey on people—they are, first and foremost, predators. They are discussed in the first and the second part of the chapter, respectively.

The other type of monsters included in this chapter are "proper monsters," namely creatures most commonly identified as monsters within the genre itself. Perhaps "monstrosity" would be more preferable, since it covers simultaneously less and more. Not all monsters are monstrosities—monstrosity refers to nature of the given creature or its quality, not just to the creature itself. Monstrosities would encompass all those beings that do not belong to any easily recognizable monster species such as vampires, werewolves, ghosts, demons, etc. and is also not a variation of a human being (e.g., undead human, incorporeal human or a human who drinks blood). Also, the term includes all those that do not have their own proper name, e.g., "ghoul," "goblin," "wyvern," "poltergeist" and so on. Most importantly, monstrosities are those creatures who are not immediately recognizable, are not associated with any existing lore, be it authentic or invented by the author(s) of the narrative—in other words, things for which the characters (and the audience) have no name for and no weapon against. Such monstrosities will be discussed in the third section of the chapter.

The last monster discussed in this chapter is the undead body, here represented by the zombie. The zombie perfectly fits Carroll's definition of a monster in that it is in its very nature interstitial: it is most certainly not alive, but it is also most certainly not dead. It is also not human and, at the same time, very human—it usurps and simultaneously wells over what it means to be human; it desecrates what would in normal circumstances naturally become human remains. The undead body stands for intimate bodily horror and the ultimate interstitiality.

According to Carroll, at the heart of monstrosity lies impurity and categorical contradictoriness; the very nature of the monster involves impurity, a conflict between "two or more standing cultural categories" (Carroll 1990: 43). Additionally, many basic shapes and forms of monstrous creatures are combinatory in nature (Carroll 1990: 43). Monsters are, as Gilmore states, "[o]ntologically intermediary, neither fish nor fowl," and therefore they do not fit into "the mental scheme people rely on to explain the world" (Gilmore 2003: 19). As such, monsters are creatures perfect for the purposes of the horror genre.

The Monstrous Predator

The central idea behind a vampire, werewolf or any other animal-derivative beast is a predator. A predator is a creature that hunts, catches and feeds on other creatures—in case of vampire and werewolf narratives, on humans. It is a superior opponent who hunts mostly to survive, but primarily because it cannot act otherwise—to kill and feed is its natural instinct. Both the vampire and the werewolf prey on people to an extent greater than any other monsters. There is, however, a more important reason for examining the vampire and the werewolf as analogous, comparable horror entities. As Erberto Petoia points out in *Wampiry i Wilkołaki,* the "metamorphosis into an animal, lying at the base of lycanthropy, accompanies the history of vampirism in numerous cultural forms" (Petoia 2004: 23). The tradition of those beliefs has held in villages across Europe to this day. "It is a specially significant fact," as Petoia argues, "that the vampire is often-times considered to be the same being as the werewolf, and both beliefs stem from the same conception of metamorphosis into an animal" (Petoia 2004: 22–23). The anthropologically similar nature of the two phenomena results from the place lycanthropy and vampirism occupy in the history of tradition of cultures; they are considered to be two aspects of the same myth: a human being transforming into Other—whether it is dangerous wolf or a creature sucking fresh human blood (Petoia 2004: 5). In some European countries, the same word is even used to refer to both the vampire and the werewolf (Petoia 2004: 24).

The werewolf and the vampire share one more interesting characteristic feature. They are the two monsters who crossed the line between terror and fascination and are now featured in many narratives not as a source of terror but as characters meant to be attractive, even desirable. In video games, the vampire and the werewolf are featured as allies, playable characters or even protagonists of the game (in games such as *Castlevania: Legacy of Darkness* [1999] or *Vampire: The Masquerade—Redemption* [2000]). People want to become the vampire or the werewolf in a game, but they rarely want to become a ghost or a zombie. It would therefore seem that the image of the vampire and the werewolf is no longer as closely related to the Other as it is the case with a zombie, a ghost or a monster.

Vampire

A predator such as a vampire kills even though it might be able to survive without depriving its prey of life. To kill, however, is a predator's instinct—otherwise the vampire would be merely a parasite, an unpleasant but not terrifying creature taking advantage of its victim but not really endangering it. Some insist that the gist of the vampire myth lies in its sexual attributes, but from the perspective of horror fiction the vampire's essential characteristic feature is that it preys on its victims and drains them, taking away that which gives them life in order to maintain its own half-life.

In *Icons of Horror and the Supernatural* Margaret Carter introduces the figure of the vampire in the following way:

> In his survey of vampire fiction, Brian Frost calls this creature the "monster with a thousand faces," the ultimate shapeshifter. Supernatural entities falling under the general classification of "vampire" include many varieties of blood-drinking demons as well as the animated dead that prey on the living, often feeding on blood but sometimes on other body fluids or simply spreading disease, draining life-force, or frightening victims to death. Some of them must return to their graves at dawn and can be trapped aboveground by scattering seeds they feel compelled to count, while at least one variety is active from midnight to noon. Some undead survive only forty days, while others maintain their quasi-life indefinitely, and still others (in one European tradition), if they survive the initial, most hazardous period of postmortem existence, eventually develop the ability to pass for human and reenter society in a community distant from their original home [Carter in Joshi 2007: 619–620].

The vampire imagery is indeed vast and versatile; the creature exists in one shape or another in many cultures. Interestingly enough, although the vampire can be portrayed in many diverse forms, it is the closest to a universal horror character among the abundant bestiary of monsters inhabiting the horror genre. In her comprehensive study *Od Gotycyzmu do Horroru* Anna Gemra sketches the origins and the earliest versions of the vampire myth, including both the morbid characteristics and the diverse nature of the creature, and sketches a number of characteristics of what could be called, for the sake of simplicity, the "traditional vampire tale," which include the insatiable hunger of the monster, its solitary nature, the repeated visits at night that drain the victim over an extended period of time, and the vampire's lack of concern regarding human life.

The vampire, in addition to being one of the oldest and most popular figures in horror narratives of all sorts, is also, as Gemra states, "one of the most eagerly exploited pop culture icons" (Gemra 2008: 237). For this reason the vampire rarely functions as the real Other and a proper source of horror in contemporary horror narratives, and instead is usually presented as a more rounded, morally ambivalent, or even praiseworthy figure (Gemra 2008: 228). Additionally, the post modern vampire is, as Has-Tokarz suggests, a figure that has undergone internal anthropomorphization (Has Tokarz 2010: 251); the vampires portrayed in productions such as *Bram Stoker's Dracula* or *Interview with the Vampire* resemble outcast romantic heroes rather than the predators presented in earlier films (Has-Tokarz 2010: 253). The vampire changed, Has-Tokarz insists, from a horrifying monster dwelling in a dreary, moldy castle somewhere in the wilderness into a visually and psychologically attractive character that the audience can sympathize and even identify with (Has-Tokarz 2010: 256). Virtually the same idea is presented by Peter Hutchings in *Historical Dictionary of Horror Cinema:*

> The film vampire might once have been a strange, exotic creature, but he or she is now much more familiar—still threatening, perhaps, but also capable of near-normality. The barrier between the monster and us has, in this instance at least, become decidedly permeable [Hutchings 2008: 322].

Therefore, although there is a plethora of vampire-themed literature, cinema, video games and graphic novels, the selection of horror narratives among them is actually limited and unimpressive, as the character of the vampire has permeated into other genres, becoming a fixture of adventure, action (*The Priest* [2011], *Daybreakers* [2009]) or romance films (*True Blood* [2008—]). Other examples include Anne Rice's *Interview with a Vampire, The Hunger* [1983], or *Underworld* [2003], where the vampires are featured as libertines, lovers or warriors—not to mention the infamous *Twilight* by Stephanie Meyer, which portrays the once terrifying monster as a sullen heart throb who sparkles in the sun.[1] The horror potential of the vampire seems to have simply dissipated over time (Philips 2005: 7).

Because the supernatural problem of the vampire is tied to the mystery of death, our fear of dying badly, and what happens to us once we have died, religion tends to be the central concern of vampire tales (Cowan 2008: 39). This is true in many cases of the earlier vampire tales, although remnants of it do resound in many contemporary vampire narratives; despite the fact that legends of creatures feeding on the blood of the living have existed within cultures predating Christianity and well as those where Christianity has not been a major cultural influence, Western cinema horror often associates the defeat of the vampire with "Christian symbols and ritual implements as the technology of salvation" (Cowan 2008: 39). The sacred arsenal includes a wide variety of items and acts: the cross that repels the vampire and drives it away, the Eucharistic wafer and prayers offered by Christian priests (Cowan 2008: 39), the holy water that sears the monster. It is simultaneously worth noting that religious warfare is virtually always accompanied by some form of folklore methods and weapons, ranging from subtleties such as garlic to more straightforward means such as a wooden stake driven through the vampire's heart.

In the majority of film and literary variations and derivatives of Bram Stoker's *Dracula* the vampire is a nobleman or at least a well-off man living in a castle or a large mansion, feared (or ostracized) by the people living nearby. Francis Ford Coppola's *Bram Stoker's Dracula* (1992) may serve as a representative of those titles, as it realizes most of the classic traits of the Euroamerican vampire tale, and is, as Cowan notes, in many ways more faithful to the novel than previous adaptations (Cowan 2008: 135). The vampire portrayed in *Bram Stoker's Dracula* meets all those criteria; he is a socially dominating figure (a count), he represents savage, profane evil (which is alluded to in the scenes when Jonathan travels into the wilderness) and, most importantly, he is an outsider—not only a damned monster but also an exotic individual (as he meets Mina in the street, he introduces himself with words "I am recently arrived from abroad and I do not know your city").

Coppola's production is also noteworthy in the context of this analysis because it includes elements of the Christian religion narrative and the concepts of being damned, unclean and forsaken. The story displays very strong religious tones from the opening; Vlad's wrath and hatred is directed towards God, not towards the living. His ultimate goal is not preying on the living, but spurning God. This is clear during the beginning scenes of the film, when the story of Vlad and Elisabeta is introduced.

Dracula initially was a man of God, a faithful warrior in the "service of the cross." When his devotion was met with the injustice of the death of his beloved, he rejected the God he had served and became (within the Christian context of the story) an Antichrist figure. When Van Helsing and others meet Dracula for the first time, they use crosses to keep him at bay, to which the vampire reacts with rage; during his confrontation with Van Helsing and his group, he calls God "their God" and contemptuously refers to their holy relics as "idols":

> DRACULA: You think you can destroy me with your idols?
> VAN HELSING: Sacred blood of Christ!
> DRACULA: I, who served the cross. I, who commanded nations hundreds of years before you were born.
> VAN HELSING: Your armies were defeated. You tortured and impaled thousands of people.
> DRACULA: I was betrayed. Look what your God has done to me.

The conflict between Dracula and God is actually one of the main threads of the film. Furthermore, if regarded as an Antichrist character, Dracula does possess a great deal of devilish attributes. The aesthetics features of Coppola's vampire correspond with the commonly accepted devil imagery—the characteristically distorted face, fur, leathery wings (Link 1995: 61). When Dracula is not in his human form, he is a visually repulsive, twisted monster; the audience catches the first glimpse of this side of him during the scenes on the ship and later, more clearly, in Lucy's garden, when Mina encounters a demon with burning red eyes, covered in fur. The Pan–like features of Dracula's face (such as pronounced brow ridges and wide mouth) resemble strongly the traditional depictions of the Christian Devil (Link 1995: 61). Later, in the time of the confrontation in Jack's hospital, Dracula reveals another, equally devilish countenance—that of a giant, humanoid bat with membranous wings.

Coppola's vampire is capable of mesmerizing people he preys upon by using mind control, but its real influence consists of awakening the darkness within his victims. Dracula reaches out to and awakens all that is savage in those he preys upon, making the victim behave as if that victim were possessed. Under his influence, Lucy's (and later also Mina's) demeanor changes dramatically. Initially playful and seductive, even verging on being improper at times, Lucy is nonetheless a good natured, charming girl before Count lies his hand—and fangs—on her. Lucy's conduct, previously merely provocative, becomes downright obscene after she is bitten by Dracula. She makes lewd remarks at all the young men in her presence, calling Quincy "such a beast" and demanding that he kiss her, and suggests that Jack, who has come to see her as a doctor, has in fact some ulterior motives (which he has not).

Visited by Dracula every night, Lucy eventually withers away and dies, despite Van Helsing's efforts to save her. But even in death she is not free from the vampire, who maintains control over her body and soul. Enraged by Mina's decision to marry Jonathan, Dracula condemns Lucy to become a blood hungry ghoul in his likeness, cursing her to "to living death, to eternal hunger for living blood." Lucy rises from the grave, but she does not resemble Dracula's brides that Jonathan encountered in the castle. She is not enticing or voluptuous but profoundly disturbing and repulsive, not human. In the scene in the tomb her ghastly white face and vicious reaction to the cross and Van Helsing emphasize the complete absence of humanity. Lucy is a ghoulish imitation of herself, a monstrous parody of a woman who could be a wife and a mother; when she enters the crypt she is cradling a baby in her arms, but to Lucy, the child is simply the blood she craves, and when she hears her name called, she drops the baby to the floor inconsiderately. She calls Arthur "my husband," and that too is a morbid reminder of all that could have been but cannot be. Lucy is not like her creator, Dracula, who can take many forms and possesses a variety of powers; Lucy is literally condemned—empty, forsaken, trapped in her unholy half-life. Van Helsing calls her "a wanderer in the outer darkness."

Coppola's *Bram Stoker's Dracula* is a particularly good example of an American vampire narrative because it has all the traits of a traditional vampire tale, while at the same time it tries to portray Dracula in a more sympathetic light and render him both monstrous and human. The film clearly demonstrates the recent trend in American vampire fiction to present the vampire not as the Other, but as the central figure of the story. Instead of epitomizing the source of unfamiliar horror, or only partially familiar horror, the vampire becomes a complicated, morally complex figure, pondering the metaphysical qualities of good, evil and its own existence (Gemra 2008: 228). Even though Stoker's original novel constructed a more brutal and more animalistic monster than the previous vampire novels (such as *Varney the Vampire* by James Rymer or Sheridan LeFanu's *Carmilla*), the American public seemed more fond of the human face of the vampire (which was visible already with Ted Browning's *Dracula* [1931], which painted a completely different picture of the vampire than Friedrich Murnau's *Nosferatu: The Symphony of Horror* [1922]). Gemra points to the fact that Coppola used the main plot line of the novel, but he effectively created his own version of "the strangest love story," where feelings overcome death, liberate and can even avert eternal damnation. This puts the character of Dracula in a new light—he is monstrous, but at the same time very human, incomprehensible and simultaneously comprehensible, of this world and not of this world (Gemra 2008: 209). In contemporary fiction, the vampire more often tends to take on the role of a tragic figure trapped between its moral nature and immoral instincts or a relentless, formidable opponent. As a character it loses its symbolic and metaphoric nature and gains an engaging, organic and temporal identity; it becomes three-dimensional, but at a cost, for it can no longer serve as the horrifying Other.

One of the most prominent and notable literary vampire horror narratives focusing on portraying the vampire as the genuine Other is Stephen King's *'Salem's Lot*. The novel is noteworthy mostly because it establishes the vampire as the primary source of horror, not as the protagonist. Nonetheless, the vampire is sketched out in detail, with care. *'Salem's Lot* attempts to give credit to the classic chilling vampire tale while simultaneously adapting the story into a more familiar, less distant context. King "transplants Count Dracula into a contemporary setting in the person of the aristocratic Barlow," playing upon the isolation of a small town and exploring the possibility of its takeover by nonhuman forces (Carter in Joshi 2007: 628, 233).

'Salem's Lot does follow in *Dracula*'s footsteps in many aspects inasmuch as it makes use of the many traditional elements of the vampire figure characterization. The vampire is active only at night; it sleeps in the coffin (shipped from overseas) and is susceptible to the arsenal of Christian religious symbols. What is more important, in *'Salem's Lot* there is just one "alpha vampire," capa-

ble of creating minions but essentially unrivaled by the others as far as strength is concerned. Even Barlow's origins remain consistent with the tradition of Dracula—the evil comes from Europe, as it always does (which is logical if the long-lived vampire is to be older than two hundred years). Barlow is not a nobleman by birth, but his character is constructed to give off an air of nobility nonetheless. In the scene where he is holding Mark hostage, the vampire is depicted not like a monstrous, hungry predator, but a well-kept gentleman. Barlow's hands are like those of a pianist (King 1991: 314) and his face is "strong and intelligent and handsome in a sharp, forbidding sort of way," although "as the light shifted, it seemed almost effeminate" (King 1991: 315). The vampire's hair is "swept back from his brow in the European manner." He is wearing "a dark suit and a wine-colored tie," which is "impeccably knotted" (King 1991: 316). Even his voice is "rich" and "powerful" (King 1991: 314).

Although significant religious undertones are present in *'Salem's Lot,* the vampire is more folkloric, older. It can be killed only with a traditional stake through the heart, and it must be invited inside to be able to feed on the human victim. Interestingly enough, the vampire's journey towards modern times coincides with its diminishing fear of the Christian God and the symbols of his church. Barlow does react violently to the sound of God's name when father Callahan is defending Mark, but later laughs at the priest, calling him a "shaman" (King 1991: 314). As Gemra points out, Callahan loses his fight against Barlow as soon as Mark is gone because his faith has eroded over the years, and the symbols of his church are just empty tokens to him (Gemra 2008: 236). In *'Salem's Lot* the ultimate battle between God and the condemned one is reduced to an encounter between individuals: a man and a vampire. Furthermore, the ability of the man to defend himself depends solely on the subjective value of faith. Barlow is confident he is going to win—and he does. He turns Callahan into his thrall, saying: "Come, false priest. Learn of a true religion. Take *my* communion" (King 1991: 317, italics in the original).

As far as the ontological status of the vampire is concerned, *'Salem's Lot* shifts emphasis from damnation and the limbo of half-life to predation and survival. The depiction of the vampire, especially of Barlow minions, is therefore slightly more brutal, concerned with the instinctive, bestial nature of the monsters. The spiritual metamorphosis is, however, still expressly accentuated. To become a vampire is to lose the human soul:

> Mike opened his eyes.
> They glittered for just a moment in the moonlight, silver rimmed with red. They were as blank as washed blackboards. There was no human thought or feel-

ing in them. The eyes are the windows of the soul, Wordsworth had said. If so, these windows looked in on an empty room.

Mike sat up, the sheet failing from his chest, and Matt saw the heavy industrial stitchwork where the ME or pathologist had repaired the work of his autopsy, perhaps whistling as he sewed.

Mike smiled, and his canines and incisors were white and sharp. The smile itself was a mere flexing of the muscles around the mouth; it never touched the eyes. They retained their original dead blankness [King 1991: 181–182].

The most important attribute of the vampirized Mike is the emptiness that had replaced his soul. He is unable to smile like a human being, but his attempt reveals "white and sharp" teeth that bring to mind a beast, an evolutionarily specialized predator. The Mike Matt used to know is dead, and this fact is also emphasized, both in the spiritual sense (Mike being empty) and in more direct, biological sense, which is brought to attention by the unshapely stitch work on his chest. It is also worth noting that Mike, as well as Marjorie and other victims of Barlow's minions, change only after they are repeatedly visited by a vampire. Their behavior grows increasingly and noticeably strange until finally they are drained to the point when they die. This element of the vampire returning to feed on his victim places *'Salem's Lot* very close to the traditional structure of the vampire narrative. King's vampires display one more interesting characteristic—they cannot simply enter their victim's house without invitation. Both Danny and Mike ask Mark and Matt to be let in and seem to be unable to get in otherwise.

Despite the fact that *'Salem's Lot* clearly gravitates towards the traditional shape of the vampire tale of Bram Stoker's *Dracula,* it simultaneously does introduce some elements typical for the modern vampire narrative. Next to the contemporary, urban setting of the story, the most critical of those elements is the nature of the vampire threat, which is significantly different in *'Salem's Lot* than in other Dracula-derivative narratives. The metaphysical aspect of the vampire horror is now subdued in favor of the inescapability of the threat. The vampires prowling *'Salem's Lot* are brutal and, most importantly, far more numerous. Additionally, each of them is capable of producing more vampires. The protagonists face, therefore, not a lone, silent, cunning predator but a whole pack of them. The vampires can simply rely on the numbers, which shapes the odds into something more along the lines of "a pack versus a herd" instead of a duel between the vampire and his victim. As a consequence, a meaningful division into "us" and "them" arises among the characters. In one of the scenes Mark warns Ben that it would be difficult for him to face Susan, whom Ben loved, saying "She's *his* now' (King 1991: 285). As a result of this "us and them" division *'Salem's Lot* takes on a similarity to a zombie narrative, i.e., it employs the motif of a "shrinking fortress"—the enemy is out there, and the dwindling numbers of protagonists need to hide and fortify against the growing number of attackers. In fashion of a contemporary vampire narrative, *'Salem's Lot* abandons the traditional slow build-up leading to a final confrontation and instead takes on more of a guerrilla warfare approach.

The urban vampire makes itself comfortable in American cinema in the 1980s. A good example of this is the 1985 film directed by Tom Holland, *Fright Night*, which also represents a "modern" vampire film inasmuch as it relies heavily on intertextuality. Holland's film, despite being a vampire horror film, is also characterized by a certain playfulness (Hutchings 2008: 164). The setting constitutes a considerable part of this frivolous quality; in contrast to *'Salem's Lot,* it completely relinquishes traditional Gothic setting or even a likeness thereof in preference of a contemporary setting, which is a "very traditional suburban house":

> *Fright Night* does not avoid the establishing shot but uses it to undermine any suggestion of reality. It emphasizes the artificiality of the filmic medium and its representation of place. The film opens on a long shot of the moon *accompanied* by the sound of a wolf howling. A man's voice is heard inquiring, "What was that?" to which a woman answers, "Just a child of the night, John." *The traditional generic quality of the opening* is however undermined by the slow tilt down of the camera onto an establishing shot of a cityscape whose bright lights and urban sprawl is reminiscent of Los Angeles. The *film is therefore not taking place* within a traditional Gothic location as the soundtrack suggests, but in a contemporary setting. As the camera tracks right, along a suburban street, the conversation continues in familiar fashion. *The camera slows down* slightly as it passes an old, decrepit house suggesting that this is perhaps the source of the voices, a seemingly suitable location because of its derelict and Gothic appearance. Once again, expectations are undermined as the camera continues to move on to a very traditional suburban house. The camera cranes up to the house and into a window to reveal that the source of the voices is a television playing an old vampire movie [Abott in Day 2006: 131].

In this manner *Fright Night* offers a peculiar but apt combination of proper horror and moments of comic relief, beginning with the vampire's rather underwhelming first name, Jerry, through the majority of Evil's actions, and ending with scenes such as Jerry deciding to retreat upon hearing Charley's mother's voice. And yet the vampire in *Fright Night* is primarily a source of horror, not humor; Charley is terrified of Jerry and desperate to convince anyone to believe him and help him. Similarly, when Peter Vincent encounters transformed Evil, the latter talks in a rather peculiar, almost funny way; nonetheless, Peter's facial expression disperses the superficial comical quality of Evil's words and emphasizes the mad like absurdity of Evil's behavior. In this respect, as far as this analysis is concerned, *Fright Night* qualifies as a horror narrative, characterized by humor conventional to the films of the time (Lewis 2006: 29 and 2006: 35).

Fright Night constructs the vampire on the basis of the traditional elements of the vampire narrative structure. After young women start disappearing in his neighborhood, Charley, the main character, begins to suspect that his new neighbor, Jerry, might be a vampire. To combat the monster, he asks for help his best friend, Evil, and the host of a TV vampire hunter show, Peter Vincent. The vampire himself is a lone predator, a powerful monster who has not been encountered before by any of the protagonists. He is capable of creating minions, but among them he is still the alpha vampire, and his powers are incomparable to those transformed by him. He can, however, turn his victims into vampires just by biting them—just one attack is sufficient and there is no need for recurrent night visits, an ability that belongs to the modern vampire narratives. Visually, in his human form Jerry is considerably good looking, neat and charming, much like Dracula or Barlow. On the other hand, his appearance when he reverts to his true form is another trait situating him closer to the traditional form of the vampire tale rather than modern vampire narratives; when no longer disguised as a human, Jerry is as unsightly and repulsive as any conventional vampire; his face is disfigured and demonic, his mouth filled with sharp, protruding teeth and his hands equipped with long claws. Notably, in contrast to vampire minions in traditional narratives, the transformed Evil and Amy are very ugly and inhuman as well. Amy is exceptionally hideous in the scene in which she attacks Charley; her eyes turn bright, sickly yellow and her mouth transforms into a giant, gaping maw (especially the fanged, distorted mouth is horrific due to its connotation of *vagina dentata*).[2]

Socially, Jerry is very self-confident and authoritative. He is cunning, predatory and arrogant, but simultaneously quite charming—for instance, he can be charismatic enough to coax Evil into submitting willfully to him. He also uses mind control, like Dracula, but again, as in Dracula's case, the control is not of the mesmerizing, enticing sort but resembles more a trance-like domination; when he takes Amy with him, she seems to hover continuously between surprise and absolute obedience that verges on erotic fascination (an attitude reminiscent of Lucy's behavior). Further traits of traditional vampire portrayal in *Fright Night* are Jerry's ability to turn into a bat and to fly in that form, as well as the lethal effect the sunlight has on him. A significant departure from this canonical depiction is Jerry's seemingly complete independence of his coffin. At variance with the Slavic-derivative lore of the Euroamerican vampire, the final confrontation with Holland's vampire does take place during the day, but the monster is not is lying powerless in his casket (although he is hiding there, locked from the inside). On the contrary, he is fully awake and able to get up and move freely, while the stake barely affects him.

Similar to *'Salem's Lot*, *Fright Night* does not rely on the religious narrative, although it does employ some instrumental elements of it. There is no motif of damnation whatsoever, and throughout the film religion remains marginal, almost non-existent. Holy water is mentioned and crosses are used in the film with varying effect—when Peter Vincent directs a cross at Jerry during his and Charley's confrontation with the vampire, Jerry merely lets out a hearty laugh and says: "You have to have faith for this to work on me, Mr. Vincent." Then he proceeds to crush the religious symbol (in this respect the character of Peter Vincent is comparable to Father Callahan in *'Salem's Lot*—like Callahan, Peter Vincent is tired and disillusioned, and the religious symbols do not provide him with any help). Only when Charley uses his own cross does the vampire recoil. It is not, however, explained why he does so; the matter of Jerry's relationship with God is not addressed in any other manner in the film and remains unexplained. It is possible, therefore, that Charley's faith in the cross as an item is enough, and belief in God is of secondary importance.

Additionally, as Stacey Abbott rightly points out in *Celluloid Vampires: Life After Death in the Modern World*, "[w]hile all genre films require a layer of self-awareness, the contemporary horror film began to textualize its conventions into its own discourse" (Abbott 2007: 182) and for its own benefit. *Fright Night* embraces the intertextuality of its genre on more than one level. The film refers to the knowledge of other vampire films (as well as the knowledge one might gain from those films), introducing a character of an actor playing a TV vampire hunter and alluding to characters known from other narratives (for instance, the characters in the TV show at the beginning of the film are called Jonathan and Mina). Furthermore, *Fright Night* belongs to the films that "privilege a horror film fan as a supreme vampire killer" (Abbott in Day 2006: 129); Charlie, a horror film fan, overcomes his modern common sense and accepts that a vampire has moved in next door—what is more, *he "goes to the* outcast and monster-movie fan 'Evil Ed' to receive instruction from him on the best ways to protect himself from the vampires" (Abbott 2007: 183). When asked, Evil graciously produces a whole variety of methods and weapons, beginning with the cross (adding that "total faith in it [is necessary] for it to work"), garlic, holy water, and finishing with information that a vampire must be invited to the house—all of which Charley accepts without reservation. More importantly, as the audience learns in the course of the film, almost all of Evil's advice actually works. Interestingly enough, in the 2011 remake (*Fright Night* [2011], directed by Craig Gillespie) it is Evil, not Charley, who must persuade his friend that the neighbor is a vampire. The "2011 Charlie" is a new horror film model of Charley, a rational, no-nonsense Charley who reacts to his best friend's news with impatience and anger.

The new dimension of the modern vampire is presented in *30 Days of Night,* a 2002 graphic novel by Steve Niles and Ben Templesmith. *30 Days of Night* is a modern vampire narrative not only in the sense of being contemporary, but in terms of the manner in which the horror is delivered. Niles and Templesmith's work casts aside the unhurried, painstaking build-up of mystery and subtle terror in favor of raw, almost obscene representation of the monster and the fear evoked by that monster. *30 Days of Night* is a brutal, bloody and savage tale that puts emphasis on the physical, mortal peril instead of the spiritual threat to the immortal soul.

In terms of the horror properties of *30 Days of Night,* one of the main assets of Niles' story is the setting, which immediately prepares the audience for an intense, claustrophobic clash of the human and the predator. The very premise of *30 Days of Night,* upon which rests its key horror quality, is an unnaturally long night. In Barrow, Alaska, the place where *30 Days of Night* takes place, the sun "doesn't rise between November 18th and December 17th," and the story starts on the last day of sunlight (Niles and Templesmith 2003: 3–4). By doing away with the natural ally of the human beings in their battle with the vampiric enemy, namely the sun, *30 Days of Night* realizes its horror potential to the fullest. The unending night removes the confrontation between the vampire and the human protagonists from its traditional turn-based mode and instead establishes a real-time battlefield. In this new reality the situation of the human protagonists is dramatic; they are faced with all the adversities characteristic to the traditional vampire tales, such as being weaker than their enemy and being more susceptible during night time, but additionally there is no break or relief they could wait for.

The vampires come for the inhabitants of Barrow as soon as the sun sets. They do not come to feed in secret, as the majority of their literary and cinematic counterparts do, they do not seduce their prey, and they do not need invitation of any kind. In *30 Days of Night* the vampires fall on the humans like locust; instead of the elegant hunters known from other vampire tales they resemble a pack of wild animals falling upon the town in a bloody "feeding frenzy" (Niles and Templesmith 2003: 33).

> The invasion came swiftly and easily. Some of the townspeople—the hunters and whalers, the tough and stubborn—tried to fight, but it was hopeless. The sun went down a long time ago and will not return for a long time more. They came

quickly, walking over the frozen tundra, cutting off communication and escape routes as they marched. Endless night, and endless supply of blood and meat [Niles and Templesmith 2003: 36–37].

The impassive captions recounting the terrifying events taking place in Barrow are juxtaposed with images of violence, blood and death. The vampires appear out of nowhere, without a warning or any previous arrangement. Their attack is neither augured nor conceivable, and there is no mercy and no hope for the human characters, who must fight for their survival against an unstoppable army of monsters "marching" towards them (Niles and Templesmith 2003: 36–37).

Embedded in the intertextual universe of existing vampire narratives and the elements of vampire lore stemming from those narratives, *30 Days of Night* gives more power to the vampire than it has ever been given before. Although stripped from its noble heritage and the capacity to transform into an animal form (features characteristic to the traditional, conventional vampire characters) and deprived of the magnetic, seductive charm and the ability to turn people into its slavish minions (features retained by the majority of modern vampire characters), Niles and Templesmith's vampire rises as a superior predator impervious to everything save decapitation. The monsters feeding on the inhabitants of Barrow are not bound by the lore effective in other vampire titles. They need not fear crosses or garlic, they are in no circumstances hindered by a cross, and they cannot be wounded and killed by wooden stakes. Only remnants of the traditional vampire lore are visible; the creatures can be killed if their head is severed, and they perish in sunlight. By eliminating or reducing the arbitrary, orthodox elements of the lore, Niles and Templesmith portrayed an old, predictable monster in a fresh, unpredictable and therefore uncanny manner, restoring the vampire's capacity to unnerve and disturb its audience.

Aesthetically, the vampires in *30 Days of Night* are also not what the traditional vampire narratives have accustomed their audience to. Incredibly fast and strong, with their mouths filled with sharp fangs and their black eyes devoid of any shade of humanity, the monsters are an intimidating pack. When the protagonists, Eben Olemaun and his wife Stella encounter the vampires, they see a "rough looking" crowd of men, women and children, "completely varied from one to the other, except for their fierce eyes"; some of the vampires have traditional fangs and some have rows of "razor teeth like a wild dog," and within each face "pure evil" can be seen (Niles and Templesmith 2003: 104). Apart from their overall, palpable monstrosity, they constitute an immensely diverse crowd. Their appearance, clothes and presence suggest a collective of all ages, sexes and social strata, as well as, presumably, different levels of influence.

Although diversified in their appearance and background, the vampires are fairly like-minded in their attitude and conduct. The character of Marlow exemplifies the disposition of the whole vampire pack. He is sadistic—the hunt for people is a game to him, and he takes pleasure in the terror of his prey, without which the feeding would be boring and unsatisfying ("let them run ... try to hide," he says); he is also arrogant, not even entertaining the thought that the human prey might be able to outsmart their chasers and hide successfully (Niles and Templesmith 2003: 27). He refers to humans as "blood-meat" (Niles and Templesmith 2003: 37). *30 Days of Night* depicts its vampires not as majestic, self-possessed and refined hunters, but as savage animals lacking self control and any traces of humanity whatsoever. Niles' vampires are not organized into a typical structure the vampire menace traditionally has, with one indisputable leader and a number of enslaved minions. If anything, they resemble a pack of wild animals with the strongest individual acting as leader (the leader can be challenged, which is clearly visible when transformed Eben chases the vampires away by defeating Vincente). They are fast, ruthless, bestial and voracious, even decadent in their greediness. There is an almost obscene quality to their uninhibited, insatiable lust for blood and their collective assault. It is this gluttony and the quantity that make the vampires in *30 Days of Night* terrifying; their ravenous group attacks make them similar to zombies in any zombie narrative or the infected in Danny Boyle's *28 Days Later* [2002]. Like in *'Salem's Lot,* the motif of "shrinking fortress" is one of the major characteristic features of *30 Days of Night,* lending the story an unpleasant flavor of realism.

As the readers later learn, Marlow's attack on Barrow was an act of insubordination. An older and stronger vampire to whom Marlow answers, Vincente, appears and vents his fury on him. There is a concrete reason for Vincente's anger, which becomes clear when Vincente reproaches Marlow:

> VINCENTE: You fucking arrogant idiot! Do you have any idea what you've done? ... I had hopes of arriving in time to stop you. I can see that I arrived too late. The damage is done.
> MARLOW: Damage?
> VINCENTE: How many centuries has it taken to become a myth? How many centuries has it taken us to mesh with the living world? To make humans no longer believe we exist? Can any of you tell me? Hundreds! Thousands! [Niles and Templesmith 2003: 52–53].

This dialogue points to another disturbing touch of realism in *30 Days of Night*—i.e., the vampires' conscious ploy to make humans believe they are only a myth. By becoming a legend and blending in with the humans, the vampires obtain the greatest advantage there is—they have made their prey oblivious of their existence, and therefore careless and unprepared, just like the inhabitants of Barrow were.

An interesting element of this particular vampire narrative is the protagonist's decision to sacrifice his humanity in order to save his wife and friends. After witnessing the fight between Vincente and Marlow, in which Marlow is killed, Eben resorts to turning into a vampire himself, with the intent of challenging Vincente. He wins, but the price of the power is the loss of humanity. Eben deems this price too high and decides to let go of life while he still feels at least partly human. Despite the protagonist's transformation into the Other, Eben's decision preserves the balance of horror in *30 Days of Night*, and the Other remains untamed and unfamiliar.

Niles and Templesmith's story is a quite original example of a Euroamerican vampire narrative. It relinquishes the slow, gradual introduction of the predator and opts for intense, shocking confrontation. The vampire, exempt from the arbitrary but merciless laws of lore, is a creature that still surpasses the human in power and desire but is as free as the human he preys upon. *30 Days of Night* is not a story of eternal damnation, monsters native to folklore or spiritual fall but a tale full of violence, despair and hopelessness.

A curious variation on the vampiric theme, worth a brief mention, can be seen in *Sleepwalkers* [1991], written by Stephen King and directed by Mick Garris, a film that expands and transforms the vampire theme practically to its limits. *Sleepwalkers* focus on imaginary shape-shifting cat-shaped vampires. Charles and his mother are a pair of vampiric monsters, human-sized bipedal werecats of sort. They blend in fully with humans and can walk in the sunlight. Their true nature is revealed only in the mirror, very much like it is the case with the conventional vampire—but not through the lack of reflection, but through disclosure of their hideous real form. When not disguised as humans, the vampires in *Sleepwalkers* resemble overgrown, deformed cats with hairless, uneven, repulsively pink skin. Their appearance is not only repulsive, but also connotes unpleasant imagery of something badly burned or freshly skinned. This much creativity pushes the monster out from the gray zone between the familiar and the unfamiliar necessary for horror fiction. To compensate for this, *Sleepwalkers* opens with internal fictitious folklore established, complete with invented source material:

> Sleepwalker *n*. Nomadic shape-shifting creatures with human and feline origins. Vulnerable to the deadly scratch of the cat, the sleepwalker feeds upon the lifeforce of virginal human females. Probable source of the Vampire legend
> —Chillicoathe Encyclopaedia of Arcane Knowledge 1st Edition, 1884.

Thus the producers prepare the audience of the film for the horror factor, introducing the necessary familiarity with the monster so that the viewers can sympathize with Tanya, the protagonist, and fear for her even before Charles displays any signs at all of being monstrous. In this way, despite transforming the subject theme to such an extent, *Sleepwalkers* operates in the same way as any other vampire narrative, relying on the slow but unavoidable advance of the predator rather than a sudden, shocking revelation of the nature of danger.

The situation of the vampire motif in Japanese horror narratives is a little more complex. There are no native legends of creatures reminiscent of Euroamerican vampires in Japan (see Bunson 2000). The vampire figure enjoys considerable popularity in Japanese fiction, but it is seen as no more than a "Western import" (Joshi 2010: 277). Just as it is the case with the Euroamerican cultural region, titles concerning vampires abound in Japanese literature, cinema, video games and graphic novels. Only few and far between, however, portray the vampire as a source of terror. In *Encyclopedia of the Vampire: The Living Dead in Myth, Legend, and Popular Culture* Joshi points out that in Japanese fiction the vampire rarely assumes the role of an evil, horrifying monster—straightforward "*Dracula*-like plots" featuring a solitary, unambiguously evil vampire are scarce in manga and anime, where vampires "frequently constitute a morally neutral society or subculture" (Joshi 2011: 202). Instead, Japanese authors and producers tend to opt for impressive, admirable vampire characters (Kōta Hirano's *Hellsing* or *Vampire Hunter D* series, written by Hideyuki Kikuchi), or compassion-worthy vampire characters (*Lament of the Lamb* by Kei Tōme). The original vampiric themes in Japanese folklore and art, on the other hand, introduce a creature bearing little resemblance to the Western predator.

One of the few titles employing the native Japanese theme of vampire-like creatures and monsters is a film directed by Kaneto Shindō from 1968, *Kuroneko* (*Yabu no naka no kuroneko,* also known as *Black Cat from the Grove*). The vampire featured in the film may seem somewhat unorthodox by Euroamerican standards: firstly, it does suck blood, but not in order to survive, and only of specific people (men belonging to the samurai class). Secondly, the precise ontological nature of the predator is unclear—although they are reminiscent of a *yōkai* called *bakeneko* (Tatarczuk 2010: 25), the creatures in the film might as well be ghosts (they do appear exactly like the murdered women, Shige and Yone) or demons (Yone mentions a hellish realm to which Shige was forced to return). Thirdly, the behavior of the vampires, as well as their powers and weaknesses, is defined by duties instead of prohibitions. There are certain actions Shige and Yone must take without fail (and in a certain manner) lest they are pulled back to the hellish realm whence they came.[3]

Bakeneko (translated as "demon cat," "spirit cat," "monster cat" or "ghost cat"), the monster to which the vampires in *Kuroneko* are similar, appears in Japanese folklore and fiction in many variations and shapes. Jeremy Roberts defines *bakeneko* as a "demon cat who can shape shift into human form" (Roberts 2010: 11). A famous story featuring a monster cat is *The Vampire Cat of Nabeshima*, one of the short stories compiled in a volume, *Tales of Old Japan*, by Algernon Bertram Freeman Mitford, in which a demon cat takes the place of the Prince's mistress to drink his blood:

> O-Toyo retired to her own room and went to bed. At midnight she awoke with a start, and became aware of a huge cat that crouched watching her; and when she cried out, the beast sprang on her, and, fixing its cruel teeth in her delicate throat, throttled her to death. What a piteous end for so fair a dame, the darling of her prince's heart, to die suddenly, bitten to death by a cat! Then the cat, having scratched out a grave under the verandah, buried the corpse of O-Toyo, and assuming her form, began to bewitch the Prince. But my lord the Prince knew nothing of all this, and little thought that the beautiful creature who caressed and fondled him was an impish and foul beast that had slain his mistress and assumed her shape in order to drain out his life's blood [Mitford 1966: 287].

The Nabeshima Cat is a scary, dangerous *yōkai,* and its story bears all the markers of a *yōkai* story. The monster appears out of nowhere and without a reason, kills O-Toyo in a brutal, vicious manner and escapes to cause further mischief. *Bakeneko* featured in films, on the other hand, is characterized by a different set of features. Almost with no exception the cinematic demon cat is born out of someone's harm and unjust death. It comes to avenge the dead, therefore acting for someone else's sake, not for its own. Extremely difficult—if not impossible—to stop, defeat or exorcise, the spirit cat carries out the revenge with no assistance from anyone else. In some stories (the third segment in the *Ayakashi* TV series [2006], as well as *Ghost Cat of Otama Pond* [1960], directed by Nobuo Nakagawa) the *bakeneko* is formed when a cat laps on the blood of someone killed unjustly or is otherwise related to the person killed. The same image is used in *The Ghost-Cat Cursed Pond* [1968], where the cat laps the blood of its mistress, thus becoming an instrument of supernatural retribution.

The *bakeneko* portrayed in Shindō's film follows the set of rules introduced by the cinematic image of the monster cat and is motivated by the desire of revenge. After having been raped and murdered by soldiers during a time of civil war, Shige and Yone, a mother and daughter-in-law, return to take revenge on those who hurt them. Interestingly enough, they are neither vengeful spirits nor are they avenged by the spirit cat, but instead they become vampiric demon cats themselves. In light of Euroamerican cinematic and literary conventions, Shige and Yone are interesting; in contrast to Euroamerican vampires, the mother and daughter-in-law are reborn as vampires because of *urami* (deep-seated grudge).[4] Yone claims that they were brought back by "evil ghosts" out of their own will and reminds Shige that "[their] vow is to kill samurai and suck their blood" (the word she uses is *ikichi,* "lifeblood"). Additionally, sucking the blood is a completely voluntary act for them since their corporeal survival does not depend on it, neither is it a compulsion (which becomes apparent when Shige refuses to drink Gintoki's blood).

Not only do Shindō's vampires suck the blood of one particular kind of people, but also they do it in a very ritualistic manner. When Shige encounters the man who led the group of warriors who raped and killed her and her mother-in-law, she does not take up the opportunity to kill him right there and then in the grove. Instead, she goes through with an elaborate trap of luring him into the house, where Yone was waiting, and pretending to be two helpless, lonely women. As Shige seduces the leader into her chamber, Yone begins to dance to a steady beat and a slow, eerie tune. The dance intensifies gradually until Shige pounces at the victim, biting his throat and sucking blood.

Visually, Shige initially resembles a ghost rather than a corporeal monster. Clad in white, almost phantasmal, she appears out of nowhere, seemingly harmless, her silhouette standing out against the dark bamboo grove. When the group leader runs into her alone in the dark, he is naturally unnerved, but intrigued nonetheless. Like an apparition, Shige leads the leader swiftly and silently into the bamboo grove. This impression is only strengthened when she disappears briefly when the leader is distracted by a cat's cry, only to inexplicably reappear by his side a moment later. The leader suspects that she is a "specter," an illusion, and he is correct; both the young woman he is seeing and the house he is invited to are merely an illusion (that is why he feels cold while being inside the "room"), created in a manner similar to that in folk legends. Shige and Yone are not supernatural creatures merely dwelling in our world, but their world merges at points with the world of the living. The moments when the spiritual world and the tangible world intersect are emphasized in the film by the use of austere lighting and shadows. The fog additionally intensifies the dreamlike atmosphere. Furthermore, Shige and Yone can apparently freely cross the border between the two worlds. When Gintoki visits the house for the first time, he realizes that he is dealing with supernatural creatures, who only had "taken the image" of his mother and wife. Confronted, Yone and Shige float away into darkness in a ghost-like fashion, disappearing entirely from Gintoki's sight and reach. It is worth noting at this point that *Kuroneko* completely forgoes all the elements related to the burial site or earthly remains of the vampires, which would be very unusual for a Euroamerican vampire narrative of the same time (or a narrative otherwise so steeped in folklore). Although Shige and Yone technically return from the dead, their ability to fade without difficulty from the material world into the immaterial one suggests that they might have no bodies that could be subjected to appropriate procedures that might lead to the vampires' destruction.

Similar to the traditional Euroamerican vampire, Shige and Yone look and behave like human beings. They are, however, slightly cat-like in nature—their carriage is delicate, majestic and subtle at times, but rough and violent at others. They move gracefully and deftly (e.g., Shige jumping over the puddles or escaping the sword strike, or Yone jumping out of Gintoki's reach). When they attack, on the other hand, they are ferocious and bestial. Further associations are triggered by subtle details and brief shots intertwined into longer scenes. For example, in one scene Yone's hair moves like a cat's tail, and Shige's hand transforms for a moment into a cat's paw when she is serving tea. Another tell-tale shot shows Yone drinking from a bucket—when her face reflects in the water, the audience can see a kabuki-reminiscent make-up (*kumadori*, specifically the make-up worn by actors playing ghosts, demons and creatures other than humans; see Żeromska 2010: 116 and 2010: 123. Also the dance performed by Yone is reminiscent of kabuki dances). On another occasion her face also reflects as a *bakeneko*'s face in a puddle, and her hand, once cut off, reverts to a cat's paw.

Shindō's vampires are ritualized and vulnerable to conventional methods of dealing with them, but their power to scare their audience lies in two very important factors. Firstly, the vampire cat is a sly and deceitful creature, capable of squirming out of any trap. Near the end of the story Gintoki, preparing to battle the remaining vampire, attempts to purify his body and mind before the fight. The vampire, being a shape-shifting trickster, manipulates Gintoki into opening the door to his solitary cell and thus undoes his preparations:

YONE: Excuse me ...
GINTOKI: Who is it?
YONE: Please open the door.
GINTOKI: Tonight ends the seventh day of solitary purification. I cannot open it until dawn.
YONE: I know that very well. I am a medium in charge of divination at the Imperial Palace.
GINTOKI: I cannot break the rules for anyone.
YONE: The Mikado is very troubled about you. Tonight is the last night, so evil

spirits may appear to thwart your plans. The Mikado sent me here. I am to seal them in, so that you may complete your seven day duty.
GINTOKI: Inform the Mikado that I am a match for any evil spirit!
YONE: You do not understand at all. Disobey him and not only you but your leader will be punished too. It will only take a little while. Please open the door.
GINTOKI: Just a little while then.

The motif is similar to that in the story *The Cauldron of Kibitsu* (published in *Tales of Moonlight and Rain* by Akinari Ueda), when a month-long ritual meant to protect the protagonist is undone by the ghost's trick. Secondly, it is debatable whether Yone could be killed or even defeated, since, as it is the case with vengeful spirits of any kind, the Japanese supernatural avenger does not leave until the retribution is fulfilled. These features, together with the eerie, ghostly appearance and fierce hatred towards their victims, account for the terrifying nature of the vampires depicted in *Kuroneko*.

A later production that also deals with vampires, but in a way more familiar to the Euroamerican audience, is Michio Yamamoto's 1971 film *Lake of Dracula* (*Noroi no yakata: Chi wo suu me*). Yamamoto's film takes a more Euroamerican approach in constructing the vampire narrative, both plot-wise and character-wise. *Lake of Dracula,* the second installment in the *Toho Dracula Trilogy,* is characterized by "distinctly Western aesthetic[s] and content" (Schlegel in Browning and Picart 2009: 263). "*Lake of Dracula,*" Schlegel argues in *Identity Crisis: Imperialist Vampires in Japan,* "is more comfortable with the material [than the first entry of the trilogy], more confident in its direction, more derivative of the Hammer model, and indeed, more fun" (Schlegel in Browning and Picart 2009: 270). The story concerns a young woman and her fiancé, whose peaceful life is turned upside down after a strange coffin is delivered to the sleepy little town they live in. The young woman, Akiko, discovers that a vampire has arrived in town and that it has begun to feed.

Since the vampire motif is not a very common horror motif in Japanese fiction, the Western "aesthetic[s] and content" may make *Lake of Dracula* a touch confusing to the Euroamerican, especially American audiences. As Schlegel suggests, when an American audience is viewing cinema of other countries, it is exposed to content and forms that are not usually included in "the mainstream diet most audiences consume" (Schlegel in Browning and Picart 2009: 264). The Hollywood audience, used to a certain aesthetic system to which they can react and relate, might experience difficulties while processing Yamamoto's film, which falls neither into the category of familiar nor into that of unfamiliar. "Audiences expect to experience uniquely Japanese vampires bound to tropes and conventions associated with Japanese mythology and folklore, yet this is not even remotely the case" (Schlegel in Browning and Picart 2009: 264). As far as the plot is concerned, *Lake of Dracula* employs a very traditional structure. The vampire arrives at a small residence in a little town and starts a methodical hunt. Even before that, the audience is treated to an atmospheric introduction sequence: the protagonist, a small girl at the time, chases her runaway dog to a secluded, creepy mansion by Lake Fujimi, which is a near replica of Hammer's often recycled castle set from *Horror of Dracula*, very close to the coast, "suggesting settlement or encroachment of a foreign invader" (Schlegel in Browning and Picart 2009: 270–271). The "foreign invader" is indeed, as the audience finds out later, not of pure Japanese origin. The monster's father was a foreigner, like his father before him, and all of them carried the cursed blood of a vampire ancestor.

The nature of the monster threatening the protagonists for *Lake of Dracula* is not named or suspected at first (the idea is referred to, but still the word is not used until the last third of the film—he is even credited as "the vampire"). The first harbinger of the vampire's presence is the caretaker's disappearance. Soon after that, Akiko's fiancé Saeki, a doctor, is called to a strange patient: a young girl almost completely drained of blood—the vampire's first victim. The caretaker Kyusaku, attacked by the monster before, also turns up changed. The Japanese vampire manages to draw from both his victims approximately the same amount of blood at once that a Euroamerican conventional vampire might do in a number of nightly visits. Both the young woman and Kyusaku are unnaturally pale, almost white, and slow in their reactions to the point of being catatonic. Their behavior is limited to very base activities and stands out in a manner far more noticeable than that of any common Euroamerican vampire victim.

When Akiko's sister, Natsuko, is apprehended by the vampire, she is portrayed in a manner more familiar to the Western audience. Akiko wakes up in the middle of the night and notices Natsuko is gone. Akiko looks out of the windows and sees her sister disappearing into the woods. The scene when Natsuko, wearing only her white nightgown, vanishes among the trees at a slow but steady pace is very similar to the scene in Coppola's *Bram Stoker's Dracula*, when Lucy Westenra, entranced by Dracula, walks down the garden. Like Lucy, Natsuko returns changed. However, whereas Lucy's behavior after she is turned into Dracula's slave is merely disturbing and confused, Natsuko is downright sinister and hateful. Not only is she the only vampire's minion who looks and behaves normally in *Lake of Dracula*, but she is also manipulative and brisk. When Akiko tries to tell her fiancé that something is wrong, Natsuko purposefully does whatever she can to make Akiko look absurd in her suspicions. It is revealed later that Natsuko had indeed been holding a grudge against her sister (she felt that she was the less-loved child), and the vampire's influence seems to have brought out all the hidden animosity in her. At other times, Natsuko seems to be fully aware of her condition—for instance, she asks Akiko to burn her body "as soon as [she] dies" so that she would not rise.

The predator whom the protagonists of Yamamoto's film must battle resembles a conventional Euroamerican vampire. Yamamoto's vampire is tall, majestic and handsome, dressed impeccably and even equipped with a gentleman's white scarf. His skin is pale and his eyes can assume a golden glow. Much like the traditional vampire figure, the vampire in *Lake of Dracula* is a dominating, majestic figure, and becomes animalistic and violent only during attack. He is not, however, afraid of sunlight (neither are his minions, Kyusaku and Natsuko), and he cannot change his form in any manner. In *Lake of Dracula*, similarly to *Kuroneko,* the motif of the vampire lying dead and vulnerable in his coffin is absent, which emphasizes the "imported" nature of the monster (since the folklore methods and weapons to defeat the vampire are as alien in Japan as the vampire itself).

Saeki and Akiko's reaction to the possibility of facing a vampire also mirrors similar moments in Euroamerican productions of that time. Having realized that something strange is happening, Saeki accepts the situation readily and assumes the role of the leader and the authority (which corresponds to the main function of the character of Abraham Van Helsing in virtually all adaptations of Bram Stoker's *Dracula*). He informs Akiko of the nature of the enemy, provides her with some history and facts about the monster and explains how it can be defeated:

SAEKI
    We're thinking the same thing. Who is this man? The people you knew changed, one after another, into devils. The marks on their necks.... The loss of blood.... The answer is [a vampire]. Some legends of vampires and cannibals sound like true stories. Even today, there are cases of cannibalism. In 1948, a man in England was executed for drinking human blood. The legends say the victims of [the vampire][5] become his slaves. He sucks their blood. Shortly after they die, they revive to be vampires themselves. Only fire and a stake through the heart can kill them.

An interesting detail worth noting at this point is that although in the subtitles the word "Dracula" is used, what Saeki actually says is *kyūketsuki,* which literally means "a vampire" in Japanese. Apart from ascribing to Saeki's character the role of both Van Helsing and Jonathan Harker, his monologue performs a number of functions in this scene. For one, it reinforces the traditional elements of the vampire narrative such as knowledge gathered from legends and stories and the monster who comes from abroad. At the same time it emphasizes the locally exotic nature of the enemy and certain vagueness of the information. Lastly, it firmly embeds *Lake of Dracula* within the same lore and universe that exist in Euroamerican vampire narratives.

Intent on fighting the monster, Akiko and Saeki go to the mansion by Lake Fujimi. What follows is another unorthodox element as far as vampire narratives are concerned; they encounter the dead body the vampire's father. In his diary they read:

> I'm going to die soon. He sucks my blood every night. There isn't much blood left in me. The horrible vampire is my own son. I'm not Japanese. The reason my father built this house in a deserted place like this was that he knew he was a descendant of the abominable vampire. His life, however, was normal and peaceful. So was mine. But the blood had been waiting for the chance. When my son was twenty-five, he suddenly assaulted a woman he loved. Then I saved a little girl and her dog who lost their way and came into the house. Still there was some humanity left in my son.

The entry provides the audience with the background information concerning the vampire. It also depicts vampirism in terms of cursed inheritance rather than the nature of existence. The sudden emergence of blood-lust (at a specific age—"twenty-five"), like an onset of a disease, and the gradual pace at which the "cursed blood" awakens (the phrase "still there was some humanity left in my son" suggests that the rest of that humanity eventually dissipated) likens the vampirism to an illness.

In the moment of final confrontation with the vampire, Saeki temporarily abandons his role of the vampire hunter and resumes the role of a rational skeptic, arguing that the vampire is simply a madman who believes himself to be a vampire and uses hypnosis to control his victims. It is a curious storytelling maneuver, which relieves some the supernatural suspense for the duration of the definitive battle, significantly alleviating its symbolic aspect (the fight between the human and the vampire usually amounts to the fight between good and evil) and lessens its sublimity (Saeki the human faces simply another human instead of powerful, immortal monster). In the end, however, the audience is of course reassured about the true nature of the monster; the scene ends with the proper, graphic, repulsive decomposition of the vampire as it dies, impaled on a baluster.

As Schlegel insists, *Lake of Dracula* is much more than "mere imitation of a successful British economic and aesthetic model"; it represents fear and anxiety of "foreign rule and interference consonant in the period under which [it was] produced" (Schlegel in Browning and Picart 2009: 275 276). Regardless of the obvious manifestations of the Western influence in both the aesthetics and the content of *Lake of Dracula,* as well as the two other films in the Toho trilogy, Schlegel argues that "these three films do in fact exist relative to the culture that produced them, but not manifestly so" (Schlegel in Browning and Picart 2009: 264). Indeed, despite the seemingly complete adaptation to the Euroamerican form, *Lake of Dracula* delivers a strictly Japanese mannerism combined with a typically Japanese interpretation of the Western predator motif.

The most recent Japanese production discussed in this part of the chapter is *Blood: The Last Vampire* [2000] directed by Hiroyuki Kitakubo. Released by Production I.G. and Aniplex, *Blood: The Last Vampire* is an animated film spanning 45 minutes, which employs a plot and aesthetic design very familiar to a Euroamerican audience. The film was released almost entirely in English (with Japanese subtitles), as the dialogues are, in most part, in English. Although the plot features American characters as well as Japanese ones, it primarily revolves around a Japanese protagonist. Kitakubo's story follows a nurse, Makiho, working in a high school adjacent to an American military base, who in the middle of her peaceful, uneventful life encounters two monstrous, shape-shifting vampires.

The animation of *Blood: The Last Vampire* is characterized by dark, subdued colors and gritty, high-end animation. The atmospheric, fast, dynamic scenes in which the vampires appear are intertwined with moments of slow-motion, blurred, nightmarish sequences (such as the scene in the infirmary or the Halloween party), additionally emphasized by the score (the jazz background music played by the band when Makiho is looking for Sharon). The combination of those elements gives the film a modern quality and an atmosphere of realism and authenticity.

An original aspect of *Blood: The Last Vampire* as a horror vampire narrative is its manner of introducing the vampires to the audience. The concept of the fight with vampires emerges in the first sequence of scenes of the film, when Saya, the vampire hunter, attacks a man whom she believes to be a vampire. The monsters are presented not as a mysterious, advancing enemy, but as an unnatural but defeatable threat. The way Saya and David, her guardian, handle the situation, likens them to wildlife control rather than vampire hunters; the more traditional form of the vampire narrative begins when the focus of the story shifts to the nurse, Makiho. When a girl feeling unwell, Linda, comes to the infirmary with a friend, Sharon, Makiho has no inkling of the danger. Because of the form the vampires have in *Blood: The Last Vam-*

pire, as well as the complete lack of the ability to mesmerize, the conventional pattern of regular nightly visits is out of the question. Once the monsters attack, the victim becomes a witness as well and must be eradicated. Due to this fact, Kitakubo's story compresses the protagonist' transition from the suspicion of the presence of the predator to the confrontation with the monster to the absolute minimum. The nurse admits the pale, taciturn girl to the infirmary and, unaware that she is actually a monster who came to feed on her blood, goes about her activities, talking to make her "patient" feel more at ease. Save for Makiho's monologue, there is no other sound in the room; unbeknownst to the nurse, Linda and Sharon communicate behind her back, mouthing words silently. Makiho's one-sided "conversation" accentuates the fact that she is, in fact, alone in the infirmary, since she is the sole human being there, surrounded by two monsters. It is only when Linda is about to lunge that Makiho is saved by Saya. An additional noteworthy detail is Makiho's light hearted question about Linda and Sharon's costumes (she asks them whether they are going to dress up as vampires), which is all the more significant as Linda and Sharon are actually vampires "dressed up" as humans.

When in their real form, the vampires in *Blood: The Last Vampire* may look unorthodox at first glance, but they do, in fact, pay tribute to classic vampires' basic characteristics. Kitakubo's monsters are called Chiroptera (translated as *yokushu* in Japanese; both denote the order to which bats biologically belong). They are huge, monstrous, unshapely bat-like creatures capable of flying, who feed on human blood. Extremely long-lived and comparable to humans in intelligence, the Chiroptera tend take human shape and are careful not to let anyone see their real form. In the scene in the infirmary, "Sharon"[6] is attacked by Saya; only then does she scream, emitting a high-pitch sound that breaks the lamps and the windows in the room, and her face becomes inhuman.

Notably, when Saya talks about the Chiroptera, she uses the word "demon" (*oni*), as opposed to "humans" (*ningen*). Indeed, the Chiroptera are so monstrous they exhibit visual characteristics attributable to demons in both Japanese and American cultural frame: large, strong body, a wide, gaping mouth filled with sharp, fang-like teeth and clawed paws. Unaffected by daylight, stakes or religious symbols, the Chiroptera can be slain only with a good quality cold weapon. The matter of the immortal soul is, it would seem, irrelevant. Saya never mentions any threat greater than losing one's life—although she does consider falling victim to Chiroptera a fate best avoided at any cost, which is clearly visible when she offers the nurse a pistol so that she can kill herself as a last resort.

Although the attack of the Chiroptera is never actually shown on-screen, the audience can assume that it was as savage as the Chiroptera's appearance. Not much is known about their behavior in their true, monstrous form. When in human form, they are fairly apt at blending in with other humans, to the point of being virtually indistinguishable. Whereas Linda is rather conspicuous—pale, silent and awkward, with her eyes almost completely hidden under her a bit too long fringe—Sharon is bright, charming and polite. Neither of them, however, including Mama-san (the third Chiropteran), can rival the overwhelming, dominating figure of the traditional vampire as he is portrayed in *Bram Stoker's Dracula*, *'Salem's Lot* or the Toho trilogy. The Chiroptera are not divided into leaders and minions; they are all equal and function like a "democratic" pack of predators. It is worth noticing that neither Sharon nor Linda are Japanese, as opposed to Makiho (the protagonist) and Saya (the slayer). "Foreign invader" takes a more profound meaning in this respect, since the action centers around the American Yokota Air Base, after World War II.

Another characteristic aspect of Kitakubo's film is that, despite being a horror narrative that established the vampire as the Other, *Blood: The Last Vampire* depicts also vampire on vampire violence. The protagonist the audience can comfortably identify with is Makiho. The nurse is lost, scared and appropriately human in her behavior and reactions. The knowledgeable, skillful vampire slayer is Saya. Saya is neither pleasant nor particularly friendly; on the contrary, she is aloof, indifferent and brusque, which makes it difficult for the audience to care about her. It is not revealed until the end of the film that Saya is, in fact, also a vampire, although entirely different from the Chiroptera. By revealing Saya's true identity only at the very end of the story, Kitakubo prevents Saya's character from diluting and taming the Other in a way similar to other narratives that use vampires as protagonists (such as *Blade* [1998] or Hideyuki Kikuchi's *Vampire Hunter D*).

Blood: The Last Vampire diverges from the traditional shape of the vampire narrative also in another significant aspect. Among the main characters' featured vampire narratives, the majority of those who manage to survive walk away from their experience stronger and more aware after having faced, fought and defeated the vampire. Kitakubo's production, on the other hand, leaves the protagonist confused and alone. When Makiho is being questioned after everything that happened in the Air Base on the Halloween night, she says:

MAKIHO
 And this is all I know. I've told you everything I've seen with my own eyes. Even though I'm not sure you believe me.... I'm not even sure what really happened. When I returned to the infirmary, what should have been Linda's.... I mean, the strange creature's remains were gone. No sign of a struggle. Everything

had been wiped clean. The principal, the teachers, nobody would believe me when I told them what had happened.

It is clear than Makiho is not the victorious heroic survivor but a terrified, uncomprehending witness. By excluding her from the fight, *Blood: The Last Vampire* upholds the horror that might have otherwise dampened the populated, well-lit modern environment.

Blood: The Last Vampire presents a dark, harsh rendition of the vampire narrative. There is nothing sexually enticing, divine or magical about Kitakubo's vampires. The story has no spiritual aspect; instead, it is a violent tale about survival. Yet it is not the survival of the human beings that is at stake but the survival of the vampire. The Chiroptera do not come after the people out of compulsion or hedonistic blood-lust. On the contrary, they appear to be hiding throughout the story, and attack only to feed before they can go into hibernation. *Blood: The Last Vampire* depicts the vampire with an impassive, almost scientific, impartiality, retaining the horror of the unfamiliar and abnormal, but completely relinquishing the traditional folklore roots of the monster.

The characteristic features that make the vampire so fascinating a monster are, as previously noted, the diversity and prevalence of its image in numerous cultures. This precisely renders the vampire so intriguing; it is immensely difficult to detect and highlight any details of definite coherence in the image of a vampire that exists within just one cultural frame (e.g., the American vampire can be classified as an early American vampire, modern American vampire etc.). Consequently, drawing sound conclusions regarding differences in portrayal of the creature across cultures is even more difficult due to its immense diversity of form and characteristics. One observation that can be definitely made as far as this particular comparison is concerned is that the vampire in American fiction exists on terms equal to any other monster creature (as it has "arrived" in America's relatively young culture and folklore together with those other monsters), whereas in Japanese fiction, among all the monsters native to Japanese folklore and existent in art for a long time, the vampire will always have an exotic, modern feel. Despite the variety of forms, whether charming or savage, the vampire will always show its predatory nature—at times more often and at times just barely.

Werewolf

The werewolf is a special kind of monster. The werewolf is a member of a broader family of creatures based on the concept of animal transformation (therianthropy). Although the wolf is the most common animal human beings transform into in the West (lycanthropy), transformation into other animals is also occasionally portrayed, as in *The Cat People* [1942] (transformation into a cat) or *Hyenas* [2011] (transformation into a hyena). A great number of werewolf narratives concentrate on the change; in those titles, the horror comes from inside. The atmosphere of fear is built on suspicion and doubt, and on fear of the unknown and the uncontrollable. In this way werewolf narratives are unique in that they balance their horror factor within the gray zone of abject—right on the line between Self and Other. Other narratives of different genres, e.g., ghost narratives or vampire narratives may use a similar device— such as *The Others* and *The Sixth Sense* discussed elsewhere in the first chapter. In such narratives, the confrontation with the Self as Other is pushed to the very edge of the story, therefore allowing the audience to fully identify with protagonist throughout the narrative and allowing for the horror to build up properly. In this way, the Other is externalized, and it does not interfere with the development of horror. The inner bestiality horror, which is the foundation of the werewolf narrative, is constructed in a converse manner, i.e., by internalizing the Other.

In contrast to the zombie or the vampire, the Euroamerican werewolf does not seem to have one original story or an original narrative that could be referred to or presented as the "most famous werewolf narrative" or "the first werewolf narrative"; additionally, werewolf narratives in cinema "have made little use of folkloric beliefs, preferring instead to conjure up their own origins" (Hutchings 2008: 329). The image of the American cinema werewolf is simultaneously diverse—ranging from a hairy countenance on a human being, to a lycanthrope to a fully-formed wolf—and at the same time easily recognizable. As Stefan Dziemianowicz argues in the section on the werewolf in *Icons of Horror and the Supernatural,* it was Robert Siodmak's *The Wolf Man,* one of the most famous American werewolf narratives, that introduced that now familiar image to the mass audience. The werewolf that the audience familiar with American cinema can easily recognize and identify is a helpless victim bitten by another werewolf. That person then changes into some sort of a wolf form during the nights of full moon, between the hours of moonrise and sunrise. The person who is a werewolf is initially unaware of the supernatural side of their life, or of their behavior after the transformation; as a werewolf they simply slaughter other beings, especially humans. Any injury sustained in the wolf form persists after the reversion to the human form (Dziemianowicz in Joshi 2007: 654). The film reached a larger audience than any werewolf narrative of the preceding century and "codified" werewolf lore—most of which originated from "folktales or werewolf fiction that itself was derived from folk legend"—in the same manner that "Bram Stoker's novel *Dracula* created the template for all vampire fiction written in its wake" (Dziemianowicz in Joshi 2007: 654).

Another feature that makes a werewolf a very special monster is its reversible nature. Although not vulnerable to sunlight, the werewolf is, similarly to the vampire, inseparably connected to the darkness. But whereas the vampire is paralyzed and susceptible to an attack during the day, the werewolf is perfectly safe and hidden—because the beast is simply not there during the day. The werewolf does not have to hide or masquerade as a human—it really *is* human. This makes him impossible to combat or track or during daytime. Even though it is not invulnerable, the werewolf's most effective defensive trait is its perfect camouflage.

The Howling, written by Gary Brandner, is one of the best known examples of a werewolf horror narrative. It employs a conventional werewolf storyline in which a human being changes into a beast of preternatural or, sometimes, supernatural strength and preys on people and animals. In this regard, the plot is straightforward enough, but with a minor alteration; instead of portraying a small town full of people menaced by a dangerous monster, *The Howling* tells the story of an innocent couple who wander straight into a town filled with monsters.

The novel establishes a customary setting of a small, isolated town and a scant, enclosed community living there who hide a terrible secret. Karyn and Roy move to Drago to help Karyn to recover from an urban nightmare of assault and rape. Their new home, however, proves to be just as unsafe as their previous one—or even more so, as they are to learn later. Drago is portrayed as a frightening place, completely isolated from the civilized world, surrounded only by forests, wilderness and animals neither Karyn or Roy are able to recognize. It is very significant that in face of that terror Karyn is alone—in many ways. Her relationship with Roy is very strained, and she is emotionally vulnerable; additionally, she must face the hostile, unfamiliar wilderness alone. By placing Karyn in a secluded house with Roy gone most of the time, *The Howling* emphasizes the man/nature opposition. Lastly, Karyn is alone when she faces the people of Drago.

Soon, Karyn discovers that Drago is not the haven they imagined it to be, but a place housing unspeakable terror. Naturally, it is not the wilderness or the wild animals that are the actual threat. The real monsters, who are the bestial inhabitants of Drago, keep their distance at first. Long before Karyn actually sees any werewolf, she can hear the monster lurking near her house, howling almost every night. When she eventually runs into the beast, the encounter is more vague and eerie than downright terrifying. The scene relies more on the uncanny, mysterious qualities of nature and the effect it may have on someone who is accustomed to an urban environment. At this point, Karyn is not even exactly sure what it is that she is afraid of. Her fear is, in a way, very primordial; it is constructed around something unseen and unnamed, around "something in the darkness." This kind of fear does not originate from the knowledge of the monster's nature, but from the lack thereof. For Karyn, who is a city person, the "thing" lurking behind the trees and bushes is not an element out of place, but merely an extension of the hostile, unfamiliar wild environment.

When the werewolves eventually show themselves, their shape further reinforces that notion; Brandner's werewolves are depicted as fully canine in their bestial form, just as they are fully human in their human form. In contrast to the most common and recognizable portrayal of the werewolf in American werewolf narratives, the werewolves in *The Howling* are not the bipedal, hybridic fusions of animal and man but creatures shifting smoothly between one form and the other. For this reason, the nature of fear they evoke is slightly different than of that evoked by the conventional werewolf who seems incomplete, stuck half way between the two forms. In the case of Brandner's werewolves, the atmosphere of terror is based on the uncanny balance of a seemingly ordinary animal form and positively extraordinary characteristics:

> Whatever was outside howled again—a wailing night cry that ended in an ominous growl. Karyn forced herself to walk back across the room to the front window. She parted the curtains and looked out. In the clearing in the front of the house, less than twenty feet from the door, hunched a dark, sinister silhouette.... It was a wolf, but bigger than any wolf should be. As the animal sat on its haunches, the big head came to nearly four feet above the ground. It did not move when the light came on, but glared defiantly at the window. The reflected light of the bulb out in front made the eyes glow like jewels. The wolf's fur was a dull gray-brown color, shaggier around the neck. The chest was full, the large forepaws planted solidly on the ground. As Karyn watched, the thin lips of the animal skinned back and she saw the teeth [Brandner 1987: 92].

On the one hand, Karyn faces a creature she can recognize and comprehend, i.e., a wolf. On the other hand, almost everything about this wolf seems wrong, beginning with its size and ending with its attitude and behavior. This combination of familiar and unfamiliar facilitates the atmosphere of terror, and defines this and other werewolf encounters; the animal features (grotesquely bared teeth, the manner of attack) are juxtaposed with human features (self confident manner of moving, the recognition of the character)

(Brandner 1987: 122). Again, there is a stark contrast between the expected, normal traits of the wolf, such as the shape of its body and its appearance, as well as the unexpected, abnormal traits such as its behavior. The werewolves of Drago may look less unnatural than conventional cinema werewolves at first glance, but that only makes them more disturbing and treacherous.

The werewolves in *The Howling* possess many traditional characteristics—they are vulnerable to silver, they prey on humans and roam the wilderness at night—but also a few unorthodox ones as well. Most importantly, they are completely independent of the full moon and can change form whenever they please (although they do feel a compulsion to do so at night). Even more significant is their nature or origin. After Karyn hears the howling for the first couple of weeks and her dog disappears, she attempts to research wolves and predators resembling wolves, but it turns out there are no wild wolves left in the United States. Her newly met friend, Inez, suggests the howling creature might be a werewolf. Karyn's first thought is lycanthropy, a form of mental illness in which a person imagines that they are a wolf. Inez, however, claims that werewolves are the servants of the Devil, who have pledged their "everlasting souls" (Brandner 1987: 60).

In this manner, *The Howling* introduces a minor, virtually negligible religious touch, significant only in the light of a far more important trait of the narrative. Whereas the conventional American werewolf tends to be constructed on a juxtaposition of the murderous beast and the innocent, unaware human, the werewolves of Drago are portrayed as inherently evil in both forms, as well as fully aware of their condition and what transpires when they become beasts. While not downright hostile at the beginning, the community is decidedly uncannily reserved and threatening towards Karyn from the moment she arrives in the town. Linda Holland-Toll indicates the significance of community in *The Howling*; the inhabitants of the original village of Dradja were so close and loyal that they would not disclose which one of them was the killer, even if it meant that the whole village would be slaughtered (Holland-Toll 2001: 138). The power of the descendants of Dradja lies in their mutual loyalty and their strong bond (Holland-Toll 2001: 139 140). This bond is something that neither Karyn nor any of the other characters can suspect or comprehend, and it is that which lies at the core of horror constructed in *The Howling*. The werewolves of Drago are not simply predators who happen to live in one place, but a uniform "werewolf community," a community that "has defined itself as non-human and actively embraced evil" (Holland-Toll 2001: 140). As Holland-Toll points out, "the antinomous and dis/easeful pairing of community values with werewolves" render *The Howling* a tremendously "disquieting" story

(Holland-Toll 2001: 140). Brandner's story creates horror not with a lonely predator, but an organized pack of predators.

The Howling features also a motif of the unwanted change into a werewolf. After being bitten by Marcia, the leader of the Drago werewolves, Roy, changes into a werewolf as well. This element, however, is not developed in detail and serves only to further estrange Karyn rather than deliver any new source of horror. Roy never experiences any anguish or terror due to the animal waking within him, merely physical discomfort and wonder; the description is graphic, but not dramatic, in the sense that it does not portray Roy's emotions. If anything, Roy seems more curious and detached—examining his hands and teeth, registering everything in detail—than fearful and shocked.

For a werewolf narrative, *The Howling* puts great emphasis on he werewolf's connection to the natural world, the darkness and the wild, untamed nature. The werewolves of Drago appear to adhere to the laws of nature in hunting, mating and following the rules of their pack. Still, they are dangerous predators impossible to kill by any conventional means; Karyn's shotgun, lethal to anything human or beastly, proves useless against the werewolf that lurks outside her house. And yet considering the way the werewolves are portrayed, they might as well be any other predators. The real horror in *The Howling* seems to be constructed not on the werewolves themselves, but on what they represent—the clash between culture and nature, between a city inhabitant and a monster from the wilderness, and also between an outsider and a community. The novel weaves a tense atmosphere of loneliness and distress, of being surrounded and hunted, allowing the readers to identify with the prey that is Karyn as she is being beset by monsters.

The next title discussed in this chapter, Stephen King's *Cycle of the Werewolf* may be regarded, in comparison to *The Howling*, as an example of the most classic werewolf scenario among the American werewolf narratives. The novelette contains three important, easily recognizable elements of the conventional American werewolf narrative: a lone beast, hunting by full moon and the use of silver. In addition, the text itself is divided into twelve short chapters following twelve nights of full moon from January to December.

Cycle of the Werewolf begins with the sudden appearance of a monster within the small community of an equally small town, Tarker's Mills. The monster wreaks havoc on the people who are first unable, then unwilling to recognize its true nature. People die, torn and ripped, on the nights of full moon, and at first no one can guess who or what might be responsible. As it is usually the case with werewolf narratives, initially only those who are killed by the beast learn its true nature. However, in *Cycle of the Werewolf* this knowledge is not withheld from the audience; the werewolf appears in the narrative immediately, in the very first chapter, and once it claims its first victim, it becomes clear what the people of Tarker's Mills are about to be dealing with:

> Before he can decide what to do about his visitor, the lowpitched whining rises to a snarl. There is a thud as something incredibly heavy hits the door ... draws back ... hits again. The door trembles in its frame, and a puff of snow billows in from the top.
> Arnie Westrum stares around, looking for something to shore it up with, but before he can do more than reach for the flimsy chair he has been sitting in, the snarling thing strikes the door again with incredible force, splintering it from top to bottom.
> It holds for a moment longer, bowed in on a vertical line, and lodged in it, kicking and lunging, its snout wrinkled back in a snarl, its yellow eyes blazing, is the biggest wolf Arnie has ever seen ...
> *And its snarls sound terribly like human words* [King 1985 : 13–14].

Instead of establishing an introduction or providing the readers with foreshadowing, the narrative firmly and plainly establishes the source of horror within the very first few pages. Arnie is murdered by something bestial but still bearing some disturbing, terrible semblance to a human being; yet even this residual vagueness is dispersed by a later statement: "something inhuman has come to Tarker's Mills" (King 1985: 14). The horror atmosphere is constructed upon two factors. The first factor is the nature of the monster, revealed to the readers beyond doubt. In this sense, *Cycle of the Werewolf* creates a discrepancy, deviating slightly from the usual strategy of horror narratives, which attempts to make the fear of the audience mirror the fear of the protagonists. Instead of introducing a mysterious killer who would turn out to be a werewolf, *Cycle of the Werewolf* forms the storyline around a human community unaware that it is being attacked by a werewolf. The suspense does not come from uncertainty concerning the nature of the threat, but, on the contrary, from the awareness that the horror will come again with the next full moon. That knowledge is the second factor on which the horror atmosphere is based. Interestingly, the werewolf itself, although unrecognized by the population, is not hidden from the eyes of the viewer. Its attacks are portrayed in full detail, and its presence is explicit—almost obscene in its openness—although its human identity remains concealed. The detailed, graphic descriptions allow the werewolf to become a concrete, powerful presence instead of an uncanny, fantastic threat. *Cycle of the Werewolf* presents its monster almost theatrically, in enough detail to haunt the readers.

King's werewolf bears all the characteristics of the conventional American cinematic werewolf image. It is a humanoid creature characterized by traits of both human being and a wolf, with a human torso, arms and legs and with a wolf's head, claws and tail:

> It stands for a moment at the base of the lawn and seems to scent the air ... and then it begins to shamble up the slope toward where Marty sits on the slate flagstones in his wheelchair, his eyes bulging, his upper body shrinking against the canvas back of his chair. The Beast is hunched over, but it is clearly walking on its two rear legs. Walking the way a man would walk. The red light of the twizzer skates hellishly across its green eyes.
>
> It moves slowly, its wide nostrils flaring rhythmically. Scenting prey, almost surely scenting that prey's weakness. Marty can smell it—its hair, its sweat, its savagery. It grunts again. Its thick upper lip, the color of liver, wrinkles back to show its heavy tusk-like teeth. Its pelt is painted a dull silvery-red.
>
> It has almost reached him—its clawed hands, so like-unlike human hands, reaching for his throat—when the boy remembers the packet of firecrackers. Hardly aware he is going to do it, he strikes a match and touches it to the master fuse. The fuse spits a hot line of red sparks that singe the fine hair on the back of his hand, crisping them. The werewolf, momentarily offbalance, draws backwards, uttering a questioning grunt that, like his hands, is nearly human. Marty throws the packet of firecrackers in its face [King 1985 : 69–70].

The werewolf in King's story is constructed and defined in terms of its indefiniteness. It is both familiar and unfamiliar, a half-formed combination of normal and abnormal. It is, as Marty thinks, "like-unlike," "nearly" but not quite. It fits perfectly Carroll's definition of a monster as something interstitial, being stuck in-between two separate species, not fully human and not fully wolf, but having the traits of both.

Near the end of the narrative the true identity of the beast is disclosed. As in the majority of American werewolf narratives, the human being that is the werewolf is unaware (at least initially) of his nature and unable to control the transformation. Reverend Lowe knows that something is "wrong" with him; he feels "amazingly *good*, amazingly *well*, amazingly *strong*" when the moon is full, and during that time he wakes up to find his clothes muddy and torn, scratches and bruises on his skin he cannot account for, and traces of blood "on his hands ... and lips" (King 1985 : 108–110). After the injury he suffers from Marty's hands, Reverend Lowe eventually comes to realize what he is, but again (just as in *The Howling*) this motif is not emphasized. Lowe is not repentant or scared, but rather mildly inconvenienced; he focuses more on the wonderful surge of energy and strength than on the fact that he regularly changes into a murderous beast.

In the final confrontation Lowe is killed with a silver bullet by Marty, who was finally able to identify the monster thanks to the injury. This and a plethora of other very recognizable, characteristic elements of what is associated with the American werewolf narrative makes *Cycle of the Werewolf* an excellent example of the horror werewolf narrative. The werewolf featured in the story is a single predator, an unnatural monster menacing a group of human beings, for a long time unaware of its cruel nature. It is a superior, supernatural killer that cannot be hunted like an animal or dealt with by the police. It attacks and disappears again in the darkness only to come back during the next full moon. This constant but elusive presence of the deadly danger of the beast's attack is the primary concept and the horror factor of *Cycle of the Werewolf.*

The last title discussed in this chapter, *Wolf* [1994] directed by Mike Nichols, presents yet another also popular take on the American werewolf narrative pattern, constructed around the concept of the struggle between human and animal nature within one person. The main source of horror of the story lies in the change itself, and the monster lurking inside one's own soul. As Anna Gemra notes, *Wolf* proposes a rather classic werewolf character, who is not responsible for his transformation and who attempts to protect the people around him from himself—i.e., from the creature he is changing into; even the make-up and prosthetics are very traditional, resembling strongly those presented in the key title of the genre, *Werewolf in London* (Gemra 2008: 395).

Wolf does indeed begin in a manner quite conventional for the genre. On his way home on a dark winter night, Will Randall is bitten by a wolf. Shortly after, he notices changes about himself: his eyesight, smell and hearing improve, and he feels—and looks—twenty years younger; his sexual drive reawakens, and he feels great. The changes are deceptively beneficial, as everything in Will's life, from his mood to his senses, seems simply better. Much more significant, however, are the accompanying changes in Will's personality. As time passes, he transforms from a well kept, temperate—almost phlegmatic—middle aged man with all the mannerisms characteristic of a middle aged man to a character brimming with self confidence and capable of taking decisive, aggressive actions.

Gradually, Will acquires more and more wolf-like traits, and eventually he himself starts to realize that something is not right. When he shares this concern with his new friend, Laura, it is clear that he is ready to accept the supernatural nature of the phenomenon, as well as its sinister implications:

> WILL: I want to tell you something. A few days ago, something happened to me. I was driving in New England and I hit an animal. A wolf.... But, this is really going to sound insane. Since it happened, I feel as though the wolf passed something on to me. A scrap of its spirit in my blood. Suddenly my senses are

so incredibly acute. I feel just so ... great. I'm just not the kind of person who walks around feeling great. I don't know—I'm different. More alive.... Stronger.
LAURA: It sounds strange, but.... If you feel great, maybe you should just accept it as a gift.
WILL: I'm afraid it will have a price.

Despite the fact that he is not ready to name his fear, Will is aware that the cost of the sudden improvement of his life and condition may be enormous. And indeed, as the full moon approaches, Randall begins rising nightly in his sleep in a semi-bestial state, showing a little more of the wolf each night and prowling the nearest parks and woods for prey. It is worth noting that although as the narrative progresses Will gains more explicit wolf characteristics, their appearance and emergence are never portrayed in a graphic way, unlike the transformation process in the previous two titles. Even in the climactic fight between Will and Stewart, another beast, the werewolf traits remain subtle and limited to pointy ears, sharp teeth, and excessive hair.

The nightly transformations are also all the more disturbing because they take place in an environment where they are completely out of place. Will does not live in a small village or deep in the forest, but in a large, busy city. He is not a creature that is one with nature and who blends in with the shadows of the wilderness, but a wild animal trapped in an urban environment. In this respect, Will as a wolf is more lost and agitated, similar to a cornered animal, than ominous and powerful like a predator in its element. This only makes Will the werewolf more uncanny and emphasizes his unnatural condition.

The horror constructed in *Wolf* rests on Will's fear of himself. He is scared of the unknown changes in his body and his personality, he is afraid of what he might do—or what he might already be doing. When he hears that his wife has been killed, he is afraid she might have been killed by him. The horror based on this notion is actually twofold. Firstly, Will is afraid he might have torn his wife to pieces like a savage animal. Secondly, he has no way of making sure that he either did or did not do it—and, if he had, that he will not do it again. Laura's alarm merely reflects Will's own suspicions. The atmosphere of terror is based on the fear of losing humanity and losing control. Will is terrified that his new instincts—whatever they might be—will make him do something inhuman and become a beast, in the full meaning of the word.

The film's most interesting departure from the werewolf lore usually employed in conventional American werewolf narratives is the nature (goal) of Will's transformation. Initially only partial, the changes gradually become more distinct, until Will completely transforms from a man into a wolf. Most importantly, however, the metamorphosis is irreversible; as a werewolf, Will becomes steadily more bestial each night until the night of the full moon, after which the animal replaces the man completely. In this way, despite seemingly following the orthodox pattern, Nichols' werewolf narrative offers, as Gemra points out, "completely new solutions" (Gemra 2008: 395). Lycanthropy is not determined by the shape of the body, but by the state of the soul; it is an inner monstrosity, held within and not acquired (Gemra 2008: 396). When at first Will gains only partial animal characteristics, it seems that he is following instincts that lay dormant deep in his heart. His slow progression through the transformation emphasizes the specific nature of Nichols' werewolf: the transformation does release the wild animal in Will, but the animal is only as savage as Will's heart is. As Gemra notes, "the somatic change is not of such great importance—although the werewolf's appearance may evoke fear, the change of shape does not entail a change of personality" (Gemra 2008: 396). For this reason, *Wolf* introduces another werewolf who, compared to Will, is a "real" monster: Stewart. Stewart, a young, ambitious man of shady morals, embraces the savage beast inside him willingly, eager to make use of the powers that come with the transformation, and giving into all the wildest instincts he feels. He murders Will's wife and many other people, and he attempts to rape Laura until he is eventually stopped and killed by Will. Significantly, in comparison to Stewart, Will represents the human and the humane; having just killed Stewart and still feeling the killing rage, Will is still both willing and able to control himself enough to get away from Laura once he sees how much he frightens her.

The horror created by Nichols in *Wolf* comes not from the confrontation with a monster, but from the unnatural, uninvited and unwanted transformation into a monster, as well as the latent monstrous potential of the human heart. *Wolf* focuses on the battle between the civilized, the normal and the natural and the wild, the abnormal and the supernatural. Nichols' main character, the protagonist and the antagonist combined into one, struggles to restrain and vanquish the beast that tries to tear its way out of his humanity. Although the beast reflects Will's heart and as such represents merely the wildness, not the darkness of his soul, the concept of an uncontrollable, wild beast lurking inside him is the driving point of the plot and the main source of horror in Nichols' film.

As for the Japanese shape-shifter motif, there are numerous shape-shifters in Japanese folklore and fiction, but they are not usually the focus of horror narratives. The most iconic Western shape shifter, the werewolf, is virtually absent in the mainstream popular horror fiction of Japan. The most common were-creatures in Japanese folklore are the fox (*kitsune*), the *tanuki* (raccoon dog) or the *mujina* (badger), all of which are not humans turning into animals, but animal-*yōkai* capable of taking human form (Foster 2009: 42). This reversal is immensely important, because it shapes the overall tone of Japanese shape-shifter narratives. The very nature of *yōkai* is transformation (Foster 2009: 29). It is the animal, a *yōkai*, that is able to voluntarily turn into a human being instead of the human in whom a beast awakens. A fox or *tanuki* can disguise itself in a human form and play tricks on people. It can seduce humans for evil purposes or interact with them with best intentions, e.g., out of gratitude (Hearn 2006: 171–172 and Werness 2007: 186). Sometimes a fox may even take on human form and get into affairs with people (Wallen 2006: 60–61). The most common fear related to the fox, however, is the fear of the power of illusion that the fox possesses. A fox can make a person see or hear or imagine whatever it wishes them to see, hear, or imagine; it is even believed to be able to divine (Hearn 2006: 172).

Shape shifters appear in Japanese fiction in large numbers, but rarely in horror fiction. For instance, Gorō Kadono's film *Ghost Stories of Wanderer at Honjo* (*Kaidan Honjo Nanafushigi*) [1957], features a *tanuki* character, but the main plot of the film centers around a motif of revenge, in which the *tanuki* plays only a marginal part. A kind samurai saves a *tanuki*'s life, and the *tanuki* vows to help him out of gratitude. When the samurai is treacherously slain, the *tanuki* attempts to bring his killers to justice at the hands of the samurai's son. The film devotes little attention to shape-shifting and instead makes use of other powers of the *tanuki* (disappearing into thin air, imitating other people, making people see ghosts, making the house appear haunted).

Two other titles worth mentioning that concern themes of the beast within and shape shifting are *The Vortex* and *The Short Night,* two short stories written by the same author, Uchida Hyakken. The first story, *The Vortex,* portrays the human-animal transformation in a slightly postmodern manner; the protagonist of the story is a man who literally transformed into a dog out of jealousy, from the inside out. *The Short Night,* on the other hand, features a classic fox bewitching motif, and will therefore be analyzed in more detail.

The Short Night (*Mijikayo*) tells the story of a man who follows a fox about to bewitch someone and ends up being bewitched himself. The main character deliberately sets out to see for himself "the place known for fox bewitching" (Uchida 2006: 45). The story therefore opens with an atmosphere of curiosity and wariness rather than fear; the protagonist wants to see a bewitching fox with his own eyes, as if it were an entertaining spectacle, not a supernatural threat. He is indeed soon rewarded with an appearance of a fox, who emerges out of a dark grove:

The fox walked around aimlessly, came to the edge of the pond, and splashed the water with its front paws. Ripples spread across the dim surface, and I could barely make out the splashing noise. The fox scooped up the thick green algae and placed the algae on its head [Uchida 2006: 46].

The protagonist is distracted briefly by fish in the pond, and when he looks at the fox again, he sees a beautiful young woman. The transformation is instantaneous and smooth, so fast that the protagonist fails to glimpse this metamorphosis. Again it is striking that the main character is neither terrified nor impressed by this display of fox powers, despite the fact that they are really remarkable. The fox can not only voluntarily and effortlessly take the shape of a young woman, but even create a living baby out of leaves and grass rolled into a ball.

The man follows the fox and discovers that she has gone to a house where an old woman apparently recognizes her as her daughter-in-law. Intent on saving her from fox trickery, the protagonist tries to warns her and offers a folk ritual to reveal the true form of the fox by means of smoking the baby "with fresh pine needles" (Uchida 2006: 47). The mentioning of this folk method exemplifies the typical way in which the fox narrative is structured. The main character seems to be in control of the situation and in possession of tools that he believes are certain to expose the trickery of the fox. The old woman reluctantly agrees to the procedure; but the baby dies during the smoking and the young woman does not revert to her fox form. The protagonist is shocked. The narrative creates a profound emotional effect, which is not, however, based on fear, but on shame and remorse. The protagonist is shaken by his own act and the consequences of it, not because of fear of the fox.

At this point, a monk appears and offers to take the responsibility for the protagonist and take him to the temple, so that he may repent. Grief-stricken, the protagonist follows the monk and soon both of them arrive at a temple, where the protagonist is told to sit in a vast hall and pray for the child whose death he caused. The monk shaves the protagonist's head and gives him a gong to strike, and then disappears somewhere. The protagonists prays and rings the gong, until the morning comes:

> Dawn broke suddenly on this short summer night.... I jumped back and looked around. The post, plaque, statue, and gong were gone. I was sitting in a hollow of roughly scattered red earth atop the bald mountain, holding the branch of a dead tree. In front of my knees where the gong had been lay a large fragment of tile, and nothing else. My scalp smarted from where my hair had been bitten off. I stood up in shock, but I had no idea where to turn [Uchida 2006: 51].

The protagonist realizes he himself had been bewitched without even being aware of it. Not only the young woman and the baby, but also the old woman (and presumably the household), the monk and the whole temple were an illusion created by the fox. What is more important, the hero knew about the danger beforehand—in fact, he visited the place he knew was famous for fox trickery. Still, the fox is able to bewitch even those people who expect to be bewitched. *The Short Night* functions as specific sort of horror narrative (rather characteristic to Japanese fiction), which does not evoke terror directly when the audience experiences it for the first time, but only after the story is complete, forming a lingering uneasiness. The horror comes not from the fox's ability to transform into a human being or manipulate the environment, but from the fact that it can trick people's senses and reason so easily and thoroughly. A fox's illusion is overwhelming and impossible to tell from reality.

One more Japanese horror shape-shifter narrative worth mentioning in this chapter is *Lycanthrope Leo (Retsu Ō Reo)*, written by Kengo Kaji. *Lycanthrope Leo* offers the readers a rationalized explanation of the story (genetic mutation) and therefore will not be discussed in detail, but it is worth mentioning because of the form of the featured shape-shifter. The manga offers an human animal metamorphosis that aesthetically resembles the iconic American cinema werewolf, although the animal in question is not a wolf, but a whole variety of different animals. The similarity is only superficial; the twist is that in Kaji's story the beasts initially turned into humans, who retained the ability to turn back into an animal form (the shape of the lycanthropes is not that of a regular animal but of something in-between man and beast). The protagonist of the manga, Leo, finds out that he is in fact a beast in a human body.

YUAKI
Ages ago, due to genetic mutations, beasts with the ability to metamorphose into humans were born. Those beasts used their strange powers to infiltrate human society and live on. *The blood tribe of the beasts* had physical capabilities *far beyond* that of *mere* humanity.... The half-man/half-beasts [sic] in the legends really existed ... [Kaji and Okamura 1997: chapter 2].

Although the transformation looks as impressive as in American werewolf cinema, it is controllable and apparently not painful. The metamorphosis is not the source of terror in *Lycanthrope Leo*. Leo accepts his new nature; what terrifies him are hunters, specialized in killing those like him, who "carried on the sacred duty" to hunt down the beasts (Kaji and Okamura 1997: chapter 2). The story's main horror factor is based not on the fear of the metamorphosis itself, or on the fear of facing other lycanthropes, but Leo's profound fear of being hunted down.

The representation of the shape-shifter motif differs greatly in Japanese and American fiction, to an extent much greater than any other motif compared in this work. The status of the monstrous predator is not the same in American and Japanese horror narratives—while in the United States the vampire and the werewolf are figures firmly embellished in European folklore, in Japan they are characters of global—especially American—pop culture. While the American werewolf symbolizes the feral beast lurking inside a human being, ready to surface, the Japanese shape shifters such as foxes or *tanuki* are merely mischievous tricksters; where the werewolf attacks his human prey ferociously, a fox or *tanuki* play tricks on people, despite the fact that they possess amazing powers. As such, Japanese shape-shifters do not represent the man/beast duality, but are a part of a greater whole, the wondrous nature-*kami-yōkai* world.[7] Whereas Western shape shifters represent the hunter/prey opposition and portray the weakness of human beings in the face of brutal wilderness, Japanese shape-shifters represent nature as an amoral, complex, powerful force to which human beings are subject.

Monstrosities

As was stated in the opening section of this chapter, a monstrosity (referred to as "monster" from now on for the sake of clarity) is that for which there is no name, that which is shapeless and unrecognizable, mangled, ill-formed, *wrong*. Monstrosities, or proper monsters, are, as Poole puts it, "beast[s] of excess, and monster stories are tales of excess" (Poole 2011: xiv). In many narratives, the physically monstrous suggests mutability, variability and instability (Bleiler in Joshi 2007: 342). Monsters are not charismatic and they are not beautiful. They are repulsive or at least deeply disturbing; they are "objects of loathing and revulsion" that violate classificatory schemes (Carroll 1990: 184).

In American horror genre, at least in the titles that meet the criteria of this work, monsters are surprisingly scarce. The truly supernatural monster rarely inhabits American horror narratives. It more often than not tends to slip into one or another rationalization scenario, which usually means that the title in question crosses over into the science-fiction genre. Examples include *The Swamp Thing* [1982], *The Fly* [1986], Stephen King's *It*, *Mimic* [1996] or *Cloverfield* [2008]. That is not to say, however, that there are no "proper monster" narratives; from time to time, a conventional monster will be portrayed in a film or a novel, e.g., in *Minotaur* [2006], *The Burrowers* [2008] or *Teeth* [2007], or many other works of Stephen King (*Langoliers*) and Dean

R. Koontz (*Tick Tock*). Those monsters remain, however, alienated in the crowd of monsters whose origins can be explained within the limits of the logic underlying the narrative.

A prominent narrative featuring proper supernatural (or at least not rationalized)[8] monsters is Stephen King's *The Mist*. *The Mist* is a short story about an unnatural, thick fog that fills a little town and hostile, monstrous creatures that dwell within that fog. After a violent thunderstorm causes the power to go out, a father and son, David and Billy, go to a supermarket for supplies. When the mist comes, they are stuck in the shop, together with the rest of the costumers that happened to be inside when the mist cut it off from the rest of the world. Soon the supermarket is surrounded by unimaginable otherworldly monsters, and the people trapped in it are terrorized by the unknown entities outside. In the end, convinced that there is nothing left for them if they stay, the father decides to take his son and flee in a car into the unknown, accompanied by a couple of other people.

The story establishes the horror atmosphere with the arrival of the mist. Although the mist serves only as an agent for the monsters hiding within, it serves a tremendously important purpose in the narrative (unlike the fog featured in a title discussed in another chapter, *The Fog*). Thick and opaque, it cuts the supermarket (as well as everything else) off from the world, both in terms of visual capacity as well as communication. It envelops the building like soft cotton wool, distorting the sounds and blocking out the sun.

The monsters proper, on the other hand, both represent the alien and the unknown as well as are depicted as such throughout the story. Even their first appearance is only relayed by a supporting character, a man who runs into a well-lit and seemingly safe supermarket, screaming: "Something in the fog! Something in the fog took John Lee! ... *Something in the fog took John Lee and I heard him screaming!*" (King 2001: 44, italics in the original). Only later do the actual, corporeal monsters eventually come. Still, they only peek out of the mist, without showing the entirety of their true form. The great portion of the horror atmosphere is created by the monsters and their terrifying shapes, of course, but also by the manner in which they appear and disappear into the mist, hidden from the human sight but apparently being able to navigate in the thick patches without effort. The people in the supermarket label them in their minds by means of comparing the unfamiliar beings to familiar shapes and creatures: David thinks of the appendage that caught the bag boy as a tentacle, and compares the flying monster with leathery wings to a pterodactyl. The crucial aspect of *The Mist*, however, is that the characters do not know what is that they are really up against. They can only guess, when they see "parts of the mist ... go darker for a minute" and when from time to time something looms in the mist: "sometimes just a little smudge, sometimes a big dark place, like a bruise" (King 2001: 97). The trapped people can discern only fragments and, what is even more ominous, sounds: "[s]omething roared occasionally from the dark, and once, shortly before midnight, there was a long, drawn-out *Aaaaarooooooo!*" (King 2001: 136). Those hiding in the supermarket can describe the sound and attempt to liken it to something familiar and imaginable, but they do not *know*. Furthermore, they cannot *imagine* because none of the creatures they have seen coming out of the fog resembles any animal or beast they would be familiar with.

Even the creatures that do appear completely, such as the insect-like monsters and the predators that eat them, are alien and bizarre. They vaguely resemble objects and animate beings that are familiar to the people, but even those associations are not of a good sort. The insect-like monster that sucks blood looks like "one of the minor creatures in a Bosch painting-one of his hellacious murals"; it is "two feet long, segmented, the pinkish color of burned flesh that has healed over" (King 2001: 98). The flying reptile-avian predators are also repulsive, with "flapping, leathery wings, an albino white body, and reddish eyes" (King 2001: 100). They are not merely unknown creatures, like unknown animals, but hostile, violent, blood-thirsty things:

> The flying creature paused on top of the lawn-food bags, glaring around, shifting slowly and malignantly from one taloned foot to, the other. It was a stupid creature, I am quite sure of that. Twice it tried to spread its wings, which struck the walls and then folded themselves over its hunched back like the wings of a griffin. The third time it tried, it lost its balance and fell clumsily from its perch, still trying to spread its wings. It landed on Tom Smalley's back. One flex of its claws and Tom's shirt ripped wide open. Blood began to flow.... The thing spread its wings and flapped them once—apparently not to fly away but to secure a better hold on its prey—and then its leathery-white, membranous wings enfolded poor Smalley's entire upper body. Then the sounds came—mortal tearing sounds that I cannot bear to describe in any detail [King 2001: 101].

The horror created by King's monsters does not come from distortion of their size or their shape, as it often the case with entities in monster narratives, but on their complete and utter strangeness. When the protagonists are later attacked by one of the smaller monsters resembling spiders, David notices briefly that "it was the size of a big dog" with "twelve or fourteen many-jointed legs," which was most certainly not an "ordinary earthly spider blown up to horror-movie size; it was something totally different, perhaps not really a spider at all" (King 2001: 129). This monstrous strangeness reaches its horrific peak when David and the others, having escaped the supermarket, encounter the last monster presented in the story:

> A shadow loomed out of the mist, staining it dark. It was as tall as a cliff and coming right at us.... It was six-legged, I know that; its skin was slaty gray that mottled to dark brown in places.... Its skin was deeply wrinkled and grooved, and clinging to it were scores, hundreds, of those pinkish "bugs" with the stalk-eyes. I don't know how big it actually was, but it passed directly over us. One of its gray, wrinkled legs smashed down right beside my window, and Mrs. Reppler said later she could not see the underside of its body, although she craned her neck up to look. She saw only two Cyclopean legs going up and up into the mist like living towers until they were lost to sight. For the moment it was over the Scout I had an impression of something so big that it might have made a blue whale look the size of a trout—in other words, something so big that it defied the imagination. Then it was gone ... [King 2001: 149 150].

The monster is so enormous that it can no longer be compared to anything familiar or imaginable—on the contrary, it "defies imagination." Its bizarre shape and size, at variance with the laws of physics and biology of the world that David and the readers know, makes the creature difficult to behold, let alone to accept.

The Mist is a story that introduces the monsters directly, while at the same time building its horror atmosphere on the concept of facing something unfamiliar hidden from the sight. The presence of the unknown monsters turns the familiar world into a monstrous, unfamiliar environment. An additional interesting motif of the story is the pressure the hostile creatures and the uncertainty exert on the people trapped in the supermarket. Despite being a monster narrative, King's story explores the behavior of ordinary people under extraordinary circumstances, as the supermarket customers become divided and begin to attack each other, adding to the oppressive, suffocating atmosphere of terror. The horror factor in *The Mist,* however, is the unfamiliar and unknown lurking just out of sight.

In contrast to the monsters inhabiting the American horror genre, Japanese monsters rarely refer to rationalization, science-fiction or otherwise. On the contrary, Japanese monsters are both amazingly diverse and fairly abundant (Gilmore 2003: 135). The monstrous imagery in Japanese folklore, as well as fiction, is "both impressive and unsurpassed in its range, diversity and oddity" (Gilmore 2003: 135). Japanese monsters range from folk creatures, such as the snake woman featured in Kazuo Umezu's *Reptilia,* monstrous *yōkai* inhabiting the urban legends, like Kōji Shiraishi's *TekeTeke* (2009) or *Wall Man* (2006), directed by Wataru Hayakawa, to monstrous reality depicted in Shinya Tsukamoto's *Nightmare Detective 2* (2008).

Japanese concept of odd, impressive monstrosity is perhaps best illustrated by *Tomie,* a manga written by Junji Itō. *Tomie* is not so much a graphic novel as a collection of short episodes, initially published separately. Due to its popularity, it has been adapted into a series of films. The stories follow a beautiful young girl named Tomie, who possesses a truly bizarre power; every man who meets her becomes obsessed with her, and every woman hates her. Arrogant and manipulative, she drives the men to insanity and violence as they kill each other and other people over her. Most importantly, at some point they almost always turn against Tomie herself, killing her in a brutal, gruesome manner. Tomie, however, never stays dead—she returns each and every time, through regeneration, transformation or possession, and her victims are subject to her influence until they die.

Tomie is composed of two volumes, each containing several stories, some of them interconnected. Each story centers on a different moment of her life, although some make up a two- or three-episode story arc. The reader first encounters Tomie when she is murdered and dismembered by her classmates. The next day, she inexplicably returns, extending her influence onto all those who killed her ("Tomie," volume one). The stories that follow introduce even more grotesque turns of events, as Tomie is killed again and again ("Photograph" and "Kiss," volume one) only to come back each time, no matter what happens to her. She can return from the dead after being stabbed with a knife, after being decapitated or after being dismembered; she can replicate her whole body from any given body part ("Painter," volume two), or from an organ transplanted to someone else ("Basement," volume two). After one of her killers throws small pieces of her dismembered body into a lake, some time later numerous copies of her emerge from the water ("The Basin of the Waterfall," volume one). Some of those copies influence men to go and kill other copies ("Murder," volume two).

Tomie's monstrosity can be illustrated adequately by means of the story "Painter" from volume two. "Painter" is a self-contained, stand-alone narrative, bearing all the trademarks of the *Tomie* stories. This particular episode centers on a young but accomplished painter, Mori, who meets Tomie and becomes obsessed with her as his model. The story opens with a splash panel showing a painting, with the painter's monologue positioned in speech bubbles around the edges of the panel:

> I am a painter. This is my masterpiece. I call it "Tomie." How do you like it? Isn't it splendid? Tomie is the best model I've ever had. But no-one accepts the beauty of this painting ... and my reputation as a painter was lost when I'd just discovered the meaning of true art.... It was all Tomie.... That terrifying girl's fault [Itō 2001: 86].

Mori's painting depicts a horrifyingly deformed head of a human girl with another, half-formed head growing out of it. Both pairs of eyes are wide and wild, white, and the skin seems scarred and diseased. The thing portrayed on the painting is ugly, twisted and unhuman.

From Mori's narration, the readers learn that Tomie appeared during at one of his exhibitions and offered to be a new model. Manipulating Mori and lying to his current model, she maneuvered him into painting her. Mori painted her to the best of his skill, but she reacted with disdain and derision: "is this a joke? Ha, ha, ha, ha, ha! This doodle doesn't capture a tenth of my natural beauty! I thought you could do it but I guess I expected too much!" (Itō 2001: 101–102). After this, Tomie left, and Mori discovered that the painting now looked dull to him as well. He slowly became obsessed with her, trying to paint her face from his memory, but he failed time after time. Desperate, Mori searched for Tomie, neglecting his work and life, and eventually found her. She allowed him to paint her again, but Mori's mind, already twisted, prompted him to paint what he perceived to be Tomie's "real beauty" i.e., her real nature, deformed and repulsive (the painting depicted on the opening panel of the episode). Tomie, furious, lashed out at him, yelling and mocking Mori, eventually pushing him to murder her—he strangled her and then chopped her body to pieces.

At this point Mori resumes his story:

> That's how I killed Tomie.... Why did this happen? For days I stared at her ruined body. After four days have passed.... My God.... Can you believe it? The mutilated limbs have begun to grow. The cells are dividing, the flesh is starting to swell ... what a constitution this girl has! Eventually it is inevitable that all of these parts will grow into identical copies of her.... Yet I probably will not see it happen.... Day by day I become thinner, and now I can't even walk.... I wait for death.... Ahh ... Tomie ... Tomie.... [Itō 2001: 122–124].

Mori's narration is illustrated by graphic images of the pieces of Tomie's dismembered body swelling up and sprouting new extensions that develop into distorted and misshaped but still recognizable limbs and heads of the girl. Those animate, sentient lumps squeal and writhe, squirming on the floor and calling to Mori.

Tomie's monstrosity is both outstanding and obscene. Her body and consciousness, while seemingly human, are in fact completely unhuman. Her face and body are beautiful beyond comparison, but underneath she is a monstrous, unnamable being. If there was ever a creature of excess, it is Tomie—ever growing and mutating, replicable, unstable and indestructible. Each fragment of her damaged body is capable of creating a new body, complete and independent. Each "copy" (since none of the Tomies seem actually to be the "original" one) has the same abilities and personality, but each acts only in its own interest. Additionally, photographs and film tend to reveal the hidden monstrosity; on those Tomie appears almost normal, but over her beautiful face there is another face superimposed—her monstrous, warped and twisted face. She is terrifying because her monstrosity is both spectacular and difficult to behold.

Tomie is a tremendously intriguing monster. Firstly, despite the fact that she is corporeal, she does not represent a physical threat. She is like an embodiment of negative emotions such as senseless lust, jealousy and malevolence, but it is not she who hurts people. On the contrary, the obsession caused by her compels the men to hurt others or themselves—most importantly, to hurt and murder Tomie herself. She drives them insane, but the destruction she wreaks is brought about indirectly. This behavior displayed by the men enslaved by her points to her second intriguing characteristic, i.e., the perverse nature of Tomie's influence. Although the men will fight over her and sometimes attack others at her request, almost every time the obsessed man kills Tomie or at least attempts to do so. In a manner of speaking, Tomie is a profoundly self-destructive creature. And yet, ironically, she always survives everything that happens to her. This incredible resilience is the third of her fascinating qualities—not only is she able to live through every possible method of murder (in one story she even replicates herself from a carpet stained with her blood), but she does so by growing unnaturally and replicating herself to no end. Considering the above, Itō's *Tomie* certainly belongs to the most interesting Japanese monster narratives.

On the other hand, Sei Takekawa's *On a Moonless Night* (*Tsuki no nai yoru ni*) delivers a more familiar monster scenario based on distortion of size, behavior and place. Takekawa's story focuses on a young woman suffering from entomophobia—the fear of insects—who one summer night is attacked by a monstrous swarm of insects. From inside the swarm, a giant, monstrous bee emerges and stings her, laying eggs inside her stomach.

On a Moonless Night is short and straight forward both in terms of volume and plot. The story takes place at the end of September. Returning home late one night, the protagonist encounters what she initially takes for a man—albeit a strange, awkwardly moving man who somehow makes her "apprehensive" (Takekawa 1991: 76–77). The terror is introduced gradually, escalating from mild concern to absolute terror. Initially, the protagonist senses merely that something is not right; then the feeling changes into certainty when she eventually sees the figure up close and can look into its face: "It wasn't a face. At least, it was not a face of a human being. It was like someone had carefully put a bunch of things together in an effort to construct a human face" (Takekawa 1991: 77).

The monstrosity depicted in *On a Moonless Night* is fairly traditional in its design. As it turns out, the face of the strange figure is composed of insects, as is the rest of his body. What she believed to be a man dressed in a coat and a hat turns out to be a monstrous swarm of various insects filling the coat and the hat. With uncanny, un-insect-like imagination, the insects align themselves to form a human form. Apart from the sheer monstrosity of a human shape made out of living insects, there are additional, subtle aspects of this particular, collective monster. For instance, the implied purposefulness—which can be gathered from the "careful effort" the insects put into constructing a human face—alone gives the swarm monstrous qualities. Also, a face composed of insects is enough to evoke fear and repulsion; the artificial, lifeless quality renders it even more terrifying.

The insects scatter and the human shape collapses as they fly and crawl away. The protagonist tries to run away, but she is surrounded by "[b]eetles, moths, centipedes, caterpillars, earthworms ... insects of every type" (Takekawa 1991: 78). Then suddenly they make way for an even more monstrous creature, a real monster among monsters—a gigantic bee:

> [It] was flapping its wings, but it stood still in midair.
> Its eyes were shiny, like metal, and I felt that they were focused right on me. Yet I didn't know for sure where and how insects focus their eyes.
> Its huge jaws. The insect's huge jaws. They looked as if though they could crush the bones of a human's finger with one bite.
> Its antennae were twitching. Its round, large stomach. And on the end of that stomach was its stinger [Takekawa 1991: 82–83].

The monstrosity of the bee is relatively plain in comparison to the human-shaped swarm. It is enormous and abhorrent, but it is still just a bee. It is certainly a monster due to its unnatural size, which reverses the balance of power between a human and an insect, but nothing about its behavior is out of the ordinary. Also, Takekawa's choice of insect is intriguing to say the least; the protagonist is assaulted not a by wasp, but by a bee, a creature commonly associated with positive traits in most cultures.

The bee attacks the protagonist and stings her in the stomach. She survives this and wakes up in a hospital, but her nightmare is not over; soon she discovers that her stomach is growing bigger, and she becomes convinced that there is life growing inside of her:

> The gigantic bee had laid an egg in my womb. Those types of bees do it as a matter of course. They lay eggs inside their prey. The eggs hatch, and the young feed

on the insides of the prey, grow, and then eat their way to the outside.... The insect will devour my entire body, and I shall die [Takekawa 1991: 86].

The odd calmness, almost resignation with which she ponders this turn of events adds to the horrific quality of this fragment. The climax of Takekawa's story is constructed around one of the most horrific and simultaneously intimate concepts, i.e., a monstrous, parasitic entity residing inside one's own body. This horror quality is also based on the fear of contamination and abolishing the border between the human and the monster. The concept of unnatural reproduction is another essential fear on which the effectiveness of the story's climax is based. That effectiveness is maximized by the fact that the protagonist is sure that the bee had laid only one egg inside her instead of countless eggs like insects usually do. A single egg has more connotations with an ordinary human pregnancy, thus amplifying the hybridic nature of the gestation.

From the Western point of view, *On a Moonless Night* is actually a relatively conventional monster story that makes use of excessive monstrosity. The excess of the insects includes their extraordinary number and anomalous size, abnormal behavior and inexplicable purpose, which is impregnating a human woman. That purpose in itself generates the final monstrosity, namely the monstrous egg and the hybridic larva bound to develop from it. The most important aspect of Takekawa's story, however, is the fusion of the imaginable and unimaginable, fascination and repulsion, referred to from the beginning of the story to the very end, where the protagonist just wonders numbly and detachedly about the egg inside her womb.

A quite different take on a monster narrative is offered in *Silent Hill 2* (*SAIRENTO HIRU 2*). *Silent Hill 2* is a 2001 survival horror video game directed by Masashi Tsutoyama. It is the second title in the *Silent Hill* game series published by Konami Corporation, the first of which was originally released in 1999. The series is significant as far as Japanese horror is concerned because of its hybrid nature, which consists in a Japanese concept expressed in an American setting. Instead of making use of traditional Japanese horror themes, the *Silent Hill* series is designed to create a more Euroamerican atmosphere, although it is still possible to distinguish elements of traditional Japanese horror concepts under the westernized surface (Pruett 2010). *Silent Hill 2* is set entirely in a fictional American town, where the player can experience quite a unique mixture of American Gothic and the modern Japanese horror genre.

Although *Silent Hill 2* is the second installment of the series, its plot is a stand-alone story, unrelated to the first game. The game focuses on the character of James Sunderland, a young widower suffering from dissociative fugue following the death of his wife, Mary. Much earlier, Mary developed a terminal disease; after three years of watching her suffer and waste away, James suffers a brief fit of insanity and smothers her with a pillow. Although it is unclear how much time actually passes between Mary's death and the events in the game, at some point James decides to travel to Silent Hill, lured in by a letter written in Mary's handwriting, whom he believes to have died of the illness three years before. The letter invites James to join Mary in Silent Hill, where she is supposed to be waiting for him.

The plot of *Silent Hill 2* is obviously layered—since finding out the truth and allowing James to come to terms with his feelings is the game's ultimate goal—which initially makes the nature of the monsters alien and obscure. Mary's letter leads James, quite literally, into the mouth of the monster—the town of Silent Hill itself. Silent Hill changes reality around James, giving his guilt, anger and fear concrete shapes and pulling him further and further into the darkness of his own soul. At the end of this painful journey, James eventually realizes the hideous truth about the atrocious sin he has committed. The town gives the sin a tangible form—in fact, multiple forms—thus creating a nightmare that summons James and swallows him.

The town in which James faces his darkest nightmare is the main source of monstrosity in the *Silent Hill 2*. It belongs to more than one plane of existence: in the world of the living Silent Hill is a small resort town located near the Toluca Lake. According to *Ushinawareta Kioku: Sairento Hiru Kuronikuru* (Lost Memories: Silent Hill Chronicle), the dark power residing in Silent Hill can lure in those who harbor darkness in their hearts (Konami 2003: 268). Silent Hill thrives on that darkness and amplifies it, creating a unique nightmare for those who stray there and reflecting and materializing anger, fear and guilt awry, like a false mirror.

The materializations of those emotions take on the form of monstrous creatures that roam the town. On a purely aesthetic level, the monsters are disturbing, ambiguously shaped beasts, with vaguely familiar but warped, twisted and alien shapes. Most of the monsters share humanoid features but are not human, thus combining the familiar with the unfamiliar—we can relate to the anthropomorphism of the monsters and at the same time their impurity repels us; "[t]hey remain interstitial as they transgress distinctions such as inside/outside, living/dead, insect/human, flesh/machine, and animate/inanimate" (Perron 2008: 129). Ekman and Lankoski further elaborate:

> Monsters in *Silent Hill 2* systematically break the categories of human and non-human: for example, the "pyramid head" monster is a humanlike creature with a block-like triangular formation instead of a head. Other monsters pertain to insect-related disgust reactions, either by movement reminiscent of scurrying

insects or by visual appearance. Synchronicity between sounds and visuals is used to create further contrast between human-like movement and sounds that go against the human: some monsters sound almost mechanical. At times, creatures change suddenly from bipedal walking to insectal scurrying. These abnormalities introduce a threat of contamination because they are blurring the categorical border between what is considered human versus non-human [Ekman and Lankoski in Perron 2008: 192].

Indeed, all of the monsters move awkwardly, twitch or writhe every now and then, or remain bent in strange positions suggesting discomfort. In addition to their bizarre movements, the shapes of the monsters are characterized by a certain ominous, ambiguous familiarity. None of the monsters have distinctly shaped faces or even snouts or muzzles. Most importantly, none of the creatures are recognizable as human (like a vampire or a zombie might be recognized as human), but nearly all of them demonstrate some sort of "a human aspect" (this is stated clearly by Masahiro Ito, the creature designer, in the "Making of Silent Hill 2" documentary included in the European release of *Silent Hill 2*), which leaves the audience with an extremely uncomfortable impression. On first sight, from afar, they do resemble human beings; when encountered up close, their silhouettes turn out to be warped and distorted: they are monstrous precisely because of that—their shapes suggest deformed human features ("Making of Silent Hill 2" documentary, Konami 2001).

Monstrosity in *Silent Hill 2* is based not only on uncanny association and visual abnormality, but also on the psychological roles performed by the creatures. Even before *Silent Hill 2* crosses over into the second layer of monstrous horror, it is clear that the monstrosities allude to dark instincts and uncomfortable sensations. As the players find out the truth, it becomes obvious that James' nightmare and the strange demons that inhabit it actually serve as a reflection of James' own subconsciousness. Each creature mirrors an aspect of the darkness in his heart. Some of the monsters carry connotations of death and violence—for instance, Red Pyramid Thing, who will be discussed in detail later, is the most distinct embodiment of those concepts. Others represent anguish, decay or putrescence, such as contorting, squirming armless Lying Figures. Without faces and only a hint of a vestigial head, Lying Figures are lumps of contorted, exposed flesh lurching on human legs. They express anguish, frustration and being trapped within oneself (Konami 2003: 313); in a way, they mirror James' emotional repression. Mandarins, lurking in dark places under the surface James is standing on, refer to exclusion and alienation from others (Konami 2003: 313). Cockroach like Crawlers embody decay and disgust, while Flesh Lips, strange creatures suspended in metal frames, carry the connotations of sickness and confinement (Konami 2003: 312). Other creatures serve to allude to James' carnal desires and presumable sexual deprivation and frustration that he experienced during Mary's illness, or are a mixture of both, like Bubblehead Nurses, who juxtapose sexual objectification of the female body with imagery of deteriorating disease (Konami 2003: 313); their slender, shapely human-shaped bodies stand in contrast with their stained uniforms and their heads, which resemble featureless balls of diseased, scarred flesh, titled at an improbable angles, infeasible for a human being. Mannequins are even more direct in their symbolism as their shape resembles two sets of female pelvises, together with lower limbs, joined in such a manner that the creature walks on one pair of legs and can swing at James with the upper pair (Konami 2003: 313). Mannequins represent the most base of carnal desires—they are basically female legs and legs only, without a torso, hands or head—that is, with no identity or personality—in most cases, not even a face. The most distinct and clear expression of sexual frustration in the game is Maria, the voluptuous, provocative doppelgänger of Mary.

Although all the demons represent one or another aspect of James' psyche, some of them are more significant than others. The most important tangible monster that James confronts is Red Pyramid Thing (*sankaku'atama,* lit. "triangle-headed," also referred to as Pyramid Head). Red Pyramid Thing is a large, violent monster. Its form is that of a tall, well built humanoid whose head is shaped like a heavy metal pyramid. Everything about Red Pyramid Thing is unsettling and menacing. It is exceptionally strong and carries massive, powerful weapons. Like other monsters prowling Silent Hill, it tends to move awkwardly, tilting its over-sized head at strange angles and clutching at it, as if in pain. Additionally, it never runs or lunges, but rather advances slowly but inevitably, grating his giant sword against the ground. This relentless but unhurried pursuit is all the more chilling because James cannot defend himself in any way; Red Pyramid Thing cannot be hurt or killed, or even slowed down—James can only run away from it. The most monstrous aspect of Red Pyramid Thing, however, is its lack of a face, or even a place that the audience could assign the role of face. Red Pyramid Thing has no face to speak of; the "pyramid" looks like a helmet, but nothing is hidden underneath. It is, by design, a monster without a face, which makes him less human and therefore more disturbing ("Making of Silent Hill 2" documentary, Konami 2001). Red Pyramid Thing does not need a face because it does not need an independent identity. He literally embodies the truth about James' sin, as well as his guilt and overwhelming desire to be punished (Konami 2003: 312).

Throughout the story, Red Pyramid Thing follows James and Maria and kills her brutally and repeatedly, extorting from James the responsibility for his sin. Each time James embraces the distraction that Maria represents, Red Pyramid Thing kills her, shattering the fantasy and reminding James of the gruesome reality. When James finally accepts what he has done, Red Pyramid Thing (appearing in a dual shape for this particular encounter) kills Maria for the third time and attacks James, only to impale itself on its own spear, having finally fulfilled its purpose. Red Pyramid Thing is not related to the concept of revenge in any way; it represents only justice. The only purpose of the existence of Red Pyramid Thing is to make James take responsibility for his sin and feel shame and pain as punishment for it. For James, facing Red Pyramid Thing means facing the darkness dwelling in his mind and heart (darkness here standing for not so much evil as weakness, selfishness and callousness).

Red Pyramid Thing as a monster is complemented by the existence of Maria. If Red Pyramid Thing is the executioner, she is the victim. Maria is necessary for Red Pyramid Thing to function, since Red Pyramid Thing performs its task not by attacking James but pursuing and hurting Maria. The spitting image of Mary (sharing her face, voice and every other aspect of appearance), cheerful, sexy Maria is the personification of James' fantasy of innocence. Maria is not real, but she is not a monster either; she is a product of James' delusion of innocence in which he is trapped. Although killed more than once, she never stays dead; she demonstrates knowledge of James and his life with Mary, and she is sexually attractive and sexually aggressive (in contrast to bedridden Mary). Red Pyramid Thing is so monstrous and effective because on an unconscious level both James and the audience recognize Maria not as a random, independent character, but as Mary. Despite the different clothes, hair and name, every time Red Pyramid Thing kills Maria, James understands that he has failed because the murder is only a reflection of the crime that had already taken place. Additionally, Maria's presence serves to further torment and confuse James, since at times Maria denies being Mary fiercely, but moments later she will behave exactly like Mary or reveal something that only Mary could know. The most important conversation between James and Maria takes place after Red Pyramid Thing kills her for the first time:

JAMES: You're alive! Maria…! I thought that thing killed you…! Are you hurt bad?
MARIA: Not at all, silly.
JAMES: Maria? That thing … it stabbed you. There was blood everywhere.
MARIA: Stabbed me? What do you mean?
JAMES: It chased us to the elevator. And then …
MARIA: James, what are you talking about?
JAMES: Just before! Don't you remember?

MARIA: James, honey.... Did something happen to you? After we got separated in that long hallway? Are you confusing me with someone else? You were always so forgetful. Remember that time in the hotel....
JAMES: Maria...?
MARIA: You said you took everything.... But you forgot that videotape we made. I wonder if it's still there ...
JAMES: How do you know about that! Aren't you Maria?
MARIA: I'm not your Mary.
JAMES: So you're Maria?
MARIA: I am ... if you want me to be.
JAMES: All I want from you is an answer!
MARIA: It doesn't matter who I am ... I'm here for you, James. See? I'm real. Don't you want to touch me?

The conversation illustrates how Maria is merely a distorted image of Mary, a device brought forth by the town to lead James deeper into the nightmare. By mentioning the videotape left in the Lakeview hotel, Maria sends James towards his eventual realization of truth. It is only in the end that the delusion that is Maria becomes a real, independent monster. When James faces her for the last time, Maria transforms into Memory of Mary—a distorted version of Mary's corpse, suspended upside-down in a metal frame, screaming. This last form mirrors James' emotional conflict he experienced during Mary's final days.

Each and every monstrous creature in the town represents some aspect of James' suppressed emotions and the underlying guilt over the murder of his wife. The creatures themselves can be called monsters; they are all brought into existence by the town and as such are merely extensions of the primary monster that is the town itself. Silent Hill calls to "those who hold darkness in their hearts ... to gather," and materializes manifestations of "each of their unconscious minds," creating a hostile, formidable world (Konami 2003: 352). This world "breathes with life," as Ekman and Lankoski put it, "suggesting that somehow the environment itself is alive, sentient, and capable of taking actions against the player" (Ekman and Lankoski in Perron 2008: 193). Silent Hill is a monstrous entity in and of itself. It has the power to concretize fears and desires, it has a purpose (leading James to the truth), and it is active and reactive, adjusting to those it has lured in. It is also cruel, as shown by the examples of Mary's letter that first prompts James to come to Silent Hill and then gradually disappears as the story progresses (first the paper turns blank, then it disappears from the envelope, and in the end even the envelope vanishes), or of Laura, the non existent little girl taunting James about him never really loving Mary. Silent Hill weaves a nightmare that physically alters the world around James, plunging him into a warped, menacing version of the original town. This distorted dimension, called the Otherworld (*isekai,* "another world"; in *Lost Memories,* it is also referred to as *urasekai,* which roughly translates to "inverse world," "inner world" or "reverse world" [Konami 2003: 268]. The nature and origin of the Otherworld is explained in *Silent Hill* [1999], which will be discussed in more detail in the analysis of that title), is monstrous in itself. Within it, there is ruin and suppuration. The Otherworld is composed of rusted metal grated floors and walls, fences and barbed wire, merged with walls or other objects made out of flesh or other organic material, often bloodstained. Both the inside and outside of it is immersed in complete darkness. Additionally, the Otherworld always reflects the psyche of those around whom it is involved, twisting the environment into their own personal hell, just like the monsters are twisted into their personal nightmares. James Sunderland's personal hell is very violent and very carnal. It is also very different from Otherworlds created by Silent Hill for other people; James in not the only person summoned to the town in *Silent Hill 2.* Wandering the streets of the abandoned town are also Eddie, a bullied young man filled with hatred, and Angela, a girl who killed her father who sexually abused her. The nightmare that Silent Hill creates specifically for Eddie is an ice-cold, quiet and hostile world that reflects Eddie's loneliness and alienation. The Otherworld created from the darkness in Angela's heart is full of ruin, blood and flames, which mirrors Angela's perception of her life.[9]

The monstrosities in *Silent Hill 2* feed on darkness and resonate darkness that dwells in people's hearts; as such, they are merely twisted reflections of the darkest human urges and desires. In other words, all the monsters come from James himself. This psychological aspect allows the monsters to perform their functions even more effectively, since they are subconsciously familiar and at the same time subconsciously threatening, abjectful. *Silent Hill's* exceptional nature stems also from the way in which the game mixes elements of American and Japanese culture and blurs the line between the traditional and the modern. The producers described *Silent Hill* as an attempt to make "Hollywood horror" (as quoted in Pruett 2010: 10). That striving for the American "Hollywood" feel is exactly what makes *Silent Hill 2* (just as all *Silent Hill* games) both effective and noteworthy (and allows for an interesting perspective of Euroamerican perception of Japanese content already filtered through the Japanese perception of American horror). *Silent Hill 2* presents a Japanese concept of what constitutes a horror story in an American setting. The story does not follow traditional American monster icon imagery or urban legends, but it does not draw from Japanese folklore or classic ghost stories either. In this sense, *Silent Hill 2* gives the audience an entirely fresh and unburdened take on a monster narrative, which relies heavily not only on pure terror, but on profound sadness, creating a unique, as well as effective, horror narrative, in which the monsters are both terrifying and tragic: the audience not only fears "Mary" and despises James, but also pities both of them. This is an aspect of *Silent Hill 2* that is very characteristic to strange tales—apart from being scary, the majority of *kaidan* are also tinted with sadness and sympathy for the characters (see Picard in Perron 2009: 108, Harper 2008:118).

The Undead Body

The fear of death is a complex one, encompassing everything from the fear of dying badly to the fear of not remaining dead (Cowan 2008: 126). As Kurt Reinzler notes, despite being aware of the inevitability of death, we do not contemplate that inevitability consciously at all times; "We do not fear death all the time, except in some remote or dark corner of our mind" (Reizler 1944: 489–498). And although we "may not contemplate death at every moment—down that road surely lies madness"—part of cinema horror's agenda is to remind us not only of the reality of death, but of the various fears that surround it" (Cowan 2008: 126). Horror fiction relies vastly on that peculiar combination of the human fear of death and fascination with it. Indeed we dare not and cannot contemplate death, but we surround ourselves with images of it. The Euroamerican audience seems to relish both the visual and implied details of death, and enjoy the oppressive presence of death in their horror. They are fascinated by that which evokes revulsion, and they delight in all of its gory detail.

Both the dead and the undead body as instances of abjectness manifest themselves very clearly in American literature and cinema. The corpse as "decaying body, lifeless, completely turned into dejection, blurred between the inanimate and the inorganic, represents," as Kristeva states, "fundamental pollution. A body without soul, a non-body, quietening matter ..." (Kristeva 1982: 109). The undead body, i.e., a corpse that will not stay dead lies even deeper within the realm of the abject than the dead body itself. As a theme, the dead and the undead in American horror fiction are handled with revulsion mixed with fascination, characteristic to dealing with the abject. Visual depictions of decaying corpses abound, similar to disfigured vampires (such as depicted in Francis Coppola's *Bram Stoker's Dracula*, Quentin Tarantino's *From Dusk Till Dawn* [1996] or a 1979 adaptation of Stephen King's *Salem's*

Lot) or werewolves (as depicted in e.g., *Wolfman* [1941] or *An American Werewolf in London* [1981]). This obsession with repulsive abjectness extends to the way the abject entity smells or what it emits, such as strange fluids or smells from the corpse's body, regardless of whether it is animate or inanimate.

The inanimate corpse is in and of itself a terrifying object of horror. It may be described in a myopic manner, as in H.P. Lovecraft's short story *The Outsider*, as being "the ghoulish shade of decay, antiquity, and dissolution; the putrid, dripping eidolon of unwholesome revelation, the awful baring of that which the merciful earth should always hide" (Lovecraft 2008: 199–200); it can also rely more on the other senses, such as smell or touch, as is the case in another short story written by Lovecraft, *The Thing on the Doorstep,* or Stephen King's *Pet Sematary,* where the olfactory aspect of the corpse is described as "a black smell, like everything inside ... was just lying there, spoiled" (King 1988: 272). Next to the bodily horror of the undead body, the place from which the abject comes is given much attention as well; the grave seemed (and still does) to be extremely appealing to American Gothic writers—even if they did not go into detailed descriptions of the bodily aspects of the undead, the theme of their fiction would still inevitably hover around, so to say, mortuaries and tombs. From all kinds of descriptions of the dead to anything connected to the grave itself as a physical location, the dead body was something fascinating and utterly repulsive at the same time, whether it lay peacefully or not, and it continues to be treated as such by the horror fiction writers to this day.

In *Celebrations of Death: The Anthropology of Mortuary Ritual* Peter Metcalf and Richard Huntington point out that the "endless shying away from confrontation with mortality is undeniably a marked feature of American culture" (Metcalf and Huntington 1979: 195). In its most basic contacts with the dead body, i.e., in its funerary practices, American culture prevents confrontation with mortality in all ways possible—the elimination of the deathbed scene (Metcalf and Huntington 1979: 202), the embalming process and the public viewing are all meant to reconstruct the very nature of the corpse; they redefine it, disguise it, as if all those proceedings allowed to somehow change the actual ontological status of the dead body. The funerals in American culture deal with death but actually express the values of life (Metcalf and Huntington 1979: 210). Japanese culture, meanwhile, assumes an attitude of resignation towards death rather than rejecting the reality of it (Hinohara in Hoshino 1994: 147). Although in the Japanese culture death is natural and unavoidable (Long 2005: 68), the dead body is unclean and ominous. This approach derives from the native religious belief of Japan, Shintō; once the soul leaves the body, the corpse is perceived as both defiled and defiling—it becomes a "phobic object" (Lifton 1996: 93).

This might be the reason for which the depiction of the dead body in Japanese horror fiction tends to be, in comparison to the American portrayal, more restrained and superficial at best, such as in Kōji Suzuki's *Floating Water* (*Fuyū suru mizu*)—where the dead body is terrifying, but the delivery of the terror lies in Yoshimi's definitive comprehension of the fact that Mitsuko is dead, not from the depiction of the corpse—or in Kei Ōishi's *Ju On* (a novelization of Takashi Shimizu's two direct-to-video *Ju-on* films and the motion picture *Ju-on: The Grudge* [2002]), which features a very dry and impassive portrayal of the dead body of Kayako Kawamata. A similarly dry and down to earth description of a corpse is given in Otsuichi's *Summer, Fireworks and My Corpse* (*Natsu to hanabi to watashi no shitai*)—in this case, however, it is more than understandable, as the narrative sets up the dead body as the object of horror in a spiritual rather than organic sense. The two child protagonists, intent on hiding Satsuki's corpse from the adults, seem oblivious to the notion of the uncleanliness of a dead body. Ken and Yayoi not only touch Satsuki's body with their bare hands, but they freely carry it around, and even take it into their home, polluting the "sacred space" of the household (see Littleton 2002). This behavior is meant to create an even more horrific setting for the narrative. The uncleanliness of the dead body is terrifying enough to serve as a source of horror, and the corpse does not need to do anything else to scare—for example, it rarely moves. In American horror fiction, on the other hand, one of the main forms taken by the abject is a body devoid of a soul—in one way or another. The dead body alone is offensive in itself to the living subject, undermining and contradicting not only the subject's aliveness, but also the point of its existence. An agent of horror in the form of a corpse that refuses to stay dead is, therefore, a heightened stage of the evolution of the body horror. The repulsive moving meat frightens the Euroamerican subject, for it represents the triumph of the mindless organic vessel over the immortal, individual soul. The "mind over matter" balance is reversed and mocked.

In his book *Sacred Terror: Religion and Horror on the Silver Screen* Douglas Cowan suggests that "[c]inema horror yields four principal archetypes for fear of death: entrapment and the inability to move on (ghost stories); condemnation and the requirement to remain (vampire narratives): bondage and eternally lost love (mummy movies) and reanimation and the need to feed (zombie tales) (Cowan 2008: 126). The zombie encompasses two of the most vivid fears regarding the biological, organic nature of death: "fear of ceasing to be, but also fear of being unable to die" (Metcalf and Huntington 1979:

196). Naturally, not every reanimated body in American horror fiction is a zombie (although the majority happen to be). Every reanimated body is, however, a source of unspeakable horror. As a monster, the undead, moving corpse is disgusting and terrifying because it grows on the natural anxiety and repulsion directed at the abject that is the corpse.

The undead body, native to folklore of many countries, can take many forms and names, but the most obvious species of the living dead figure in contemporary horror narratives is the modern zombie, who embodies all of the repulsive aspects of the undead abject. As Kim Paffenroth notes, the zombie stirs many fears and emotions related to death:

> Besides being on the threshold between human and nonhuman, zombies also clearly straddle the line between living and dead in a perverted version of the Christian idea of bodily resurrection. Like other monsters, such ambiguity, or the hybrid or oxymoronic nature of being "living dead," means that zombies violate the natural order, both of the physical world and of human society. In zombie movies, human society is in a shambles not only because there is a deadly threat, but because there is a threat of turning into something that is neither alive nor dead. Such a prospect of becoming neither alive nor dead diminishes the human characters' ability to deal with mortality, which is already a deep enough psychological strain for most of us [Paffenroth 2006: 12].

Indeed, there is a profound connection between the figure of the zombie and the aforementioned shying away from death in American culture. In *American Zombie Gothic: The Rise and Fall (and Rise) of the Walking Dead in Popular Culture* Bishop calls the zombie a creature "new to the twentieth century and fundamentally American in its origins" (Bishop 2010: 5). In addition to being an American creation, the zombie might be, according to Bishop, "the most unique member of the monster pantheon"; although other creatures such as ghosts, werewolves, vampires, and the undead originate from the folk tradition, the zombie is "the only supernatural foe to have almost entirely skipped an initial literary manifestation," one that has passed directly from folklore to the screen (Bishop 2010: 12–13).

S. T. Joshi points out that the earliest representations of the zombie in American culture derive from Haitian folklore and voodoo practices (Joshi 2007: 726), whereas Morgan suggests that "much of the particular imagery and detail in horror invention, especially as regards the zombie or living-dead figure, derives from racial memory of plague and infectious disease victims— things such as their vacant demeanor, lack of facial affect, paleness, and shambling walk" (Morgan 2002: 55). Bishop, on the other hand, notes that the central features of the living dead narrative are apocalyptical scenarios and the collapse of societal infrastructures (Bishop 2010: 26). He does, however, also point to the fact that "[s]ince the release of Victor Halperin's *White Zombie* in 1932, Americans have regularly enjoyed the horror, terror, and at times excessive violence of many successful zombie movies, most departing drastically from the creature's humble and ethnographic origins" (Bishop 2010: 13); as Bishop notes, the Hollywood filmmakers have essentially "divorced" the zombie from its religious and cultural roots the moment they appropriated the creature for mainstream entertainment (Bishop 2010: 63). Cannibal and zombie myths do originally stem from the same stories—tribal ritualistic cannibalism was not related to the soulless corpses of the living dead controlled by black voodoo magic—however, Romero's franchise, beginning with *Night of the Living Dead* [1968], merged the traditional zombie and the cannibal figure into one composite living corpse (Balmain 2008: 114–115).

The "divorced zombie" has made itself quite comfortable in the mainstream entertainment, becoming one of the most popular movie monsters. Naturally, as a popular and familiar kind of monster, the living dead is doubtlessly affected by the same affliction as Frankenstein's monster, the vampire and the mummy; it is so well-known and so familiar that is has already shifted not only to being the characteristic feature of an action film (such as *Doom* [2005], and the last five installments of the *Resident Evil* series) but also to being a subject of ridicule (in titles like *Shaun of the Dead* [2004]). It is, however, undeniable, that it is the character of the American horror film zombie that formed the figure of the living dead in the mainstream Euroamerican horror—the unique combination of a dead body resisting peaceful rest and hungering for the flesh of the living.

In order to analyze and discuss that fundamentally American mainstream horror zombie one doubtlessly needs to turn to George Romero's *Night of the Living Dead* [1968], an independent film that introduced that particular monster. In this respect, *Night of the Living Dead* is *the* zombie film, the film that established the American (and, consequently, Euroamerican) concept of a zombie. In *Icons of Horror* June Pulliam argues that Romero established a certain canonical image that permeates the horror genre:

> In the twenty-first century, the word "zombie" conjures up a familiar figure of a decaying corpse shuffling in a somnambulistic state, eyes glazed and arms held stiffly forward, in the mindless pursuit of human flesh. We owe this iconographic image to filmmaker George A. Romero's 1968 low-budget black-and-white movie *Night of the Living Dead,* which transformed the zombie in much the same way that James Whale's 1931 film *Frankenstein* altered Mary Shelley's creature or Tod Browning's 1931 film *Dracula* changed Bram Stoker's count. Today, writers and filmmakers who take zombie as their subject must acknowledge Romero's inter-

pretation of the creature, if only to argue within the reality of their own fictional universes that his portrayal was inaccurate [Pulliam in Joshi 2007: 723–4].

Apart from cinema, the horror genre includes a wide variety of media, including literature, graphic novels, animated feature films and series, video games and role-playing games. The interesting fact about the canonical image of the zombie, created by Romero, is that it functions not only aesthetically, but also within the narrative dimension and the acted one. In his article *The Rules of Horror: Procedural Adaptation in Clock Tower, Resident Evil, and Dead Rising* Matthew Weise comments on the practical aspect of Romero's influence in this way:

> The modern zombie is associated with a clear set of behaviors, which could just as easily be called "rules." According to these rules a zombie is a creature that: violently attacks any human in sight, eats human flesh, cannot move quickly, cannot use tools, possesses no reason or higher intelligence, and cannot be killed except by a blow or shot to the head. The final rule is that any human bitten by a zombie will eventually die and become one themselves. These rules are clearly laid out in *Night of the Living Dead,* partially by example and partially by dialogue [Weise in Perron 2009: 252–253].

In this sense, Romero brought into being the cinematic zombie as we know it today (interestingly enough, the word "zombie" does not appear in the film at all). The "flesh-eating ghouls" introduced in *Night of the Living Dead* are not very repulsive as far as looks are concerned. They are not putrid monsters dropping body parts, but seemingly normal looking humans when they are introduced to the audience; they move stiffly and awkwardly, and sort of aimlessly (until they spot a victim), with wide open eyes and vacant, slack expressions on their faces. They are, however, profoundly disturbing, all the more so because they are a completely unfamiliar threat. Only gradually do they evolve into what the zombie is directly associated with today, as near the end of the film they are described as "just dead flesh"—an impersonal, biological term, denoting shapeless matter, a substance rather than individual organism. And it is that absence of individuality that constitutes the horror of the zombie. In *Writing Horror and the Body* Linda Badley notes that what the zombie reflects in the horror genre is dehumanization, very often on a vast scale (Badley 1996: 74). Romero's zombies embody the sheer horror of a body devoid of soul since, as Badley states, they provide images for "the persistent vegetative state of 'brain death'"; in addition, they are motivated by "visceral reflex functions"—in other words, they breathe and they eat, but they are in fact cognitively and legally dead because they have lost the functions that conventionally designate individuality and personhood (Badley 1996: 74).

Badley puts great emphasis on the issue of loss of individuality, pointing to the fact that the collective but diverse mob of zombies represent the image of an "ambulatory mass grave" (Badley 1996: 74). The zombie is not a person, but a thing; it is formidable in the mass and simultaneously anonymous in it. The mass hinders and empowers at the same time; it is characterized by one instinct. The zombie have no names; they are regarded in the context of numbers, not in the context of individuals. Therefore, the zombie will be always defined in the negative, as something that is not alive, not sentient and not a person.

Romero's *Night of the Living Dead* introduced the plot pattern of a zombie narrative that would be reconstructed to a large extent in virtually every zombie narrative to follow: the protagonist(s) encounter the undead being unaware, at the time, that the strange-looking humans are in fact dead humans; they run and find shelter, which is eventually overrun by a steadily increasing number of the undead. In *Night of the Living Dead* the living protagonists are initially a brother and sister, Barbara and Johnny, who are visiting the grave of their father in a secluded cemetery. As they are about to leave, Johnny is attacked and killed by an odd-looking aggressive man. Barbara manages to get away and lock herself in a seemingly deserted house on the hill. Soon other people come seeking shelter in the house, and all of them eventually learn that the aggressive attackers surrounding the house are actually the living dead.

Plot-wise, Romero's living dead represent an evil of fresh, unknown nature—not only within the story, but within the cinematic context of the time as well, leaving both the characters and the audience (of the time) at a loss. At the beginning of the film, when Johnny delivers his famous line "They're coming to get you, Barbara," we can naturally presume he means the dead, but the word is left unspoken. He continues: "They're coming for you, Barbara. They're coming for you. Look! There comes one of them now." Whoever "they" are, they remain formally undefined and unnamed. Therefore Barbara's first encounter with the living dead is, in fact, a struggle with an unknown. The man attacking her might as well simply be mad or delirious. Ben refers to them as "those things":

BEN
    You know a place back down the road called Beekman's? Beekman's diner? Anyhow, that's where I found that truck I have out there. There's a radio in the truck. I had jumped in to listen to it, when a big gasoline truck came screaming right across the road. Well, there must have been ten, fifteen of those things chasing after it. Grabbing and holding on. Now, I didn't see them at first. I could just see that the truck was moving in a funny way. And those things were catching up to it. Truck went right across the road. Slammed on my brakes to keep from hit-

ting it myself. It went right through the guard rail. I guess ... I guess the driver must have cut off the road, into that gas station by Beekman's diner. It went right through the billboard. Ripped over a gas pump, and never stopped moving. By now it's like a moving bonfire. Didn't know if the truck was going to explode or what. I can still hear the man, screaming. This thing is just backing away from it. I look back at the diner to see if there was anyone there who could help me. That was when I noticed that the entire place had been encircled. Wasn't a sign of life left, except ... by now, there were no more screams. I realized that ... I was alone. With fifty or sixty of those things. Just standing there, staring at me. I started to drive. I ... just plowed right through them. They didn't move. They didn't run, or ... Just stood there, staring at me. Just wanted to crush them. They ... Scattered through the air, like bugs.

Despite the palpable horror conveyed by the story, Ben's narrative does not shed any light on the monsters' nature or origin—on the contrary, it only makes the situation more baffling. The radio announcer initially calls the creatures "unidentified assassins." It is only later, when the radio reports that "[a] widespread investigation of reports from funeral homes, morgues and hospitals has concluded that the unburied dead are coming back to life and seeking human victims," that the horror factor manifests itself fully. The claustrophobic setting of the narrative is complete—the living cannot either hurt or outrun the dead, as the dead cannot be killed, and they outnumber the living by far. It is also at this point that the dehumanization of the undead begins; they are no longer "dead persons" or "attackers," but just "flesh." The characters are urged by the authorities to carry the bodies to the street, so they can be immediately soaked with gasoline and burned. The scientist invited to the studio goes even as far as saying: "The bereaved will have to forgo the dubious comforts that a funeral service will give. They're just dead flesh. And dangerous."

Rationality is one of the most important factors of the applied dimension of any zombie scenario. The living characters may attempt to fight (and they usually do), but they do not stand a chance, so their only choice is to run. As they run and try to separate themselves from the attackers, they establish what Weise calls "the shrinking fortress"; the human protagonists run, hide and attempt to create a stronghold for themselves (Weise in Perron 2009: 252–253). This is first shown in *Night of the Living Dead* where the survivors barricade themselves in a farmhouse in order to escape the walking dead. They use boards, nails and furniture to block all the doors and windows, but those barricades are eventually overwhelmed, and the survivors retreat to smaller, individual rooms and are forced to rely on weapons and close combat again; this concept—the "shrinking fortress"—is a "mainstay of the subgenre, finding expression in virtually every zombie film" (Weise in Perron 2009: 252–253). The formula is so recognizable that sometimes even films that do not feature zombies may be recognized as "zombie films" (e.g., *28 Days Later* [2002]). It is also the reason for which zombie narratives tend to be far more repetitive than ghost narratives, monster narratives or narratives that focus on religious horror: the formula is solid, but it is also rigid.

That does not mean, naturally, that all zombie texts are the same. Although they may feature very similar scenarios, the zombie itself can differ from narrative to narrative. It can be depicted as either slow and shuffling (*Night of the Living Dead, Resident Evil* [2002]) or capable of regular, fast movement (*Dawn of the Dead* [2004]). While usually the zombie is mute, on occasions it is depicted as capable of speech (*The Return of the Living Dead* [1985]). It is, more often than not, unintelligent (*Resident Evil, Dawn of the Dead* [1978]), although intelligent zombies also exist in fiction (*Land of the Dead* [2005]). It is, however, the heritage of Romero's living dead that created the shape of the modern zombie: aggressive, fierce, voracious. Unable to talk or otherwise communicate any abstract ideas and share information, the zombie are just an unstoppable, mindless force. The most horrifying attribute of the zombie, however, one that characterizes this particular monster in virtually every single portrayal, is the relentless tenacity with which the zombie pursues its victim. This obstinacy is what characterises the zombie in the most distinct manner; the dead body, refusing to stay dead, never stops. It can be damaged, but not injured. It can be destroyed, but not really killed. The slowly shuffling zombie is the anticipation of a gruesome end. And its abject, contagious nature means the zombie is never alone, but surrounded by other zombies; when the human protagonists eventually run out of ammunition, when they are tired, hungry and exhausted, and all their weapons are lost or broken, the zombie is still there, waiting, in a crowd of awkward, staggering, hungry undead. The undead body is not only a terrifying monstrosity, but a lurching horror that is impossible to escape, ignore or wait out. And although the protagonist cannot wait out the undead threat, the living dead can wait for a long time, indifferent to material adversity and mental discomfort—for there is nothing inside the mindless undead. Morgan refers to this feature as an "awful straight-ahead vector," combined with an "absence of personality" (Morgan 2002: 102). What makes zombie a zombie is its lack of selfhood, which allows it to proceed forward without doubt or thought, focused only on its goal, oblivious of adversity or any impediment (Morgan 2002: 102). An additional, closely related dimension of horror represented by the undead body is the inability of the human subject to fight against the descent into blind, inhuman savagery. The futile struggle against this descent, i.e., against becoming an undead, is one of both most common and simultaneously resonant points in the majority of zombie narratives. The human protagonist will struggle desperately, but ultimately in vain to remain among the living, and will always inevitably succumb to the monstrous transformation.

The evolution of the cinema zombie is very appropriately illustrated in Tom Savini's re imagining of the original *Night of the Living Dead*—a remake by the same title [1990]. Savini's *Night of the Living Dead* presents a story approximately identical to the original. Significant differences, however, concern the figure of the zombie; Savini's living dead deviate from Romero's living dead in a number of important characteristics. The 1990 zombie is not merely dead—it is ostensibly and irreversibly dead, as its appearance gives to understand. The stiffness of movement and the blank expression has been replaced by far more straightforward imagery of decay and damaged flesh. The zombie is now uncomfortably unsightly and putrefying, but also more vicious and animalistic, growling rather than moaning. This image of the living dead seems to remain prevalent in American zombie narratives. Although the visual aspect of the zombie tends to vary from narrative to narrative (some depictions center on the putrefaction and disintegration of the body while others lean more towards the haggard, diseased look), it is most often concerned with the repulsive aspect of the dead, whether they are putrid, grunting monsters dropping decayed body parts or almost normal looking humans who move stiffly and awkwardly, with wide vacant eyes and slack expressions on their faces. This imagery works in a twofold way. On the one hand, the uncomfortably unsightly damaged flesh points to the inevitable fate of all organic remains once the person is dead. On the other hand, the vicious, animalistic creature that is no longer human and cannot even speak—instead it is only capable of moaning, hissing or howling—represents the immediate threat of dying. A great many films set up essentially exactly this image: from the mainstream franchise such as the *Living Dead* films (from the sequel to the *Night of the Living Dead*, *Dawn of the Living Dead* [1978], to *The Land of the Dead* [2005] and *Diary of the Dead* [2007]), as well as independent or low budget titles such as *Re-Animator* [1985], *Beneath still Waters* [2005], or more recent (and undeniably more disturbing) *Deadgirl* [2008]. As Kim Paffenroth argues, "[w]hen one speaks of zombie movies today, one is really speaking of movies that are either made by or directly influenced by one man, director George A. Romero" (Paffenroth 2006: 1). She also notes that "Romero's landmark film, *Night of the Living Dead* (1968), has defined the zombie genre since its release, and has even spilled over into the depiction of zombies in any medium, including books, comic books, video and board games, and action figures" (Paffenroth 2006: 1). In that sense the American zombie is the Romero zombie—the most universal representation of the living dead in American horror.

As for Japanese horror cinema and literature, the zombie is not a very common monstrosity, neither is it a popular cinematic motif. When it does appear on screen, it bears striking resemblance to the Euroamerican living dead, as Colette Bailman points out, stating that "[t]he shuffling zombies in the Japanese zombie film tend to be recycled revenants of the zombie films of the 1970s..." Balmain 2008: 115). Balmain also suggests that "these zombies owe as much to the contemporary popular culture, both American and Japanese, as they do to their earlier prototypes" (Balmain 2008: 115). Indeed, as many other popular culture characters and concepts in American and Japanese culture, the Japanese representation of the zombie is characterized by certain cultural hybridization (Marak in Bohorodycz et al. 2012: 259). A great example would be one of the most prominent Japanese titles to deal with the zombie theme, namely the *Resident Evil (BAIOHAZĀDO)* video game franchise, which later spanned the European and Canadian series of film adaptations, beginning with *Resident Evil* [2002], directed by Paul Anderson. The zombie depicted in the original Japanese *Resident Evil* is the Euroamerican zombie, but the Japanese execution lends the game a certain unmistakable flavor. *Resident Evil* presents an American concept executed by Japanese creators, which in turn later inspired Euroamerican producers.

The first *Resident Evil* (initially released in Japan as *Biohazard*) game was a survival horror video game published in 1996 by Capcom. What sets it apart from other video games is its exclusive focus on the zombie. Bishop refers to *Resident Evil* as "the first true zombie video game," explaining that although zombies did play bit parts in other games, the first video game actually completely devoted to that creature was *Resident Evil* (Bishop 2010: 16). *Resident Evil* effectively was the "true zombie video game" inasmuch as it not only used the zombie as its main opponent for the player, but also due to its faithful recreation of the Romero's living dead experience. The previously mentioned "zombie film conventions" which are, according to Weise, laid out in *The Night of the Living Dead* are also "rudimentally modeled in *Resident Evil*" (Weise in Perron 2009: 253). Moreover, *Resident Evil* visibly strives for the Euroamerican feel; it uses a Western-style mansion located near a fictional small American town, Raccoon City, and a team of American characters. The living dead that the player must go up against are also presented in a form and way consistent with the Euroamerican tradition insofar that their movements are awkward and sluggish, and they are motivated by their hunger for the living flesh. And yet at the same time the way in which *Resident Evil* portrays the zombie feels distinctively Japanese.

The plot of *Resident Evil* begins with a special police team "Alpha" being sent to investigate bizarre murders with signs of cannibalism after contact is lost with the first team on the task— "Bravo" team. The "Alpha" team locates the helicopter of the "Bravo" team, but there are no signs of survivors. While searching the area the "Alpha" team is attacked by savage dogs and escapes to a nearby abandoned mansion. Inside the mansion, the team splits up to search for one of their team members, separated from the others during the chase. Depending on whether the player is controlling the character of Chris or Jill, either Chris or Jill wanders the spacious, empty mansion until they run into a dead man devouring the body of a "Bravo" team member.

This first zombie scene in *Resident Evil* introduces the zombie as a slow, ungainly creature, perhaps not very repulsive as far as appearance is concerned, but most certainly dead beyond doubt; the player encounters the undead as it is devouring one of the characters. This introduction establishes an image of the zombie that is very familiar to the Euroamerican audience. There are, however, subtle qualities that make the first zombie of the *Resident Evil* franchise distinguishable. They do wander the mansion in blood-splattered clothes and attack the player, but they do that in a far less aggressive manner then the living dead portrayed in American horror cinema. They do not groan or growl but rather moan softly and sorrowfully, shuffling indecisively in the general direction of the player. Their apathetic manner of movement and the vague gloominess, combined with the somber, unsettling soundtrack of the game includes an additional dimension into the horror they evoke. Although *Resident Evil* precedes Kiyoshi Kurosawa's *Pulse* [2001] by five years, the zombies in *Resident Evil* are actually very reminiscent of the dead portrayed in Kurosawa's film. This, combined with the specific score, creates an overall atmosphere of lifeless, empty spaces bearing an overwhelming sense of the loneliness in death.

Similar to the Euroamerican zombie, the living dead in the *Resident Evil* franchise undergo a certain evolution in consecutive installments. In the second installment of *Resident Evil, Resident Evil* 2 and its sequel, *Resident Evil 3: Nemesis,* the zombie gradually become faster and more aggressive, as well as visually repulsive, denoting more advanced stages of decomposition. In this respect the modern Japanese zombie does not differ immensely from its Euroamerican prototype, which permeates the zombie narratives all over the world. Interestingly, in one of the few Japanese zombie films, *Junk* [2000], the zombies are not only faithfully modeled after the American zombie, but also they are played in the most part by Caucasian actors, thus emphasizing the close relation between the zombie and its Euroamerican origins. Jim Harper notes that "[d]espite the popularity of the zombie movie in Europe and America following George's Romero *Night of the Living Dead* (1968), the walking dead never became a staple feature of Eastern horror films" (Harper 2009: 43). He suggests that "the main issue facing Japanese zombie films is a religious one. In keeping with Japanese funerary practices, corpses are usually cremated, leaving very little behind to resurrect" (Harper 2009: 43). The Japanese titles portraying the living dead I intend to provide next tend to circumvent this problem in both creative and profoundly Japanese ways.

Another prominent Japanese survival horror video game dealing with the theme of the living dead is *Siren* (*SAIREN*, released in Europe and Australia as *Forbidden Siren*), published in 2003 by Sony Computer Entertainment. In contrast to *Resident Evil*, which attempts to emulate an American setting and furnishes that setting with an American monster, *Siren* is, in words of Chris Pruett, "steeped in traditional Japanese horror ideas and motifs" (Pruett 2010: 4). The story is set in a small mountain village called Hanyuda, and all the characters who appear in it (both playable and non-playable) are Japanese. Pruett points out that *Siren* and games similar to it (such as the *Zero* franchise, known in the United States as *Fatal Frame*) "draw upon imagery and stories that are common throughout Japan, and are therefore excellent candidates for cultural analysis" (Pruett 2010: 4). *Siren*, saturated with Japanese native horror elements, introduces a completely avant-garde image of the living dead.

For a title focusing on the living dead, *Siren* pays little to no respect to the "zombie film conventions," creating instead its own, original monster. The living dead featured in *Siren* are *shibito* (lit. "corpse people"). The *shibito* are pale figures with bloody tears streaming down their faces and hollow-looking eyes. As opposed to the traditional Euroamerican living dead, they are well-coordinated and capable of moving fast, even running. They do not moan but instead make peculiar and deeply disturbing half-human and half monstrous sounds. They do not feed on people in any manner, although they do attack them, attempting to make them drink the crimson water. They retain intelligence (for instance, after having turned into a *hanshibito*—a half-corpse man—Akira recognizes Takeuchi and talks to him briefly), perform simple tasks (open doors, like Risa's sister during her attack, or operate wagons) and handle tools such as sickles and guns. One of their most important features, however, one that marks them as highly original among the living dead, is their ability to communicate. The *shibito*, if attacked or in need of assistance, will utter a sound resembling a howl to call other *shibito*. What is more, they are organized and capable of coordinated work for a common goal (which is, in the end,

Datatsushi's resurrection). Still, it is strongly emphasized that they are not human. In one of her moment of being oblivious to her own identity, Hisako warns Kyoya about the *shibito;* while teaching him how to sightjack, she asks him to try and "feel" her.[10] When Kyoya catches a glimpse of a *shibito*'s field of view, Hisako says "Did you feel anything else? They are no longer ... human."

The true nature of *shibito* and their most fascinating feature is revealed only later in the story. As the player finds out in the progress of the game, the people of Hanyuda have been cursed by what they refer to as a god (a creature from another world) after having eaten its flesh. The villagers developed a cult surrounding this being, whom they called Datatsushi. The *shibito* are simply villagers who have sought union with their god; for this reason, whenever the siren sounds the people of Hanyuda go into the red ocean and become *hanshibito*. The *hanshibito* then undergo *umi-okuri,* during which they submerge themselves in the crimson water and come back as perfect, complete *shibito* during *umi-gaeri,* their return from the water. At one point during the game, Akira Shimura and Yoriko Anno stumble upon this ceremony, witnessing the villagers emerging from the red sea, at which point Akira remarks that those villagers are not human anymore, and tells Yoriko "It's over. I'm going to get out of here. Before I turn into a monster as well."

The *hanshibito* returning from the sea are not human any more because, just as Akira points out, the "crimson sea" is not an ordinary ocean, but a barrier between this world and other world, i.e., the dimension from which the god came. The crimson water is in fact god's blood,[11] which can heal any wounds and bring the dead back to life. Whenever the villagers hear the sound of siren—which is, in fact, Datatsushi's cry—they submerge in the crimson water to get closer to their god. The whole underlying concept of the *shibito* character has very strong religious undertones. The living dead presented in *Siren* is the complete opposite of the Japanese representation of a vampire; the traditional Euroamerican vampire is always imbued with religious narrative, whereas the Japanese representation of a vampire is not. Similarly, the American zombie has no religious context (at least no context within the predominant Christian religious outlook) of abomination, sacrilege or curse. In *Siren,* on the other hand, the very nature of the *shibito* is both religious and ritualistic, which renders them "clean," more spiritual than organic. Even when incapacitated by the player, they are not really killed but merely sink into something resembling a praying position.

Although called "corpse people," the *shibito* do not necessarily start out as dead; if someone dies and then comes in touch with the crimson water, he is resurrected. When at the beginning of the story Kyoya regains consciousness after being mortally wounded, Hisako explains to him: "This red water is now coursing through your veins.... In place of all the blood you lost." Also, those who have become *hanshibito* but do not complete their transformation eventually wither away and decay. The majority of *shibito*, nonetheless, begin their transformation because of their devotion; they drink the blood of god and forsake their own human blood in order to get close to Datatsushi. This actually makes the *shibito* even more horrifying, mainly because, as Christian McCrea points out in his article *Gaming's Hauntology: Dead Media in Dead Rising, Siren and Michigan: Report from Hell,* they are "all the more monstrous because they seem willing participants in their undeath" (McCrea in Perron 2009: 225). Becoming a *shibito* may be regarded as a curse or as blessing, depending on the devotion or lack thereof that a character may hold for Datatsushi; those who have not yet become a *shibito* resist the metamorphosis, and those who are at any stage of change welcome it. In this respect, the living dead are indeed "corpse people," with no regard for the earthly word. Their human souls are gone.

A similar manner of presenting the undead, both as far as the religious aspect and the characteristics of the living dead are concerned, can be found in a 1999 film *Shikoku*, directed by Shunichi Nagasaki. In order to construct its horror, *Shikoku* relies—similar to *Siren*—on a native Japanese setting and genuine (at least partially) Japanese beliefs and folklore. The story takes place in a secluded little village on the smallest and least populated of Japan's four main islands, Shikoku. Like *Siren,* the film makes use of religious elements and is heavily imbued with folklore. The main difference between the titles is that *Shikoku* is less other-worldly and more straight forwardly traditional; the world of *Shikoku* is incorporated smoothly into an existing reality of rituals and the religion of Shikoku Island.

The title of the film is a homophone to the name of the island (lit. "four provinces"), but the *kanji* characters used create a word that literally reads a "land of the dead." This play on words reflects the basic concept of the film. The plot revolves around the authentic practice of the 88 temple *seiseki* pilgrimage tracing presence of the holy person of Kōbō Daishi (Reader 1991: 10), but *Shikoku* changes the meaning of this custom, giving it a darker side. The audience is introduced to the central idea of the film when Fumiya explains to Hinako the role of the pilgrimage—the pilgrim should visit the eight temples, the first one at Tokushima, and then go all the way around the island and end up at Kagawa. Although the pilgrimage can start at any point, it must be made in order. According to Sayori's father, the centuries old custom was meant to turn the island into a holy precinct, a barrier between the world of the living and the world of the dead. If the line were to be broken, the barrier would fall and "the four lands" would become "the land of the dead."

Within the presented world of *Shikoku* the function of the pilgrimage is to help the dead reach the afterlife peacefully and preserve the barrier between the world of the living and the world of the dead. In this way the film smoothly interweaves the genuine folklore and beliefs of Japan with fictitious ones, thus establishing a firm base for the horror narrative. The attempt to create a believable holy practice is well executed as the pilgrimage of the 88 temples is a factual religious ritual, consisting of visiting the consecutive temples while maintaining the correct spiritual attitude (Reader 1991: 17). The ominous practice of "reversing the order," on the other hand, referred to as *gyaku uchi* is, in fact, harmless (Reader 1991: 16). In *Shikoku,* however, the consequences of *gyaku uchi* are portrayed as ghastly:

> SENTO: To the left is the path to the dead. The one which breaks the seal. The other path you circle Shikoku once for each year of the dead persons age. The dead of Shikoku ascend Mt Ishitsuchi and are purified there. But one too strongly attached to this world may not ascent Mt Ishitsuchi. It is these souls who grow restless. They know that by the other path they may return to this world.
> FUMIYA: And what happens then?
> SENTO: If the gate to Yomi opens the spirits of the dead take on flesh and return. It won't just be the girl. All the dead will return in the flesh of this world.

Sayori's mother expected her daughter to become the next Hiura priestess. She needs her daughter back to maintain the Hiura bloodline, so every year for sixteen years she has been making the pilgrimage in the reverse order. The possibility for a girl who has been dead for sixteen years to return to life in the flesh is provided by the fact that *Shikoku* localizes and couples the terror with the depicted surroundings by means of placing a very important place in the vicinity of the village—a cave with a reputed entrance to the underworld, which the villagers do not like to talk about and which they do not approach. "In the myths," Fumiya explains to Hinako, "the gateway is always a cave," and it leads to a land of the dead in which the dead still have bodies.

This is a crucial point of Sayori's mother's plan. She does not want to conjure up Sayori's spirit; she needs a living, breathing Sayori to continue the house of Hiura. And so after the sixteen *gyaku uchi* pilgrimages made by her mother Sayori does come back in the flesh. This makes Sayori a very specific representative of the living dead, and an immensely interesting one. Once she emerges from the pond in the cave, Sayori is initially rather slow, both in the intellectual and physical sense. She moves awkwardly, and makes low, incoherent sounds, which makes her comparable to a traditional Euroamerican zombie. Later, however, she begins to speak, and although she slurs her speech and seems detached most of the time, she improves with time, eventually gaining the ability to communicate clearly. She also possesses supernatural strength she seems to be unaware of. Her reasoning is simple and very base, but also very emotional—the only thing she really cares about is seeing Fumiya again. As she becomes more articulate and graceful, she also becomes ever more fervent about him, which gives her an air of obsessiveness that nears madness.

Sayori is a resurrected being, an undead, but she differs from a regular living dead in that she is capable of speech and experiencing feelings. Still, she does not belong among the living, even though the consciousness inhabiting her body, brought back from the Land of the Dead by her mother, really belongs to Sayori (unlike in the case of those resurrected in *Pet Sematary* or *The Rising.*)

The most essential aspect of Sayori as the living dead figure in the context of Japanese horror narratives is the fact that she transgresses the natural order of things. Her presence in the world of the living is wrong; when attempting to send her spirit back to the Land of the Dead, Sento shouts: "The dead must not return!" Sayori must go back to Yomi because she is "no longer of this world." The constitutive feature of the Japanese living dead is their state of being deceased. They are dead not aesthetically, but ontologically, and it is that ontological nature of their living death that evokes the horror. The sheer fact that they are dead constitutes their status as horror figures, and their appearance and behavior are actually of secondary importance. The living dead in the form of American zombie, as featured in *Night of the Living Dead* are identified as dead because their biological functions have ceased. The living dead in *Siren* are recognized as dead because they are dead as human beings; their human souls have departed, leaving behind only a phobic object, the body. In *Shikoku,* Sayori evokes terror because her existence itself is unacceptable, since the dead do not belong with the living. If the American living dead violates the natural order of life and death, the Japanese living dead is a source of horror because it does not belong.

The undead body embodies the horror of experiencing the process of dying and death itself while still being alive. It horrifies the living subject and at the same time deprives the human remains of human dignity; the human corpse is replaced by "moving meat" and is treated like "moving meat," a subject and character-less threat that must be destroyed. The zombie symbolizes the horror of helplessness in the face of physiology, the inability to resist disease and death. And in its dreadful, sluggish "unlife" (Morgan 2002:176), the zombie represents the death itself, first stopping the biological functions of the victim and then again death, the ultimate end of the mind subject. The undead is not a person brought back to life from the dead. It is the triumph of the until now docile, obedient body over the mind-subject, the ultimate rebellion of the ruled against the ruling.

The concept of monstrosity and monsters is a complex issue. When regarded from one perspective, the majority of horror entities are monsters— or, like Carroll claims, all horror entities are monsters: all the undead, vampires and ghosts, all the werewolves, goblins and demons, and every other creature ever to evoke fear in human beings. And yet, within this impressive, multifarious parade there are so few authentic, "proper" monsters. "Proper monsters," as they are defined in this chapter, are even more complicated as horror figures. They are the most primal, most familiar and intimate form of fear; they are the things without a name. Simultaneously, there seems to be less and less place for them because the taxonomy of fear grows ever broader, as does the tendency for rationalization, leaving little to no place for the unnamed and unnamable terror.

3
The Divine and the Unholy

All horror narratives tend to have some sort of connection to a religious system of beliefs. For example, the mere consideration of the soul entails the necessity of some spiritual frame of reference. As Cowan points out, whether not at rest, tormented or being fought over by conflicting forces, the soul itself is an "explicitly religious concept, one that makes little sense apart from the various religious frameworks in which it comes embedded" (Cowan 2008: 6). The titles discussed in this chapter do not merely touch upon, but are founded on the concept of the sacred order of the universe (see Cowan 2008). Those narratives concern fears related to beliefs, whether religious beliefs or beliefs concerning some other supernatural causality—in other words, the aspects of the sacred or the magical/occult that must observe the laws of the given spiritual system (a partial exception here are the Japanese demons, who are portrayed in a variety of ways; some of them perform functions related to religious concepts, and some of them are merely a part of the natural world, and they do not represent any kind of moral conflict, nor are they related to any).

Just as the vampire and the werewolf are related concepts, so are religious fears and demons. They may seem disparate at first glance, but are in fact closely connected in the contemporary world-view, both American and Japanese. Religious horror narratives deal with fears related to religious mythologies containing laws and rules—specifically to the rituals, values, and powerful beings existent within those mythologies. Demon narratives concern powerful supernatural, often malevolent beings that most commonly exist within some mythologies and obey certain laws and rules. Demons as entities are also at least partially related to the concept of Hell or hells, i.e., religious places of punishment. The American demon most common in horror narratives is the Christian demon; within the Christian mythology, demons are servants of the Devil, associated with hatred and lies (Russell 1987a: 71). The Japanese demon, on the other hand, roams the world freely, interacting with it and being subject to earthly needs and desires, but it may be also associated with hellish functions. In fact, the traditional image of Japanese *oni* comes from the Buddhist concept of horrifying creatures who dwell in the abyss of Buddhist hell to terrify and torment sinners (Reider 2010: 10–11). This differentiates demons from other monsters; they have a place and function in the sacred order.

Demon

A demon is very specific monster, but in a manner different from the werewolf. Demons are a complex, diversified and manifold monster species, especially in the Euroamerican cultural frame. Matt Cardin, sketching the silhouette of the demon as it is known in Euroamerican popular culture, emphasizes that demons were not originally what we now recognize them as. The English word "demon" (which derives from the Latin *daemon,* which in turn derives from the Greek *daimon*) denotes any spirits, both good or evil, that are not divine and not mortal, and which inhabit the "intermediate realm between gods and humans"; therefore even angels belong to the general class of beings known as demons. However, somewhere between roughly 200 BCE and 200 CE, the word "demon" came to indicate only the evil entities within the category (Cardin in Joshi 2007: 34). Cardin further mentions three most important currents of thought that formed the now iconic image of the demon. Those included the "beliefs and ideas about spirits that saturated the Middle East from the earliest antiquity," "the angels and evil spirits of ancient Judaism" and the Greek concept of *daimones* (Cardin in Joshi 2007: 34). It is important to note that the *daimons* were, at least originally, neutral spirits, neither good nor evil, but rather potentially both; only later more concrete categories of good *daimons* and evil *daimons* were developed (Cardin in Joshi 2007: 35 36).

The diverse nature of the demon and its manifold manifestations makes it a very powerful horror figure, and simultaneously one that is tremendously difficult to describe and define. While in literature demons tend to remain in touch with their ancient cultural background, cinema oftentimes disposes of that background and depicts demons as a nearly contextless monsters. Despite the fact that there are notable films that take into account demons' historical context, in many other cases demons are presented as mindless, vicious killing machines (Cardin in Joshi 2007: 43). Therefore, supernatural horror narratives featuring demons may be, according to Cardin, divided into three categories, depending on which of the following they emphasize: the narratives featuring demons as "fallen angels" (religious context), the narratives featuring demons as "moral tempters," and the narratives in which demons appear as "afflicting presence" (which tend to range from physical and/or psychological harassment to proper demonic possession) (Cardin in Joshi 2007: 43–44).

The easiest and most useful, in terms of this work, distinction to be made is the affinity of the demon. A demon in a horror narrative may be a demon associated with the religious framework of the culture within which that narrative was created, or it may simply be a powerful, dangerous entity. In an American narrative, this means that the demon may be a Christian demon or a demon completely unrelated to religion. As Cardin notes, this latter kind of demon became more common with time:

> The postmodern demon is not a fallen angel who can be commanded in the name of Christ or driven away by any version of the iconic Angel, but is instead an unaccountable spirit of viciousness that arrives for no reason and cannot be driven away. As such, it may be taken as a kind of apotheosis of the iconic Demon as the afflicting, possessing presence [Cardin in Joshi 2007: 53].

American demon narratives may be approximately divided into two classes, represented in this chapter by the titles *The Exorcist* and *Paranormal Activity*. *The Exorcist* portrays a demon belonging to the Christian mythology, whereas *Paranormal Activity* depicts a non–Christian, occult demon ("occult" being used here in the sense "related to the paranormal," related to practices and lore associated with magic, spiritualism, and divination). Other demon titles usually fall into one of those two categories; they either present the demon as an adversary of the Christian God (*The Exorcism of Emily Rose* [2005] or *The Last Exorcism* [2012]) or present the demon as a non human, malicious entity, not necessarily connected to the Christianity mythos (*Insidious* [2010], *Drag Me to Hell* [2009], *Killing Ariel* [2008]). The non–Christian variation of the demon is naturally more diverse; James Wan's *Insidious* presents the demon as a malevolent being occupying the same otherworldly realm as the spirits of the dead and wanting to possess a human body. *Drag Me to Hell*, directed by Sam Raimi, leans more towards a mixture of folklore and occult lore, where the only chance for the protagonist to save herself from the demon is to resort to folk magic. In Fred Calvert's *Killing Ariel*, on the other hand, a man is haunted by a young woman whom he kills over and over again, only to wake up by her side again, which eventually drives him to madness and suicide.[1]

In American demon narratives, the demon works mainly through possession (although not always, as it can be seen in *Drag Me to Hell* and *Killing Ariel*); it may move objects or cause strange noises, but eventually it will want to possess its victim and destroy his or her life—regardless whether the narrative makes use of Christian mythology or not.[2] In the case of the non–Christian demon, it is almost impossible to chase it away without killing the person possessed by it, as seen in *Session 9* [2001], *Killing Ariel, Jennifer's Body* [2009] or *Insidious*. On the other hand, possession by the Devil or a demon in the Christian sense (*akumatsuki*), as it is usually presented in Euroamerican narratives, is practically non-existent in Japanese narratives. A title worth mentioning here is Kaneto Shindō's *Onibaba* [1964], where a woman repeatedly puts on a demon mask only to discover at some point that she cannot take it off any more. Nonetheless, Shindō's film is more a symbolic psychological drama than a horror story. The old woman is not so much possessed by a demon as she turns into a demon herself. Examples of possession in Japanese culture include the possession by the spirit of a fox (*kitsunetsuki*), which resembles a demon possession to some extent (Chamberlain 2007: 123)[3] or possession by a spirit of another person (such as Lady Aoi in Murasaki Shikibu's *Tale of Genji*, who was possessed by the spirit of jealous Lady Rokujō. See Bargen 1997: 10). Neither of those, however, are structured like horror possession narratives; the possession is not as violent and may even be comical in the case of the fox. Additionally, neither of those is associated with evil:

> There are ... very important cultural differences in the responses to witchcraft and spirit possession. In the comparatively recent witch hunts and trials of medieval Europe and colonial America, spells and "demonic possession" were attributed to the actions of persons who were diabolically empowered to do evil. After their confession, often obtained by torture, witches were condemned to death. In contrast, Japanese practices were relatively benign. Buddhist exorcist rituals allowed *mono no ke* to reveal themselves and disperse. The evil spirits were immune to prosecution because they, as a rule, belonged to the dead. Thus, unlike persons accused at European and American witchcraft trials, those thought to be the source of *mono no ke* were not blamed for the harm and pain they caused the possessed.... The mildness of the response can be attributed to the belief that neither the spirits of the living (*ikisudama; ikiryō*) nor the spirits of the dead (*shiryō*) were thought to form the kind of intentionally evil alliance that the witch forms with the devil [Bargen 1997: 9–10].

This may explain why the possession motif, whether in the native Japanese form or in the Euroamerican one, is not as popular in Japanese horror fiction; lacking the important elements of physical and spiritual danger, it simply is not effective horror material.

One of the most prominent representatives of American demon narratives featuring the Christian demon is beyond doubt *The Exorcist*, a novel by William Peter Blatty. Not only representative, but also immensely famous, *The Exorcist* owes a lot of its renown to the acclaimed 1973 film adaptation directed by William Friedkin, which, similar to Polanski's adaptation of *Rosemary's Baby*, is almost identical with the original novel. As a horror narrative, Blatty's story is remarkable for a number of reasons, but for the purpose of this chapter we shall focus on its most obvious and most powerful aspect, i.e., the religious plot-line. As Cardin proposes, the strong point of *The Exorcist* was its explicit and obscene (in more than one sense) depiction of the main source of horror—the demon. The demon in *The Exorcist* is horrific and visceral; it is an afflicting presence that possesses a person's body and personality, and such portrayal made a strong impression on the audience of that time. Damien Karras, with his initial skepticism and reluctance to accept the supernatural explanation, served effectively as a stand-in for a "spiritually skeptical but existentially fearful American public" (Cardin in Joshi 2007: 48). It is also worth noting that, as Cowan points out, the primary plot of *The Exorcist* is structured around Christian—specifically Catholic—mythology, and therefore the story is "rather difficult to follow if you are not aware of Roman Catholic demonology" (Cowan 2008: 170). And yet, Blatty's text does not exclude the audience unaware of that mythology; in the context of horror the narrative makes use of a much wider, more universal conflict of good and evil, which in the novel happens to be represented by a demon and by servants of God.

Blatty's book tells the story of Regan, a young girl possessed by a demon, and her mother, who goes from skepticism and doubt to open-minded desperation as she turns from doctors to priests in hopes of helping her daughter. The demon steals into a suburban house where a mother and daughter are leading a happy, peaceful existence until Regan starts displaying most bizarre patterns of behavior. Chris, who initially shared a very strong, intimate mother-daughter bond with Regan, suddenly feels as if her child were a stranger. There is something wrong with Regan, but it is not clear what it might be. The escalation of horror in *The Exorcist* is remarkably subtle and deliberate. Most significantly, initially, there are no clues at all that would point the readers to an assumption that the source of the problem is something supernatural and related to religion.

The demon depicted in *The Exorcist* bears all the characteristics of a Christian demon. Because of its place in Christian mythology, it is vulnerable to the name of its God and the symbols of faith, including the holy water and crosses. It is also not corporeal and therefore not subject to carnal desires such as hunger, lust or blood-thirst. It does, however, display very human traits such as malice, cruelty, self-confidence or hatred. It is insidious and sexually obscene (it deprives Regan of her virginity with a crucifix, masturbates in front of the doctors), heretical (it offers to worship Merrin's anus), ruthless and brutal (it kills people), lying but all-knowing, vulgar and cruel (it lies in order to hurt people). It is also worth noting that in its cruelty and power the demon is arrogant and pretentious, behaving excessively at times, for example speaking backwards and levitating just to scare the priests.

Another aspect of *The Exorcist* very characteristic to American demon narratives featuring Christian demons is the physical absence of the demon. There is actually very little that the demon does outside of Regan; the horror is created through its control of her. The demon takes over her from within, invades her inexperienced, innocent soul, and makes her do things she would never dream of doing, hurting herself and others. It never materializes as a visible, corporeal monster, for that would defeat the purpose of its presence; Chris, Regan and everyone in their vicinity would simply accept the demonic threat as real and seek refuge in church. By making humans doubt its existence and hiding its face, the demon is able to fulfill its goal; it drives them away from God.

Thus, the first dimension of horror is physical. The demon's complete control of Regan's body allows it to make her hurt herself and attack others. It gradually changes her body and her face—not in a supernatural way, but through emaciation and self-injury—until it is Regan who becomes a monster. Even Karras, initially unconvinced of the legitimacy of Regan's possession, is struck by her appearance:

> Then his eyes locked, stunned, on the thing that was Regan, on the creature that was lying on its back in the bed, head propped against a pillow while eyes bulging wide in their hollow sockets shone with mad cunning and burning intelligence, with interest and with spite as they fixed upon his, as they watched him intently, seething in a face shaped into a skeletal, hideous mask of mind-bending malevolence. Karras shifted his gaze to the tangled, thickly matted hair; to the wasted arms and legs; the distended stomach jutting up so grotesquely; then back to the eyes: they were watching him ... pinning him ... shifting now to follow as he moved to a desk and chair near the window [Blatty 1971: 203].

Although Regan has not changed drastically—she has not grown another head or horns and a tail—the way she looks is striking. As Karras talks to the demon, he realizes it is a separate entity, and, despite himself, he begins to refer to the demon as "it" (Blatty 1971: 206) or "the Regan thing" (Blatty 1971: 207). Aware of Karras' wavering faith, the demon toys with the priest; instead of just manifesting himself to Karras, it makes him sway between belief and cynicism.

The second dimension of horror is obviously the moral and spiritual dimension. The tragedy taking place in *The Exorcist* is actually emotional in nature. The demon cannot affect Regan's soul, but it can hurt her and the people close to her; it can cause pain. It thrives on maliciousness and on cruelty as it reveals secrets people want to keep hidden and reminds them of painful moments in their lives, such as with Karras's mother. Although the demon possesses substantial telekinetic power and is capable of moving or raising into the air various objects (from drawers to the heavy bed Regan is lying in), its main power lies in its words. This is tremendously important, if not the defining feature of the Christian demon; all-knowing and able to manipulate the information freely, the demon speaks to cause pain. It talks incessantly, jeers and mocks, curses and taunts, disclosing enough truth to seem credible and simultaneously mixing it with lies, all in order to cause doubt and erode faith. For this reason, Merrin forbids Karras to converse with the demon, saying "The demon is a liar. He will lie to confuse us; but he will also mix lies with the truth to attack us. The attack is psychological, Damien. And powerful" (Blatty 1971: 299).

Although it is beyond the demon's power to simply snatch a soul away from God, it can do its best to undermine the faith of those it attacks. By causing despair and pain the demon raises doubt and attempts to sever the connection between God and man. Most importantly, however, the demon attempts to subvert that connection:

> "Then what would be the purpose of possession?" Karras said, frowning. "What's the point?"
> "Who can know?" answered Merrin. "Who can really hope to know?" He thought for a moment. And then probingly continued: "Yet I think the demon's target is not the possessed; it is us ... the observers ... every person in this house. And I think—I think the point is to make us despair; to reject our own humanity, Damien: to see ourselves as ultimately bestial; as ultimately vile and putrescent; without dignity; ugly; unworthy. And there lies the heart of it, perhaps: in unworthiness. For I think belief in God is not a matter of reason at all; I think it finally is matter of love; of accepting the possibility that God could love us ..." [Blatty 1971: 311].

Indeed, the demon in *The Exorcist* observes the laws of Christian mythology, according to which the purpose of demonic possession is to distort and destroy the divine likeness of man, i.e., the image of God within a man (Lane 1974 and Walvoord 1983), which, as Christians believe, is inside every person. The horror comes from the shocking, horrifying transformation Regan undergoes, as she changes from a smiling, innocent twelve-year-old into a violent, cursing, lewd travesty of herself, tearing at people's hearts. By making Regan seem unworthy and abhorrent, the demon casts doubt on one of the most important truths of Christianity.

3. *The Divine and the Unholy* 165

As a horror narrative, *The Exorcist* performs its function very well, owing to the vivid, clear opposition of good and evil, the righteous and the wicked. Regan is clearly an innocent victim, and her mother and the priests are all good people. The evil is entirely external. What is more important, it has a face, although unseen, and it is personified in the demon tormenting Regan. As a religious horror narrative, *The Exorcist* is predictably perverse. In the end, the Christian rituals are shown to have no power over the demon, and it is Karras' sacrifice that saves Regan, not his or anyone else's religious faith. This renders *The Exorcist* terrifying not only as a religious horror text, but generally as a religious narrative.

The second most common type of demon featured in American demon narratives is a "household demon": an entity having no spiritual or moral agenda other than haunting a specific person (in American demon narratives, demons virtually never haunt places). A film featuring this kind of demon is *Paranormal Activity* (2007), directed by Oren Peli. Originally developed as an independent feature, the film proved to be immensely popular and was acquired by Paramount Pictures after festival screenings. Marketing included a rather interesting viral campaign consisting of videos depicting the reaction of members of the audience to the film. The popularity of *Paranormal Activity* spawned the four following installments: *Paranormal Activity 2* [2010], *Paranormal Activity 2: Tokyo Night* [2010], *Paranormal Activity 3* [2011], and *Paranormal Activity 4* [2012].

Like the majority of characters found in American demon narratives and religious narratives, the protagonists of *Paranormal Activity,* Katie and Micah, are portrayed as either indifferent to or skeptic towards religion. No religious or spiritual angle whatsoever is introduced until the second half of the film. Both Katie and Micah (Katie from the start, Micah eventually) accept that ghosts and demons might exist, but they do not tie this concept to any broader spiritual understanding of reality. The film presents a very skeptical attitude of the characters: everything has to be documented. Micah relies on technology, research and experiments to solve the problem, dismissing the psychic, the demonologist and the exorcism. Katie believes that professional spiritualist can help, but she gives in under Micah's pressure.

The story begins with Micah attempting to catch some of the supernatural phenomena surrounding Katie on camera, in hope of finding out more about them. Initially, Katie displays a rather indulgent attitude towards Micah's enthusiasm (as she explains, the phenomena may be new to him, but they are not new to her). Her leniency, combined with Micah's light-hearted curiosity, set up a relaxed, casual atmosphere for the beginning of the narrative.

This atmosphere is supported by the nature of the entity haunting Katie. The main source of horror in *Paranormal Activity*, the demon, is essentially the antithesis of the arrogant, loud-mouthed Christian demon depicted in narratives such as *The Exorcist*. It lurks in the shadow without ever showing its face, if it does have one, that is. It stays just out of sight, in the corner of the eye; neither the nature nor the purpose of its presence are explained. The demon does not take corporeal shape at any point, but it is capable of affecting the environment at will. Initially, the things happening in the house, the ones that prompted Katie and Micah to begin recording are, in comparison to the actions of some Christian demons, subtle and rather innocuous: the lights flicker, the kitchen taps turn on and off inexplicably, doors and small objects move on their own. There are, however, also more disturbing occurrences, such as the sound of banging on the walls, scratching sounds, footsteps. When Katie talks to the psychic whom she had asked for consultation, she mentions the entity addressing her directly: "I've heard whispering. Sometimes I can't understand it, sometimes it's saying my name."

None of those manifestations are life-threatening or even spectacular (in the way Regan's shaking bed was). As horror factors accompanying the household demon they need not be, since the fact that they occur at all is far more important. Those minor nuisances are in fact a demonstration of the demon's constant presence and its complete dominance over Katie and her life. Despite the fact that the demon could kill or hurt both Katie and Micah in an instant, it does not. Instead it plays with them, leaving marks and footprints by the side of the bed where Katie and Micah lie fast asleep. Their unawareness and vulnerability in the presence of danger are the key horror factors in *Paranormal Activity*.

The concept of the demon within the depicted reality of *Paranormal Activity* is introduced by the psychic, Dr. Fredrichs. He explains to Katie the nature of the powers persecuting her:

> DR. FREDRICHS: My area of expertise is dealing with ghosts. That's what I've built my career on, helping people get in touch with people who have died. Communicating with ghosts. The spirits of dead human beings. A demon is something different. That's an entity that relates to something that is non-human. A lot of debate and discussion about what that could be, but it's not a person.
> KATIE: OK.
> DR. FREDRICHS: OK? Dealing with demons is not my area. I'm very uncomfortable with it, and I'll tell you, quite frankly, I sense there's something going on in this house. You cannot run from this. It'll follow you. It may lay dormant for years. Something may trigger it to get ... become more active, and it will, over time, reach out to communicate with you.

The origin of the entity pursuing Katie is unclear, but it is clear beyond all doubt that it is connected to Katie and has been following her since she was eight years old. No explanation is given as to why or how. This emphasizes the ambiguity characteristic of the household demon. The vague nature is further stressed by Dr. Fredrichs' description of the demon as "something that is non human."

Neither Katie nor the psychic make any reference to the Christian mythology or methods, such as seeking the help of a priest or undergoing an exorcism; instead, Micah suggests using a Ouija board. Instead, the course of action suggested by Dr. Fredrichs is ignoring the demon's presence:

> MICAH: What if we just get this Ouija board, right? We find out what it wants, then we give it what it wants and then ... gone.
>
> DR. FREDRICHS: Because what it probably wants is Katie. And if you do pick up a board and try to play games with it, the entity will sense that you're trying to communicate with it, and that's opening the door, inviting it in. Do you understand me?

This is an important point of the profile of Peli's demon and a crucial element of the storyline. Dr. Fredrichs explicitly states that the thing following Katie must not be antagonized. Although Dr. Fredrichs says that the demon wants Katie, he does not specify why the demon might want her or for what purpose exactly. In fact, the demon's goals are actually impossible to guess. It is even conceivable that it might have no agenda at all. This is supported by the information delivered later in the film. As Micah reads about demons, he finds out that demons are "malevolent, evil spirits that only exist to cause pain and commit evil for their own amusement."

Paranormal Activity employs an interesting point of view, with each of the main characters presenting a different attitude. While Katie is genuinely scared and willing to follow Dr. Fredrichs' advice, Micah is overconfident and conceited. He seems to perceive the whole situation as a game and enthusiastically enters the role of an amateur ghost hunter. Ironically, he believes that the experts Katie relies on are frauds and rejects help from the demonologist, declaring: "I'm going by the evidence. I'm doing my research and I'm gonna find out what it is." He refuses to relinquish control even when it becomes obvious that Katie is terrified and that the situation has become grave. Additionally, despite Dr. Fredrichs explicit warnings against doing so, Micah engages the demon on more than one occasion; he talks to it, and he taunts it, shouting: "You're worthless!" He even experiments with a Ouija board, provoking the demon further. Micah's almost personal attitude to the presence of the demon is one of the defining aspects of the narrative as well as the driving device.

Things go from bad to worse as Micah aggravates the demon. The noises become louder and more threatening; items begin to appear out of time and place, like Katie's childhood photo. Katie suffers from spells of apparent sleepwalking, and on one of the final nights she is dragged out of the bed by an invisible force. Again, the most important aspect of the situation is the utter powerlessness of the characters in the face of the powerful but invisible force. It is also significant that the demon is an external force, i.e., until the final night it follows Katie but does not invade her mind and body, save for the brief episode in which it influences her to get up and go outside. In comparison, the power of a Christian demon is more localized; it mainly relies on controlling the body of the possessed person and its immediate surroundings, as well as on verbal torment.

Near the end of the story, Micah finds information on a woman who suffered from the same haunting as Katie, and was exorcised. Micah explains that the Christian exorcism had in fact exacerbated the situation to the point where the possessed woman died of self-inflicted injuries. Shortly after, however, Katie turns to a cross anyway, but in her stupor-like state she clutches onto it so hard that she cuts her palm, and Micah takes it away. It is unclear whether the cross would have helped or made things worse. Katie and Micah's lack of religious beliefs of any kind is very significant. Micah thinks that technology, rational thought, and research can solve the problem, and dismisses exorcism as too risky, while Katie trusts experts such as psychics and demonologists. Therefore, the possible effectiveness of religious methods—or lack thereof—is not addressed at all. It is, however, safe to assume that Peli's demon is not susceptible to religious symbols.

Quite traditionally, *Paranormal Activity* ends in possession, although it is done in a much more subtle way than in classic demon stories such as *The Exorcist*. At some point, Katie simply suddenly changes her mind and refuses to leave the house at all. At this point Micah leaves the room, frustrated, and Katie mutters "I think we'll be OK now." As she speaks, staring blankly in front of her, another voice can be heard, speaking the words with her, implying that the demon is either influencing her or possessing her at this point.

Demon narratives relying on the non–Christian demons tend to end tragically; while the Christian demon is successfully conquered in the majority of cases, the non–Christian demon seems to be invincible. Following this pattern, *Paranormal Activity* ends with the demon finally possessing Katie and killing Micah. The ending suggests that the demon's goal was simply the possession of Katie, just like Dr. Fredrichs suggested in the first place. "Possession" in this context refers not only to the control over her body but the control over her

3. The Divine and the Unholy

life, as the demon torments Katie, brings her to the verge of mental breakdown, kills her lover and spirits her away into the unknown. What makes Peli's demon even more terrifying is the complete lack of possibility of communicating with it. The demon in *Paranormal Activity* has absolutely no human characteristics; it does not talk, it has no face, and it has no understandable purpose. It may be very well the most inhuman creature of all the creatures inhabiting the horror genre.

The main difference between the American and the Japanese image of the demon in the horror genre is the demon's ambivalent nature. *Oni*, the Japanese demon, is not even exactly the same entity as the Euroamerican demon. In her study, *Japanese Demon Lore: Oni from Ancient Times to the Present*, Noriko Reider explains:

> In an English language treatment of *oni* it is tempting to seek comparisons in Western demonology. Indeed, the concept of *oni* and the history of development of their representation have some striking affinity to the demonic entities that populate Judeo-Christian myths and the various figures from older Greco-Roman, Celtic, Anglo-Saxon, Germanic, and Norse traditions that became "demonized" as Christianity spread through the European continent, the British Isles, and finally Iceland.... It suffices to say that the Western adjective *demonic*, while the closest Western term to describe *oni*, falls short of capturing the full idea of these creatures [Reider 2010: 1].

Indeed, in comparison to the Euroamerican demon, the Japanese *oni* is extraordinarily diverse and complex, and not just in terms of its appearance or powers. The Japanese demon has many faces. It can be cruel (Reider 2010: xxiii) but it can also be kind (Reider 2010: xv), it can be born already as an *oni* (Reider 2010: xxiii), or it can be born as a human being who only later becomes an *oni* (Reider 2010: xxiii). It belongs to the same layer of the sacred order as *kami*, gods (Reider 2010: 11). Nonetheless, because of its connotations in popular Japanese thought, as well as its Buddhist origins, the *oni* is a perfect horror figure:

> In popular Japanese thought, the word "*oni*" conjures up images of hideous creatures emerging from hell's abyss to terrify wicked mortals. Some scholars assert that the concept of the Japanese *oni* is a purely Buddhist one, while others argue that it is not exclusive to the Buddhist cosmos. Komatsu Kazuhiko, for example, notes that the term oni was used in *onmyōdō* (the way of *yin* and *yang*) to describe any evils spirit(s) harmful to humans ("Supernatural Apparitions and Domestic Life in Japan"). Some scholars find the root of *oni* in Chinese thought while others claim the creatures are indigenous to Japan. Each theory of origin and formation seems plausible, even though some theories contradict each other. *Oni,* as a subject of study, thus represent rather eclectic supernatural creatures [Reider 2010: xviii-xix].

Apart from its versatility, the Japanese demon is characterized by one more tremendously significant trait, one that defines its nature; in contrast to the Euroamerican demon, the traditional Japanese demon is corporeal. Therefore, it is naturally subject to needs and desires, such as lust, thirst or hunger. Its appetite is associated with the *oni*'s infamy, since in many tales and narratives the *oni* hungers after human flesh (Reider 2010: xix). Additionally, since it possesses a physical form, it can be physically defeated or tricked. The *oni* is also independent of religious warfare; it cannot be exorcised, but can be slain, in contrast to Western demons. Interestingly, an *oni* will not necessarily lie; on the contrary, often times it will be truthful and honor agreements (Reider 2010: 29).

The Japanese demon rarely appears as the main source of horror in Japanese horror narratives. Although demons are featured in many fantasy titles bordering on horror, such as Yōjirō Takita's *Onmyōji* [2001], Hideyuki Kikuchi's *Demon City Shinjuku,* or Nagai Go's manga *Devilman* and *Devilman Lady*), they are merely an element of the world depicted and are never the main source of horror; they are not the terrifying Other. When it does appear, it appears physically in its own form, as in Hideyuki Kikuchi's novel *Demon City Shinjuku* or *Kikōshi Enma* [2006–2007], directed by Mamoru Kanbe. For this reason, in this section, similar to the one concerning the American demon narratives, there are only two titles. One of them, *KakuRenBo: Hide and Seek*, depicts the demon in a form closest to the traditional Japanese demon imagery. The other one, *Paranormal Activity 2: Tokyo Night,* is a Japanese rendition of the American portrayal of the demon.

Paranormal Activity 2: Tokyo Night (*PARANORUMARU AKUTIBITI Dai 2 Shō TOKYO NIGHT*) [2010], directed by Toshikazu Nagae, is a demon narrative featuring a foreign demon design. This title will be discussed outside of the hitherto assumed chronology due to its strong connection to the previous discussed title, Peli's *Paranormal Activity*. *Paranormal Activity 2: Tokyo Night* is a direct sequel to Oren Peli's independent hit. The story is an immediate continuation of the events depicted in *Paranormal Activity*. Although the analysis of *Paranormal Activity 2: Tokyo Night* might be similar to an analysis of a remake, it is crucial to keep in mind that while Nagae's story adapts and localizes Peli's concept—and adjusts the plot elements accordingly—the two films actually tell two separate stories that merely follow one pattern.

The plot of Nagae's film is simple and naturally bears striking resemblance to *Paranormal Activity*. Haruka Yamano returns home from her trip to the United States with both legs broken after a car accident. Her younger brother, Kōichi, is taking care of her. With their father away on a business trip, they are alone in the house. The striking differences in the films consist in the char-

3. The Divine and the Unholy 171

acters' attitudes and reactions. To begin with, Kōichi films Haruka and the strange occurrences happening around her out of curiosity, but at the same time he immediately resorts to traditional Japanese methods of dealing with hostile forces. Additionally, Kōichi's approach is never offensive, but only protective at first (*morijio*), and defensive later (*o-harai*).

At first, concerned and curious about Haruka's wheelchair moving at night, Kōichi places a pile of salt in Haruka's bedroom, claiming that there is "something that can't be seen with the naked eye" in there. The salt put by Kōichi in Haruka's room is *morijio,* a pile of salt placed at the entrance to ward off evil spirits (see Murakami and Richie 1980). The *morijio* not only gives a distinct Japanese atmosphere to an otherwise Euroamerican concept, but also immediately validates the legitimacy of the haunting, since an unknown force scatters the *morijio* on the very same night. The destruction of the *morijio* prompts Kōichi to monitor Haruka, who sleeps, after all, in a separate room, more closely. Initially reluctant, Haruka gives in to the idea as the strange phenomena become more ominous. Cups and photo frames break, heavy footsteps can be heard at night, and Haruka can feel something touch her. Worried and scared, Kōichi calls a priest to come and conduct a purification, *o-harai,* in their house. The priest comes and performs the ritual. In contrast to an exorcism, which is basically a struggle between a demon and an exorcist to drive the demon out, *o-harai* is intended to purify a place or a person,[4] not combat entities or forces. Even the rhetoric of the scene is more impartial and less aggressive than in the case of Christian exorcism:

KŌICHI: What happened to the evil spirit?
PRIEST: Be at peace. It will trouble you no longer.
HARUKA: Does that mean ... our house is safe?
PRIEST: Yes. The evil that once was, has now disappeared forever.

Despite the fact that the ceremony proceeds uninterrupted, the purification fails. Instead of being chased away, the demon is only aggravated, and as a result the priest who conducted the purification ritual dies on the very same night. Although Nagae's characters choose the most sensible options available to them, their actions prove useless. The demon depicted in *Paranormal Activity 2: Tokyo Night* is completely independent of Japanese religion, as much as it was from Euroamerican religion.

Interestingly enough, the word "demon" is initially not used in *Paranormal Activity 2: Tokyo Night*. Instead, periphrastic constructions are used, such as "something that can't be seen with the naked eye" (*me ni mienai nanka*), "evil spirit" (*akuryō*), or "seems like [it] is still here" (*mada iru mitai*—in Japanese, this phrase is in fact a subject-less sentence). The word "demon" (*akuma*) appears for the first time only when Haruka reveals that the woman she had run down (Katie) was haunted by a demon.

Nagae's story is characterized by a typically Japanese karmic touch; after the exorcism fails Haruka realizes that she is followed by the same entity that had haunted the woman she run down. The woman hit by Haruka's car dies, so Haruka is now haunted by the demon:

> HARUKA: Strange things were happening when I was in hospital in America, too. Even though there was no-one there, I heard footsteps, and things started moving by themselves.... But I thought it was something to do with the hospital, not because of my accident. But now it's happening here.
> KŌICHI: You serious?
> HARUKA: Yeah.... When I got back, I started looking up stuff on the Internet ... about the girl I hit in America. Her name was Katie. Before she killed her boyfriend, there was strange stuff happening with her too.
> KŌICHI: What are you trying to say?
> HARUKA: This evil spirit.... It's not just in our house. It's coming for me. Same as it did for her.

Haruka's way of thinking is much in line with the Japanese outlook. She experienced uncanny occurrences in the hospital, but assumed they were connected to the hospital, not to her. As such, the phenomena did not terrify her. Once she realizes that she is being haunted by a demon in an environment she believed to be safe and unpolluted, she is really scared.

Confronted with an alien demon, Kōichi resorts to alien methods of protection like the cross (which is used as "*mayoke*," a charm against evil spirits, not as an item denoting conscious faith in Christian God), which proves to have no effect whatsoever. Significantly, all steps taken by Kōichi are non-offensive; they are meant for protection, not provocation, unlike Micah's actions. In contrast to Micah and Katie, Haruka and Kōichi initially believe that leaving the house should help them. Only later, as Haruka discloses what had happened to her in the United States, they realize that would be futile since neither karma nor a curse can be escaped.

Then the story heads for the same tragic ending as *Paranormal Activity*; the demon possesses Haruka and kills her brother. This sequence is longer than the abrupt, tense climax of *Paranormal Activity*. It takes time for the possessed Haruka to get up and walk over to her brother's room in a disturbing scene where she limps awkwardly forward on her broken legs, the plaster cracking as she moves. The denouement of *Paranormal Activity 2: Tokyo Night* is also more drawn out, as Kōichi gets away from the possessed Haruka and manages to put some distance between himself and the house but in the end is nonetheless found by the demon and dragged into darkness.

3. The Divine and the Unholy

In comparison to *Paranormal Activity*, which moves forward *because* Micah refuses to let Katie seek professional supernatural help and taunts the entity, *Paranormal Activity 2: Tokyo Night* moves forward *despite* Kōichi's best efforts and logical strategy. He places protective charms around his sister and asks for a purification ceremony. He does not address or offend the demon at all, but the entity is nevertheless set on (and able to) ruin their lives. The demon created by Nagae is virtually the same entity that is presented in *Paranormal Activity*; it is inhuman, and it is impossible to understand or defend against. It personifies the threat of "the unknown."

A diametrically different image of the demon in Japanese horror is presented in *KakuRenBo: Hide & Seek*. *KakuRenBo: Hide & Seek* (*Kakurenbo*) is a Japanese 2005 short cell-shaded animated film, written and directed by Shūhei Morita. The film is an explicit demon narrative, connecting modern setting and characters with traditional Japanese demon folklore. Morita's story centers around a group of children playing a game "o-to-ko-yo," a variation of hide and seek, which requires the players to wear masks and play in the ruins of an abandoned old city. "O-to-ko-yo" is rumored to be very dangerous, and those who play it are said to disappear, spirited away by demons.

KakuRenBo: Hide & Seek opens with conversation between a number of unseen characters, one of which explains:

> *O-to-ko-yo* is a secret game they play in that town, a game of hide and seek. Sometimes, the lights of the town get brighter in a spooky way, and the whole town becomes a maze. But there are marker signs. If you follow the neon lights of *o, to, ko,* and *yo,* then you can find your way. When you get to the end, you will arrive at the *o-to-ko-yo* square, and when seven kids arrive, the game begins. All kids must wear a fox mask to play. *O-to-ko-yo* is not a normal game of hide and seek. It's very ... dangerous. They say that all kids who play the game disappear. Yes, in the game of *o-to-ko-yo,* real demons appear and steal the children away.

Despite this warning, the characters—seven children—decide to play the game, unaware that in the old town there are real demons out to get them. The concept itself, especially the manner in which it is expressed in the last sentence, is connected to an authentic concept of *onikakushi* (lit: hiding by demons), which describes a sudden disappearance of a person, usually a child, as having been spirited away and hidden by demons (a concept closely related to *kamikakushi,* lit. "hiding by gods"—i.e., being spirited away by gods).

The story follows mainly Hikora, a boy who joins the game solely for the purpose of finding his missing sister, Sorincha, who has gone missing while playing the game with other children. He sets out to look for her as soon as the seven players gather. The game of hide and seek begins, and the children break up and explore the confusing maze of decrepit gates and abandoned streets. On their way they encounter statues shaped like demons, but they do not know that the statues are actually real demons lying in wait. Also, they do not know that one in their midst, a young girl, is in fact a demon as well.

Morita's *oni* do not inhabit mountains and forests, but a place closest to wilderness to be found in an urban environment—an abandoned, ruined part of the town. Just like the urban setting, the demons themselves are also a combination of the old and the new, with a particularly interesting twist; Apart from the last demon, they are all depicted are automatons. Although composed of mechanical parts, they still bear a striking resemblance to traditional Japanese demons and display regenerative capacities that surpass those of mere machines. This juxtaposition of sentience and traditional design with robotics is truly uncanny and constitutes an interesting, modernized take on the image of *oni*. The demons are living but mechanical entities, and they appear to feed on electricity. It is therefore only fitting that in order to survive they steal children and use them to create new sources of energy. In the very center of the city there is a tall battery tower that the demons guard and where every child they catch is taken. It is an intriguing way of presenting the *oni,* but it is still firmly rooted in traditional folklore, since Japanese demons are frequently associated with lightning (Reider 2010: 23)—which is, naturally, electricity. Morita's demons are related to electricity in a twofold manner, as they both collect electricity from the children's bodies as well as affect it, making the lights and neons of the ruined city blink and go out. When Hikora makes his way to the center of the town, he discovers that all of his fellow players have been captured and connected to the strange electric tower that powers the town and, presumably, the demons themselves.

The demons chasing the children are not only formidable and dangerous, but also diverse in shape and form. There are four individual different demons chasing after the children. One of them is a red, vaguely humanoid demon with three arms and four legs, holding a mechanical wheel on its back and a huge club in his hand. Another one is a demon resembling an ox, whose head is crowned with two sets of impressive horns. Yet another demon is actually a pair of small demons riding an enormous cart—which is, incidentally, also shaped like a monster. Lastly, there is an eight armed demon with no visible legs that resembles a spider. The faces of all the demons are contorted in hostile, fearsome expressions with knit eyebrows and bared teeth. All of demons are fantastic in shape and menacing; all of them are also of imposing physical statue, which is yet another traditional trait they all exhibit (Reider 2010: 8). The sounds they make range from mechanical sounds, rattling and grating, to animal-like growls and panting. Morita's demons are terrifying half mechanical contrivances behind the guise of traditional monsters from Japanese fairy tales.

In fact, there are more traits that are remarkably traditional that characterize the demons depicted in *KakuRenBo: Hide & Seek*. To begin with, they constitute a group, in comparison with the majority of American demon narratives that feature only one demon in the storyline. As far as their appearance and behavior are concerned, they display supernatural (or, depending on the definition as mentioned earlier, preternatural) attributes such as regeneration, strength, speed or resistance. In accordance with the most common portrayal of *oni*, Morita's demons have yellow, red or blue-tinted skin, and tend to be horned and scantily clad (Reider 2010: 7). Furthermore, their actions, i.e., abducting the children, are carried out for personal gain, which is also a fairly traditional characteristic. Even their names are surprisingly traditional, keeping in mind that Japanese demons are frequently associated with devouring human flesh (Reider 2010: 14). In *KakuRenBo: Hide & Seek* the children are devoured only symbolically, but the names of the demons are still related to the concept of eating human flesh: *kimotori* (*kimotori-oni*, lit. "liver taking demon"), *chitori* (*chitori-oni* lit. "blood taking demon"), *aburatori* (*aburatori-oni*, lit. "fat taking demon") and *kotori* (*kotori-oni*, lit. "child taking demon"). The audience learns those names when Hikora reads them aloud from an old scroll he and Yaimao find in one of the buildings. The scroll itself, stylized for an old ink drawing, depicts the demons in an old-fashioned manner.

In contrast, the name of the last demon, as given on the scroll, is not related to human flesh at all—instead, it indicates the demon's role. The title *oni'ou* (lit. "demon king"), together with its central position among the other demons, suggests leadership. On the scroll the last demon is portrayed as a nine-tailed fox, but it is never seen in the film in this shape. *Oni'ou* assumes the shape of the last child who wins the game of "o-to-ko-yo" and reveals its true form when the next child is about to win. When no longer disguised as an "o-to-ko-yo" player, the last demon resembles a human figure with a bluish tinge to the skin and claws, and face covered by a large-horned demon mask contorted in a fearsome scowl, bearing striking resemblance to traditional demon masks in *nō* theater (see Żeromska 2003: 216–219). At the end of the story, Hikora asks the extra player whether she is in fact Sorincha (who, incidentally, must have won the game before Hikora), but she turns out to be a demon impersonating his sister. "Sorincha's" mask, until now a regular fox mask, suddenly splits, shifts and rearranges into the face of a demon, and Hikora realizes he's been deceived:

HIKORA: You are the [last] demon.
THE DEMON: (*sings*) "Who'll play hide-and-seek with me?" When we play the

game of *o-to-ko-yo,* the town gets brighter. However, that doesn't last for long. That's why we must play again. The game of hide-and-seek called *"o-to-ko-yo!"* ... (*sings again*) "Who'll play hide-and-seek with me? Come meet me here..." Everybody has been caught.... You are the last one.... Now, you are the demon.

This conversation, apart from marking the climax of the narrative, is also interesting because of its double meaning. The line "now you are the demon" (*tsugi wa anata ga oni*) is significant due to the nature of *kakurenbo*, the Japanese hide and seek. Similar to the game of *onigokko*, in the Japanese tag, the person who is "it" is called *"oni,"* a demon.[5] In *KakuRenBo: Hide & Seek,* the children set out to play hide and seek, but once the game begins, it seems to blur with tag, where, instead of other players, they are chased by real demons. When the last demon gives Hikora the mask, it says "Now you are the demon," which means "now you're 'it'"—but in the same way "demons" chasing the players were real demons, so does Hikora become a real demon. This, incidentally, emphasizes another traditional element of Morita's *oni,* i.e., the power of transformation (Reider 2010: 16) and the ability freely to change sex (Reider 2010: 17).

By changing the harmless children's game of "demon" chase into a horrifying real demon chase, *KakuRenBo: Hide & Seek* presents a fresh, intriguing take on the demon narrative. Morita's story depends on the merging of old superstitions with modern fears. The story takes place in a regular but abandoned place that borders with another realm of the universe; similarly, the demons are creatures residing simultaneously in the land of everyday reality and the world of fairy tales. They roam the streets and hunger for electricity, but their scary appearance relies on old-fashioned fearsome expressions, fangs and fantastic shapes. *KakuRenBo: Hide & Seek* combines old Japanese folk legends with a contemporary urban environment, thus admitting the *oni* into the reality of contemporary audience, which allows the film to perform remarkably well as a horror narrative.

The demon is a particularly effective horror figure because apart from being a very powerful supernatural entity, it carries strong religious connotations even if it is not presented in the context of religious mythology. Fears related to religion, as will be presented in the next section, are one of the most powerful and complex horror devices.

Religion

Spirituality is a tremendously powerful, even formidable concept. Religions and belief systems provide intricate narratives and symbols that are sup-

3. The Divine and the Unholy

posed to give meaning to life. Morality and ethics, as well as the understanding of human nature, are oftentimes based on the ideas provided by organized spiritualities. Religion touches upon universal questions and issues, and by definition involves supernatural elements. First and foremost, however, religion is a social phenomenon (see Pickering 1984), and this is perhaps why it works so well in horror narratives.

Euroamerican horror narratives naturally tend to focus on the Judeo-Christian religious reality. The fears referred to and evoked by those works are defined by the Judeo-Christian system of beliefs. In Judeo-Christian religious reality, there are Good and Evil with capital letters, and to distinguish one from the other is the moral duty of those living in that reality; the difference between right and wrong is clear, as is the difference between true and false (Yukawa in Moore 1968: 64). That which is good, right, and true belongs in the light of God, whereas that which is evil, wrong and false belongs in the darkness where his adversaries dwell. Most importantly, there is a distance between the mortal human beings, who were created by God and grovel on earth, and God himself, who judges the mortals from heavens (Yukawa in Moore 1968: 64). Against God man can commit sin, and the sin is an offense in the eyes of God, condemning man to damnation (Yukawa in Moore 1968: 64). In Euroamerican religious world-view, there exists one decidedly evil, extremely powerful, sentient supernatural force that is morally evil, in contrast to Japanese gods and demons, who are largely dual, even amoral. That force, or rather entity, is the Devil—a personification of evil (Russell 1987b: 36). The Devil actively opposes God and influences people to do evil—a concept not present in Japanese religious reality.

On a technical note, religious horror narratives—at least Euroamerican religious horror narratives—tend to be the most complex among the thematic narratives discussed in this work, since they involve many aspects. For this reason, religious horror narratives are usually layered and oftentimes also dimensional.

Perhaps one of the most recognizable Euroamerican horror narratives based on religion is *Rosemary's Baby*, written by Ira Levin. *Rosemary's Baby* is a tale that relies purely on the religious aspect of the story in order to construct the horror factor; the plot of the novel revolves around a young woman pregnant with the Devil's child, and the main horror potential is consequently built upon the significance of the baby's nature and Rosemary's unawareness of that nature. The key elements of *Rosemary's Baby* as a horror narrative are the ominous fetus within Rosemary, the insidious elderly neighbors and the manner in which Rosemary is tricked into carrying the Devil's child and deprived of free will. At the core of Levin's novel lies the concepts of the end of days and the corruption of belief—themes common in religious horror narratives, as will become clear during analysis of subsequent titles in this chapter.

A young couple, Rosemary and Guy Woodhouse, move into an old yet elegant and spacious apartment in Bramford. They soon meet an elderly couple living next door, the Castevets. Rosemary and her husband—as well as the audience—are unaware that the Castevets are in fact the leaders of a Satanic cult, and they worship the Devil. Beneath the gaudy, clamorous guise of a noisy but innocuous and a touch silly elderly husband and wife, Minnie and Roman Castevet are calculating, resolved individuals, who work methodically to achieve their sinister goal. Unaware of the danger lurking next door, Rosemary is beyond herself with happiness when her husband suggests they have a baby.

The majority of American horror narratives which include religious elements, such as religion horror narratives and demon narratives, feature characters who have very vague or weakened spiritual beliefs or none at all—at least initially.[6] *Rosemary's Baby* follows this pattern to an extent, but not entirely. Asked whether she is religious, Rosemary answers that she was brought up to be religious, but now she is agnostic (Levin 2003: 70). Her Catholic upbringing plays an important part in her understanding and experience of the horror that surrounds her; it is something that is ingrained in her so profoundly that she relies on it without thinking, as in the scene where she sees Terry's dead body in front of the building and automatically crosses herself (Levin 2003: 45).

As a horror narrative, *Rosemary's Baby* is constructed in three distinct dimensions, which for the most part correspond with the layers of the story: Rosemary's alienation and entrapment, the plot against her and her child, and the identity of her child. Initially the story operates within just one dimension of terror, as the readers have access only to the first layer of horror, based on the atmosphere of a vague, unspecified threat.

This sense of indistinct dread begins to come into focus at the same time Rosemary and Guy decide to try to conceive. After a romantic evening and a supper crowned with desserts brought over by Minnie Castevet, Rosemary begins to feels strange and falls into a shallow, troubled sleep. The dream sequence works in all three layers and all three dimensions of the horror narrative employed in *Rosemary's Baby*. Rosemary drifts away into sleep before she and Guy have a chance of making love, and experiences strange visions. The sequence begins with a blend of haphazard, seemingly unconnected images of the dead president, a party on a yacht and, later, Rosemary's family. Then the images become even more outlandish. "It was the first time the Sistine Chapel had been opened to the public and she was inspecting the ceiling on a new elevator that carried the visitor through the chapel horizontally, making it possible to see the frescoes exactly as Michelangelo, painting them, had seen them" (Levin 2003: 107–108). Further images, such as the underside of the closet, reveal that Rosemary's "dream" is in fact a shallow trance-like drowse. Now the readers can recognize the reality of the novel mixing with the dream, but the extent of Rosemary's detachment makes it impossible to distinguish clearly the real course of events from under the veil of narcotic fantasy. Something ominous is happening, but it is not clear what; within the strange hallucinations there is subtle but sinister foreshadowing, such as the ship heading for disaster. Significantly, one of the images Rosemary sees in her dream is *The Creation of Adam,* which naturally connotes the beginning of life.

As the vision progresses, more and more distinct chunks of reality force their way into Rosemary's visions; the dream becomes less abstract and more menacing:

> Below was a huge ballroom where on one side a church burned fiercely and on the other a black bearded man stood glaring at her. In the center was a bed. She went to it and lay down, and was suddenly surrounded by naked men and women, ten or a dozen, with Guy among them. They were elderly, the women grotesque and slack-breasted. Minnie and her friend Laura-Louise were there, and Roman in a black miter and a black silk robe. With a thin black wand he was drawing designs on her body, dipping the wand's point in a cup of red held for him by a sun-browned man with a white moustache. The point moved back and forth across her stomach and down ticklingly to the insides of her thighs. The naked people were chanting-flat, unmusical, foreign-tongued syllables-and a flute or clarinet accompanied them. "She's awake, she sees!" Guy whispered to Minnie. He was large eyed, tense. "She don't see," Minnie said. "As long as she ate the mouse she can't see nor hear. She's like dead. Now sing" [Levin 2003: 108–109].

The scene that follows is the most important scene of the whole dream and, plot-wise, the turning point of the whole storyline. Guy comes and begins making love to her, but there is strangeness about him. Again, Rosemary initially readily accepts the bizarreness of the situation; her mind fabricates a reason for Guy's strange appearance—a costume party. However, from her hallucinations and confused reasoning a grotesque, monstrous figure emerges, with clawed hands, coarse skin and an enormous, beastly penis. The color of the monster's eyes, described as "yellow furnace," together with the smell of sulphur, is the first indication of the nature of both the monster itself and the horror Rosemary is about to experience (Levin 2003: 109–111). Something about this sight awakens Rosemary's dormant Catholic upbringing, for it is only when she looks into the eyes of the figure atop her that the reality pierces through her narcotic vision, and for the briefest moment she is aware of what is happening. Then, however, the drugs take over again, and she descends back into her tangled dream visions, where she meets the pope, who forgives her for not coming to see him.

The dream sequence marks the moment in which the narrative of *Rosemary's Baby* changes over to the second layer of horror. The imagery of Rosemary's visions is rather straightforward: the black mass, a demonic figure using her body. The atmosphere of previously indistinct dread is condensed into an atmosphere of terror clearly based on religious grounds. Although it is not apparent within that layer of the narrative, the events in the "dream" are an inversion of the Catholic concept of Immaculate Conception, where Mary is visited by the Holy Spirit and becomes pregnant as a result of divine, incorporeal intervention—a blessing. In *Rosemary's Baby,* the Devil's heir is conceived through non-consensual, physical contact—the opposite of the blessed virgin birth.

Soon after that evening Rosemary discovers that she is pregnant. Once the news reach her neighbors, she suddenly finds herself the center of their attention. Both Castevets and their friends seem uncannily interested in the baby, to a point where they even recommend her to a doctor she would not be able to afford otherwise. The pregnancy proceeds fine until Rosemary gets a terrible pain in her abdomen, a pain of terrifying relentlessness and intensity. Everyone around her—her doctor, her husband, the Castevets and other neighbors she is in regular contact with—seems to play down the magnitude of her ordeal or to be blind to it, leaving Rosemary alone with her suffering. The loneliness and fear that Rosemary experiences are crucial in this part of the narrative; the sense of isolation and Rosemary's complete lack of control over her life contribute to the heavy, suffocating atmosphere of the novel.

The pain grows, eating away at Rosemary, until it becomes clear that something is very wrong. The pain is monstrous; it is too great for an ordinary pregnancy symptom, too great even for an alarming pregnancy symptom. The severity of the pain serves not only to illustrate Rosemary's torment, but also to emphasize the unnatural and abnormal character of her pregnancy. Together with pain, Rosemary's strange cravings grow. She cannot stand salt, which in many cultures is associated with purification and repelling evil. She eats virtually nothing but meat, first rare, then nearly raw. This behavior is deeply disturbing in the light of the previous dream sequence, and becomes even more disturbing once Rosemary as a character acknowledges it. One night she catches a glimpse of her own reflection as she is chewing on a raw, bloody, dripping chicken heart. The changes in her terrify her so much that she rebels against the Castevets, against her doctor and everyone else's apathy—she decides to see another doctor and refuses to drink the cocktail Minnie has been making her every day.

However, just as Rosemary is about to break free of the control she is not even aware of, the pain disappears, and with it Rosemary's qualms. She remains calm until she receives a book her friend Hutch had intended to give her— right before he mysteriously fell into a coma after taking interest in Rosemary's bad shape and the Castevets' attention. The revelation within the book brings into focus the religious aspect of the novel, although the perception of that aspect is still limited within the current layer of horror. Rosemary assumes that her neighbors, together with their friends, are a coven of witches. She realizes that her strange dream was real and that she had indeed been an unwilling participant in a sabbath. At this point, the main religious dimension of horror is the cult who, in Rosemary's eyes, are merely insane fanatics who want to hurt her baby and use it in their unholy rituals; the actual capability of the coven members to inflict any kind of damage is irrelevant. The coven represents a religious threat insofar that they are religiously motivated.

Rosemary soon learns that Guy is a part of what she believes to be a plot against her baby. She is intent on protecting her baby at all costs, unaware of the true nature of the life growing inside her. She tries to escape, but wherever she turns, she discovers she is surrounded by the coven members. She is caught, and her baby is taken away from her. Rosemary manages to slip out of the coven's grip once again and finally finds her baby. Within this layer of horror, her fear is *for* her baby, and the threat is a corruption and harm from the outside:

> Across the room, in the one large window bay, stood a black bassinet. Black and only black it was; skirted with black taffeta, hooded and flounced with black organza. A silver ornament turned on a black ribbon pinned to its black hood.... The silver ornament was a crucifix hanging upside down, with the black ribbon wound and knotted around Jesus' ankles.
>
> The thought of her baby lying helpless amid sacrilege and horror brought tears to Rosemary's eyes, and suddenly a longing dragged at her to do nothing but collapse and weep, to surrender completely before such elaborate and unspeakable evil [Levin 2003: 287].

The decorated crib is both sacrilegious in terms of Christian (Catholic) faith and cruelly taunting at the same time, considering the fact that Rosemary chose bright, sunny yellows and whites for the nursery and the layette. Rosemary approaches the crib, and as the second layer of horror crosses over into the third layer, she is (together with the readers) subjected to the final, most profound dimension of horror: her own child. Rosemary's son has not been sired by her husband, but by the Devil himself. She has been impregnated by Satan and given birth to his son. It is her baby that is the source of harm and corruption, not the other way round.

The members of the coven have prepared for this "inversion of naziresis"[7] with great care. The fact that Rosemary's baby was delivered safely and unharmed brings a horrific finality to the narrative. The damage is done; what is more, it is irreversible, un-imagined and unimaginable. As Rosemary descends into despair and terror, Roman gloats and triumphs:

> "Oh God," Rosemary said.
> "God's dead," Roman said.
> She turned to the bassinet, let fall the knife, turned back to the watching coven. "Oh God!" she said and covered her face. "Oh God!" And raised her fists and screamed to the ceiling: *"Oh God! Oh God! Oh God! Oh God! Oh God!"*
> "God is DEAD!" Roman thundered. *"God is dead and Satan lives! The year is One, the first year of our Lord! The year is One, God is done! The year is One, Adrian's begun!"* [Levin 2003: 292].

The coven has won. God is dead insofar that he has been defeated, proved to be weak and powerless; the "year one" denotes the beginning of new era. Rosemary calls "Oh God!," but it is unclear whether it is simply an exclamation or whether she is actually calling to God.

The third dimension of horror is actually accessible to the reader only in the story's finale. At this point, previously introduced elements take on an ominous note and together create a sinister, disturbing whole. The three layers overlap, and the complete shape of the religious horror narrative emerges. Rosemary has been trapped from the beginning. Betrayed and alienated, despite being an innocent, good person, she has become an instrument of evil nonetheless, unknowingly bringing on the end of days. The fact that this calamity was orchestrated by a seemingly innocuous, eccentric elderly couple next door and a group of their elderly friends only adds to the horror. There was no revolution and no war to be fought; the end of the world has come quietly, by means of deception and a trap.

The primary horror in *Rosemary's Baby* is based on the concept of a threat concealed within. The undetected and unexposed presence of the coven right next door, capable of controlling Rosemary's life and getting rid of anyone who stands in their way, is horrifying, as is the ulterior motive of the coven, namely bringing the Devil's child into the world. Most importantly, the core of the narrative, which is the life growing inside Rosemary, is literally horror incarnate. The combination of those elements makes Levin's story a notable example of a religious horror narrative.

A tremendously interesting fact to be noted is that although Rosemary entertains the thought of killing her baby, she does not go through with it. An evil Nazirite or an Antichrist tends to meet very little resistance in horror narratives as long as they are unborn or are small children, as seen in *Rosemary's Baby,* and Stephen Hopkins' *The Reaping* or *Blessed,* directed by Simon Fellows. In comparison to an unborn or child Antichrist, who enjoys invincibility, an adult Antichrist never triumphs, as can be seen in Janusz Kaminski's *Lost Souls, End of Days* directed by Peter Hyams or Darren Bousman's *11–11–11*. This might point to the fact that killing a child on-screen, even an evil one, would verge on a cultural taboo. Another character following this pattern is the Antichrist portrayed in *The Omen*.

The Omen was directed by Richard Donner in 1976. The main horror potential of the story is based, just like *Rosemary's Baby*—and for that matter, practically all Euroamerican horror narratives concerning religion—on the Christian concept of the adversary of God and those who aid him. A large portion of dialogue revolves around the Bible and religious dogmas, although very little of it is actually genuine. The narration structure of *The Omen* is not as consistent as that of *Rosemary's Baby*. Apart from the ambassador, the story follows also the ambassador's wife, the priest and the photographer. Although such a structure allows for less emotional impact, at the same time it establishes a more realistic atmosphere.

The Omen builds its horror factor on the most common scenario as far as Euroamerican religious horror is concerned, i.e., the coming of the Antichrist:

> *The Omen* is a powerful horror film because it knowingly and cleverly interprets aspects of Christian belief regarding the ascent of Satan's son.... By including such signs, and opening the film with a quote from the Book of Revelation, *The Omen* seeks to unnerve moviegoers, and tap into that irrational "belief" zone in all of us. What if the Bible is correct? What if all the signs of the Antichrist are happening around us, right now? Would we believe them? [Muir 2007: 429].

The title sequence of *The Omen* makes use of imagery belonging to a Christian frame of reference; a silhouette of a boy throwing a shadow in the shape of an inverted cross is cast against a red background, accompanied by choral music reminiscent of a Christian church choir. In this way, the film establishes an expressly religious frame even before the plot proper begins.

The film centers around a deeply unsettling source of horror, i.e., a child—

a five-year-old son of Ambassador Robert Thorn, Damien, who was taken in by the ambassador when his and his wife's child was stillborn. Damien appears to be an ordinary, charming little boy, but there is a certain uncanny quality about him. The story begins to gather momentum when Damien's nanny suddenly hangs herself during his birthday party. With a wide smile on her face, she calls to him from the roof of the house, saying "Damien, I love you. Look at me, Damien. It's all for you!" These few words bear great significance and serve as foreshadowing of the events to come. The nanny's plea for Damien to look at her, her affirmation of love and the declaration that "it is all for him" suggest that there is something very special about Damien, something special beyond belief, and indeed there is.

Things go wrong around Damien. A black dog follows him around, animals flee or go berserk at the sight of him, and his new nanny vows to protect him the first time they see each other. Damien himself, meanwhile, remains calm and cheerful, saying very little and smiling constantly. As different people, such as the priest present at Damien's birth and a photographer who sees omens of death on the photographs he takes, attempt to tell the ambassador that something is wrong with Damien, Robert Thorn slowly comes to realize that something strange is happening.

When the priest tells Ambassador Thorn that Damien is the Antichrist and he shall bring about the end of mankind, the ambassador dismisses him as crazy. The priest also foretells that the ambassador's wife will become pregnant and that Damien will do anything to prevent the baby's birth. This is also dismissed by the ambassador until his wife's doctor tells him that his wife is indeed pregnant. This is a turning point in *The Omen*; upon hearing about his wife's pregnancy, the ambassador begins to consider the idea that Damien might in fact be something more than he appears to be. He is skeptical but willing to hear more. In fact, the majority of film's atmosphere in this transitional part between the suspicion that Damien might be evil and discovering Damien's true nature is based on a subtle balance between the possibility of explaining all the bizarre events as coincidence and the fact that such a number of coincidences is improbable. This is clearly visible in many scenes and dialogues, such as the ambassador's conversation with the photographer:

> JENNINGS: These are supposed to be the events that signal the birth of the Antichrist. The Devil's child. It's making more sense. The Jews have returned to Zion and there has been a comet. As for the rise of the Roman Empire, scholars think that could well mean the Common Market, the Treaty of Rome.
> AMBASSADOR THORN: Bit of a stretch.

JENNINGS: What about this? In Revelations it says: "He shall rise from the eternal sea."
AMBASSADOR THORN: That's the poem again. "From the eternal sea he rises, creating armies on either shore." That was the beginning of it.
JENNINGS: Theologians have interpreted the "eternal sea" as meaning the world of politics, the sea that constantly rages with turmoil and revolution. So the Devil's child will rise from the world of politics.

Despite the fact that the narrative retains the possibility of a rational explanation, at this point Damien is no longer a strange child giving the audience the sensation of indistinct uneasiness, but an uncanny, potentially fantastic figure—the boy who might be the Antichrist.

As ambassador Thorn investigates, he finds out that his own child was actually murdered, not stillborn, and Damien's real mother was not a human woman, but a jackal. The plot enters into the second layer of religious horror, the previously vague sense of threat is replaced by a common Christian end-of-days scenario, in which a child (living or planned) is meant to overthrow the dominant (usually Christian) religious order. It becomes clear that Damien represents an ancient, unimaginable evil; he is the Antichrist, whose goal is the destruction of humanity. Ambassador Thorn makes an attempt to kill the Antichrist, but he is thwarted by Damien's guardians and eventually killed by the police before he can save the world. As John Muir puts it, in *The Omen* "the Antichrist is born into the world, but 20th century man is too distracted by political ambition, deception, and pragmatism to notice. Those who do notice die first, before they can fight Satan's child" (Muir 2007: 428). The Antichrist cannot be defeated; the fall of humanity cannot be averted. God must yield before evil and the Antichrist shall walk the Earth, wreaking havoc.

The Omen performs so well as a horror narrative for two main reasons. Firstly, Damien's triumph appears to be unavoidable. The bizarre coincidences not only defy the laws of rationality, but are also impossible to defend against or to be avoided, and in the end, Ambassador Thorn's desperate act is prevented. Secondly, the young age of Damien's character adds to the atmosphere of terror. Children are culturally coded as innocent, and they are conventionally portrayed as the victims of a horrific Other (Cowan 2008: 216–217). Indeed, a pretty, smiling boy like Damien looks like an image of innocence. It is the treacherous nature of that innocent look that contributes to the horror factor of Donner's story. Damien looks like an ordinary boy; there is, however, a sinister quality about him, which manifests itself clearly when the boy is threatened. The scene in which the Thorns are on their way to church is a good, however subtle, example of this. As the senator's car draws closer to the church, Damien becomes visibly tense, almost rigid, until he suddenly and inexplicably goes berserk, screaming and writhing. The very sound of his scream is low and screechy, almost inhuman. A very similar thing can be observed when Ambassador Thorn carries him over to the church in the climax of the film. Damien sounds not like a scared child but like a cornered predator.

The Omen is, in Hutchings' words, "a key example of apocalyptic horror and, even by the cynical standards of 1970s horror, unusually bleak, with the forces of good left comprehensively defeated" (Hutchings 2008: 236). As Hutchings further points out, this defeat is portrayed as preordained and unavoidable, mainly through implementation of Biblical prophecies, an element unusual within the horror genre that rarely engaged explicitly with Christianity before (Hutchings 2008: 236). The most striking element of Donner's story, however, is the character of the main antagonist. Monstrous children[8] were not an uncommon theme in horror of the time, but in *The Omen* this portrayal was executed with "real conviction" (Hutchings 2008: 236). The fact that the Thorns are not special in any way—in the sense that they are not knowledgeable about the occult nor do they worship the Devil—but merely happen to facilitate the Antichrist's rise to power by accident lends *The Omen* an additional dimension of realism and universality.

One more title worth mentioning is *The Reaping,* directed by Stephen Hopkins in 2007. Like most religious horror titles, it features an end of days scenario, but with a number of subtle differences. Firstly, there is no ambiguity in the story—the plagues are real beyond doubt. Secondly, the plot moves the balance of struggle from beliefs and actions of individuals to actual physical phenomena. Thirdly, the plot of *The Reaping* features one noteworthy element not present in almost any other religious horror title, i.e., God's intervention.

The protagonist of *The Reaping,* Katherine, a disillusioned former Christian devoted to debunking false miracles, is called to Haven, a small town suffering the ten biblical plagues. The local people believe that a little girl, Loren, has killed her brother and turned the river into blood. Presented as a very rational, no-nonsense person, Katherine is skeptical and confused rather than afraid in the face of the inexplicable events, and she refuses to accept a supernatural explanation:

> KATHERINE: You wanna talk plagues? Let's talk plagues.... In 1400 BC, a group of nervous Egyptians saw the Nile turn red.
> BEN: Oh, God. Come on.
> KATHERINE: But what they thought was blood was actually an algae bloom which killed the fish, which prior to that had been living off the eggs of frogs.

Those uneaten eggs turned into record numbers of baby frogs who subsequently fled to land and died.... Their little rotting frog bodies attracted lice and flies. The lice carried the bluetongue virus, which killed seventy percent of Egypt's livestock. The flies carried glanders, a bacterial infection which in humans causes boils. Soon afterwards, the Nile River Valley was hit with a three-day sandstorm otherwise known as the plague of darkness.

BEN: Katherine ...

KATHERINE: During the sandstorm, intense heat can combine with an approaching cold front to create not only hail, but electrical storms which would have looked to the Egyptians like fire from the sky. The subsequent wind would've blown the Ethiopian locust population off course and right into downtown Cairo. Hail is wet, locusts leave droppings. Spread both on grain, and you've got mycotoxins. Dinnertime in Egypt meant the first-born got the biggest portion which in this case meant he ate the most toxins, so he died. Ten plagues. Ten scientific explanations.

However, in contrast to films such as *Rosemary's Baby* and *The Omen,* the events in the film cannot be ascribed to simple coincidence (additionally, Katherine's down-to-earth attitude further eliminates the matter of the unreliable narrator). The events in the film are in no way subtle, neither are they easy to write off as odd instances of bad luck, in the way the death of the priest or the photographer in *The Omen* or Hutch's coma in *Rosemary's Baby* could be interpreted. In *The Reaping,* the water in the local river turns into human blood and fire rains from the skies, for which no coincidence or chance can account.

In terms of plot, *The Reaping* is not so much dimensioned as it is layered. In the context of religious horror layers, the story is rather straight forward, and the only misdirections are of minor importance. The only dimension of the narrative is the attempt of the people of Haven to create a child in the Devil's image and the ensuing wrath of God. When the initial reluctance to accept the supernatural crosses over into acceptance, Katherine becomes genuinely scared and awed as she bears witness to vengeance. In the climactic part of *The Reaping,* this imagery is very clear as flames and lightning come down from the sky, killing the people of Haven and destroying the town.

The Reaping's main horror potential is based on its scale. The town is struck with plagues of proportions impossible to ignore or misunderstand. They are real, powerful, abnormal, and they are enough to evoke end-of-days fear even in someone who is not religious. The most interesting element of *The Reaping,* however, is the inclusion of God. God is not an absent spectator, as in the majority of religious horror narratives, where the Devil or his worshipers are able to do their work undisturbed. Hopkins actually allows for the presence of God in the film about God. It is no longer a narrative about people who do evil and want to bring about the end of days, but it is a narrative about people who disobey God and face his retribution.

Japanese religious horror, on the other hand, is scarce at best. Very few narratives concern religious matters such as end of days or moral offenses. They do feature religious elements, such as people haunted by ghosts asking to be exorcised by priests, but few of them are focused solely on religion. A notable drama-horror film focusing solely on religion is *Sinners of Hell* (*Jigoku*), directed by Nobuo Nakagawa in 1960. *Sinners of Hell* is famous for its graphic imagery of Hell and the souls being tormented there. It is not included in this work because despite its horrific imagery, it does not aim at evoking fear but rather moral reflection.

Japanese religious horror will naturally be shaped by and operate within the world of Japanese system of beliefs—the unique mixture of Shintō and Buddhism. The Shintō/Buddhism understanding of the world is dualistic—all things bear good and evil inside. Japanese Buddhist thought assumes a dualistic concept of man as good and evil, whereas Shintō assumes the essential potential for good in human being (Lebra 1982: 98, Yamakage 2006: 44). The distance between gods and men is also not as great—the gods are more human-like, and since all beings carry sacred spirits, it is possible for anything and anyone to become a *kami,* and enlightenment is the goal of each spirit (see Reader 1991). Furthermore, Shintō is free from notions of sin and guilt (Yamakage 2006: 44) (although it does recognize pollution), while in Buddhism the concept of karma exists—a notion of just causality, where an evil deed needs not to be named or labeled in any way, but will simply lead to consequences, as time brings about evil to the evildoer. Overall, as Ian Reader suggests, the Japanese religious system is a system that does not involve "fear and trembling" but evokes "a sense of healthy interaction" instead (Reader 1991: 175).

A title that connects Japanese and American religious horror, or rather gives a good idea on how Japanese and American horror work most comfortably within the same premises, is a video game, *Silent Hill*, and the American adaptation thereof, *Silent Hill* [2006], directed by Christophe Gans. *Silent Hill* is, just like *Silent Hill 2,* a hybrid horror, set entirely in an American setting. *Silent Hill* is the first installment in the previously mentioned *Silent Hill* game series, directed by Keiichiro Toyama and published in 1999 by Konami.

The structure of *Silent Hill,* like most religious horror narratives, is layered, and the story is revealed gradually. The protagonist of the game, Harry Mason, regains consciousness after a car crash to discover his eight-year-old adopted daughter Cheryl gone. He sets out to search for her in the small town of Silent Hill, which they were passing when the crash happened. Wandering the abandoned town, Harry experiences what appears to be a bizarre nightmare. It is snowing lightly, despite the fact that it is April; the town, shrouded in heavy fog, occasionally plunges suddenly into complete darkness. Out of the fog and darkness strange, hostile monstrous creatures emerge, and a little girl bearing an uncanny resemblance to Cheryl keeps appearing and running away from him. All those creatures and events are incomprehensible for him, and for the audience as well, until the very last moments of the story. Eventually Harry runs into a woman named Dahlia, who during their subsequent meetings tells Harry that his daughter is about to become a sacrifice to a demon, Samael, who is veiling the town in darkness. Terrified for his daughter, Harry accepts an object Dahlia claims can help him and hurries off to find Cheryl.

In this manner *Silent Hill* establishes the first layer of religious horror. Harry's first meeting with Dahlia takes place in a Christian church (Konami 2003: 256). It is safe to assume that Harry himself is a Christian, since the story takes place in an American setting, or at least he is permeated with Judeo-Christian lore and symbolism. Therefore Dahlia's words exert a powerful effect on him:

> DAHLIA: The demon is awakening! Spreading those wings! ... Was it not as I said? I see it all now. Yes, everything. Hungry for sacrifice, the demon will swallow up the land! I knew this day would come! ... Even in daytime darkness will cover the sun. The dead will walk and martyrs will burn in the fires of hell. Everyone will die.
> HARRY: So what am I supposed to do? I've got to save Cheryl.
> DAHLIA: It is simple. Stop the demon. The demon taking that child's form. Stop it before your daughter becomes a sacrifice. Before it is too late. Stop it. Stop it.

Dahlia also explains to Harry that the strange markings he saw throughout the town are Marks of Samael. Upon hearing phrases such as "sacrifice," "darkness," "demon spreading his wings" or "fires of hell," the audience, together with Harry, is plunged into a terrifying but familiar reality of comprehensible religious horror. For all Harry knows, his daughter is going to be taken by the demon Samael if he does not save her in time.

Harry wanders the nightmare for some time, running into few people, equally alone and equally confused, until he meets the mysterious girl again. At this point the second layer of horror unveils and Harry learns the truth; once the contraption Harry received from Dahlia earlier activates and constraints the girl, Dahlia appears again. It is then that Harry learns that Dahlia has been deceiving him, and that it is in fact she who wants to sacrifice Cheryl to the demonic God she serves. Most importantly, she has already done so once, and Cheryl is not really an independent person, but half of the soul of the girl sacrificed once. Dahlia is a former priestess of a cult that used to reside in the town and worship an ancient deity. Seven years earlier Dahlia eventually grew impatient with waiting for the second coming of God, which was supposed to bring about a paradise on earth, and used an occult ritual to impregnate her own daughter, Alessa, hoping to "birth" God through her. However, the ritual did not go as planned, and Alessa's soul fractured and created Cheryl (who took the form of the baby Harry and his wife found on a road outside of Silent Hill). Alessa's soul was split; she was trapped in a nightmare of her pain, which both nurtured the God within her and was simultaneously fueled by God's power. When Dahlia finally managed to restrain Alessa's will to oppose God's birth, the whole town has collapsed into the nightmare that is the manifestation of Alessa's pain and God's power. Alessa reunites with the other half of her soul—Cheryl—and God is eventually allowed to mature in her body. Fully subjugated by the demonic entity, Alessa begins to transform into God, but is defeated by Harry before the transformation can be complete.

The first dimension of religious horror in *Silent Hill* is centered around Dahlia and the cult. As the priestess of the cult, Dahlia represents all the horrifying aspects of the religious practice taking place in Silent Hill.[9] In order to speed the second coming of God, Dahlia offered Alessa as a sacrifice in an immolation ritual, impregnating her with the seed of God. When the ritual failed, leaving Alessa incomplete, burnt and in agony, Dahlia used magic to keep her alive in hope that her daughter's soul might yet be restored and she might give birth to God. In doing so, she condemned Alessa to unending pain:

DAHLIA
    It's been a long seven years.... For the seven years since that terrible day, Alessa has been kept alive suffering a fate worse than death. Alessa has been trapped in an endless nightmare from which she never awakens! He has been nurtured by that nightmare, waiting for the day to be born. That day has finally come! The time is nigh! Everyone will be released from pain and suffering! Our salvation is at hand—this is the day of reckoning! When all our sorrows will be washed away, when we return to the true Paradise! My daughter will be the Mother of God!

In her quest to bring paradise to earth, Dahlia has no regard for the life of Alessa, Harry or anyone else. It is also clear that her vision—and, consequently, the cult's vision—of God is specific, since she assumes that God requires nurturing by "an endless nightmare." As Perron points out, the real monsters in *Silent Hill* are not the creatures born of Alessa's nightmare, but the believers. The cult either worships an evil demon god, or warps and twists their belief in God who created Paradise. In case of the former, the religion is built around a fearsome object of worship. In the case of the latter the religious practice Dahlia and the rest of the cult follow "completely displaced the path to deliverance and salvation" (Perron 2011: 49). In *Silent Hill,* the conventional symbiosis between the demonic and the divine, which allows one to be recognized when juxtaposed with the other, is subverted; Dahlia and the cult have completely mixed up this symbiosis by "trying to return to the true paradise through fear, hate, and an endless nightmare, by releasing everyone's pain and suffering" (Perron 2011: 50). Whatever the object of their worship is, what is important is the manner in which they decide to summon their deity. Even if Dahlia did think of salvation for all people, her monstrous means of achieving that (burning her daughter alive in an occult ritual) still render her and her followers as monsters and the true source of terror.

The second dimension of religious horror concerns the object of worship of the cult, i.e., the twisted ancient power, coming from the sacred ground of Silent Hill. Long before the town was built, the place in which Silent Hill is located was worshiped as a sacred place (Konami 2003: 257). The power of the sacred place is what nourishes God, who clearly is a demonic being of some sort. The same power weaves a dark, agonizing, twisted nightmare around Alessa's susceptible psyche, physically influencing the environment, creating a darker, more disturbing reflection of the town, retaining roughly the same physical outline but housing hell itself—the Otherworld in which Harry must wander. Alessa's pain and fear take tangible forms of the monsters he encounters. Those monsters are not there to serve her purpose, however, but merely embody Alessa's anguished, tortured dreams from which Alessa herself can't escape. The holy place worshiped by the cult is in reality a dark, cruel and evil place.

The third dimension of horror in *Silent Hill* is represented by God. The exact nature of the entity is unclear; God may very well be a demon that Silent Hill's founders worshiped or simply a tangible embodiment of the dark power dwelling in Silent Hill. Despite her divine name, she is at best a morally ambiguous, and at worst a cruel, destructive being that draws power from the demonic energies abounding in Silent Hill. God's horror potential naturally stems from the fact that it represents an alien realm of sacrum, but it is symbolic also because of its ambiguous nature. God originates from and embodies the demonic power residing in Silent Hill, but the cult believes she is capable of transforming earth into paradise, not hell. In the story, God appears in two forms through Alessa: as the angelic Incubator and the hellish Incubus. The Incubator has the appearance of a beautiful, dark haired woman glowing with a heavenly light, wearing pristine white robes. The Incubator reflects Alessa's mental image of God capable of bringing Paradise. However, due to an interference the process is interrupted, and the Incubator transforms into the Incubus, a hideous monstrosity with a horned goat's head, hermaphroditic body and wings.[10] This form reflects both the nature of the power of the holy place and Dahlia's twisted comprehension of God. With this duality of form, God represents the potential of any deity for kindness and cruelty, benevolence and monstrosity.

The American 2006 adaptation of *Silent Hill*, directed by Christophe Gans, deviates significantly in some aspects from the original Masons' story arc. Some plot elements were entirely removed from the plot due to the obvious time limitations of a cinematic production; other elements were changed to an extent that they are no longer recognizable, beyond even ordinary adaptation freedom—even if the film were to be treated not as an adaptation of the first game but as a hybrid of the first three games of the franchise.

Although the plot of the film begins on a note similar to the original story, the main premise is completely different. A mother and daughter, Rose and Sharon DaSilva, are on their way to Silent Hill. In the film, Silent Hill is a small ghost town in West Virginia, infested with toxic fumes from underground coal mines. Despite the danger, Rose decided to take Sharon to Silent Hill because her sleepwalking daughter kept repeating the town's name in her sleep.

The turning point of the plot—the sacrifice of Alessa intended to induce the birth of the cult's god—has been changed and simplified into a scenario bearing distinct Puritan tones. In the film, Alessa is an illegitimate child of a harmless, weak-willed woman named Dahlia. A group of religious fanatics, led by Dahlia's sister, Christabella, burns Alessa in order to "restore innocence." Alessa survives and is visited by a demon, who offers her revenge on those who hurt her. Alessa accepts and the whole town, including its inhabitants, is transferred into another realm, reflecting Alessa's "darkest dreams." The revenge is the pivotal point of the plot and the climax of the film. Since Alessa's soul was never fractured, in the film Alessa and Sharon are not two parts of the same soul; instead, Sharon is the "goodness" extracted from the soul of the original Alessa and incarnated into a new being, hidden safely away.

The human nature is presented within a typical Euroamerican binary convention. The realm of darkness is no longer the product of Alessa's tortured nightmares, but vengeful desires. In this way, the darkness is presented as completely unrelated to the "good" part of Alessa. This separation is facilitated by means of introduction of a completely new element—the demon, or the Reaper. Although physically resembling Alessa, the Reaper is an outside entity and an outside force, who has "many names," which also alludes to distinctly Judeo-Christian motifs:

DARK PART OF ALESSA
    Now the dream of this life must end and so, too, must the dreamers within it. For over thirty years they've lied to their own souls. For thirty years they've denied their own fate. But now is the end of days and I am the Reaper.

As such, Alessa is in fact portrayed in the film as three separate entities sharing one appearance: the bitter, resentful part of Alessa (the now adult victim of burning, confined to a hospital bed), Sharon Da Silva (the good part of Alessa) and the Dark Part of Alessa (the Reaper).

The cult itself is also portrayed in a completely different manner. The congregation that burns Alessa in the film consists of religious fanatics, descendants of witch hunters. Alessa, as a bastard child, is in their eyes "sin incarnate." The act of burning the girl is meant to purify the sin that is her existence. This presents a stark contrast with the game, where burning is not meant to eradicate and vanquish the profane, but to summon the sacred.

Apart from the plot changes, the film adaptation of *Silent Hill* was a fairly faithful portrayal of the game's imagery and general atmosphere, which makes it a valid point for comparison. It begs the question, why did the producers decide to completely remove the alien God from the equation, replacing it with a group of cruel, insane fanatics of a "proper" religion, Christianity? In this way, Gans' rendition of the story moves the weight of horror from the unfamiliar, alien sacrum to the familiar one. The terror comes not from strange religious values but from the perversion of familiar ones.

Another title worth mentioning is *Kakashi*, a film directed by Norio Tsuruta in 2001. The plot revolves around a small, secluded village located deep in the woods, and the strange religious practices of its people. The primary religious horror factor of *Kakashi* is, in comparison to *Silent Hill* and other titles discussed in this chapter, very subtle. Tsuruta constructs the horror atmosphere not around an elevated showdown of good and evil or around the end of the world, but rather by stratifying small, uncomfortable and uncanny distortions and pollution of innocuous, commonplace rituals. *Kakashi* follows a young woman, Kaoru, who in search for her missing brother, Tsuyoshi, comes to the isolated village of Kozukata. Kaoru believes Tsuyoshi has gone to Kozukata because of a mysterious letter from a former schoolmate, Izumi Miyamori. She finds the village, and inside she discovers a world she cannot comprehend. The plot of Tsuruta's film is incomplex and operates mostly within only one layer and one dimension of horror.

In the opening sequence of the film, the audience is informed that in the undefined past, people used *kakashi*[11] (here: scarecrows) to scare away evil spirits. People believed these scarecrows embodied various divine spirits. Unfortunately, the spirits called by the *kakashi* were not always benevolent. With this introduction, Tsuruta sets the mood for the transition from the mundane and familiar to the distorted and unfamiliar.

As Kaoru enters the village in hopes of finding her brother, the villagers speak little and seem to shy away from her. It is obvious that no one wants her there and, more importantly, she should not be there, which creates a heavy, disheartening atmosphere. Kaoru feels alienated and lost; the behavior of the population of Kozukata is not comprehensible to her. The people behave in a strange, secretive and threatening way, and throughout the town she sees evidence of some strange local belief celebration and belief system at work. In fact, the whole village of Kozukata seems to be preparing for some sort of annual scarecrow festival. As Kaoru inquires about the festival, she receives only vague and unnerving answers. The nature of the festival itself is equally enigmatic and unnerving, as no one is willing to explain to Kaoru its exact purpose or course. She is, however, able to steal a glimpse of the site of the *kakashi* celebration, which is bizarre and, at the same time, vaguely sinister; in a small field an enormous windmill is erected, around which the villagers are putting up life-size straw figures.

Kaoru does not manage to find either her brother or Izumi, but Izumi's parents offer to put her up for a couple of nights. She is haunted by bizarre nightmares about the villagers, her brother, Izumi, and scarecrows coming to life, which serves both to intensify the atmosphere of indistinct terror, and as foreshadowing, symbolizing the presence of the dead. Eventually, Kaoru learns from Mr. Miyamori that Izumi died some time earlier, and her parents came to Kozukata because of the peculiar scarecrow festival. The celebration of the scarecrow festival, as Mr. Miyamori explains, offers the possibility of reunion with the dead; as it turns out, the people of Kozukata live closer to the dead than the people anywhere else. They in fact "co-exist" with the dead:

KAORU: What on earth is this village?
MR. MIYAMORI: We co-exist with death here.
KAORU: Co-exist with death?
MR. MIYAMORI: Here they summon the souls of the dead to scarecrows.

In Kozukata, as Kaoru learns, around the time of the scarecrow festival, people build straw effigies of their dead, which become inhabited by the spirits of the loved ones. The spirits are drawn back partly by the grief of those left behind and partly by the power of the scarecrows; other spirits want desperately to come back out of their own volition. At this point, it is important to emphasize that the most significant aspect of *Kakashi* as a religious horror narrative is the significance of the scarecrow festival and the manner in which it is presented to the audience. Among the people of Kozukata, the resurrection of the dead is not perceived as some unprecedented, shocking undertaking, but as something done regularly, a ritual practice. This renders the whole celebration profoundly chilling and disturbing, especially considering the fact that the villagers seem to practice some strange travesty of genuine Shintō rituals, in which instead of representing Tano-kami, a god of fields, the scarecrows are supposed to accommodate the spirits of the dead (see Joya 1985). As Jim Harper notes, the roots of this ritual reflect the Shintō belief that all objects have souls. The villagers have called upon benevolent spirits to possess the *kakashi* and look after their fields for centuries, but later they started summoning the spirits of their loved ones; unfortunately, some of those spirits were not benevolent and could not be controlled (Harper 2008: 152). The power that the people of Kozukata are harnessing is very unnatural, as it upsets the balance of the cycle of life and death, and, naturally, it can only lead to a tragedy. Scared, Kaoru decides to leave the evening before the festival, but the villagers of Kozukata attempt to stop her now that she knows their secret. Kaoru runs into her brother, and together they try to escape, unaware that the scarecrow ritual has actually started. As they go past the windmill, an Izumi shaped scarecrow transforms into Izumi and makes Tsuyoshi kill himself, bursting in flames seconds later. Elsewhere in the village, scarecrows attack living people.

Kakashi aptly constructs the atmosphere of alienation and fear resulting from being an outsider in a hostile world, the rules of which one does not understand. Although the scarecrows represent a concrete, real threat to the characters, Tsuruta's film relies primarily on the psychological horror stemming from the knowledge that harmless everyday rituals of a small village have gone incredibly, perversely wrong. The fact that the rituals are presented as a religious practice, not a black magic ritual, merely intensifies the impact of the concept. The terror in *Kakashi* is based on the steadily increasing awareness of the nature of the religious practices of the people of Kozukata and the very basic fears connected with death.

Because religion concerns such great concepts as the struggle of good and evil, life after death and the moral value of human deeds, the narratives concerning religious fears are especially effective. Euroamerican religious horror narratives naturally deal with elevated motifs and scenarios, since the Judeo-Christian religion addresses elevated ideas. One of those ideas is the existence of supreme evil so strong that no human being can make a stand against it.

Such an idea is alien to the Japanese religious view of the world, where all beings and events tend to be dual; therefore, no creature or force can be regarded as entirely evil or entirely good. Japanese religious horror narratives are consequently scarce and center on alien spiritual elements or on obscure rituals. Regardless of their focus, religious horror narratives are one of the most intriguing horror narratives in the genre.

Conclusion: Different Shades of the Universal

The purpose of this book was to indicate and juxtapose the horror factors in in American and Japanese horror fiction, as well as some characteristic elements of composition and plot. This book deals with only a selection of narratives, as comprehensive, exhaustive representation and analysis of a larger number of texts would be nearly impossible; instead, the focus of this work is certain ideas and patterns. By highlighting the similarities and differences between American and Japanese horror narratives, I hoped to put them in the context of elementary characteristics of both cultures—including aspects of aesthetics, religious, social and folklore nature. The differences that emerge from the analysis of the texts include differences in perception, expression and interpretation, as can be seen in consecutive chapters.

The cultural differences revealed in the discussion on monstrosity narratives are the differences in expression of horror invoked by the unthinkable and in the connotations the monsters bear. Supernatural monstrosity, while rare in American horror fiction, knows no boundaries in Japanese horror fiction and includes many varieties and shapes of strangeness. This also applies to the monstrous predator, whose forms—and functions—tend to be less conventional in Japanese narratives than in the American ones. Whereas in the American horror fiction the focus is on the moral aspect of the monster (in case of the vampire) and on the man/beast dichotomy (in case of the werewolf), in Japanese horror fiction the vampire and the werewolf are just monsters like any others, included in a wider landscape of strange monstrosity. The discussion concerning the undead monstrosities, on the other hand, points to differences in perception of the dead body and death. Just as the dead body is itself associated with disparate concepts in both cultures (i.e., crossing the line between Self and Other in the American cultural frame, and with pollution (*kegare;* see Bernstein 2006: 27) in the Japanese cultural frame), the horror of the undead body in American horror fiction is associated with the disintegration of the Self and personhood, which shifts focus onto the problem of death itself—while in Japanese horror fiction the emphasis is placed on the violation of the spiritual and social order to which the living and the dead belong, pointing to the matters of affinity and social obligations.

The differences highlighted in the chapter discussing ghost narratives are the differences in perception of human relations and social principles. Although both cultures have a developed concept of afterlife, those concepts, as well as their employment in horror narratives, are quite disparate; in contrast to American haunting and retribution narratives, where both the storyline and the horror factor is based on an individual, personal conflict between the victim and the perpetrator, the horror factor in Japanese haunting and retribution narratives is constructed within a wider perspective—the characters are not simply individual entities, but members of groups and communities, dependent on and responsible for others. Additionally, Japanese haunting and retribution narratives tend to deal with matters such as empathy, duty and moral obligation, which again points to the disparate perception of the concepts of individual and community in both cultures.

The differences that emerged in the chapter discussing demon narratives and religion narratives concern the interpretation of good and evil. In American horror fiction, defined by Christian mythology, demons are generally associated with evil, regardless of their portrayed origin; in contrast, Japanese horror fiction depicts its native demons as amoral—if ever. Similarly, the horror factor of American religious horror narratives is based on the ultimate triumph of evil (the Devil) over good (God), while Japanese religious horror narratives tend to focus on distortion of otherwise innocent beliefs or rituals, blending good intentions with evil will. This points to the understanding of good and evil in respective cultural frames—in American cultural reality, is it constructed as a binary opposition, whereas in Japanese cultural reality good and evil are perceived to be close to one another and intertwined.

While the preceding chapters juxtaposed a variety of diverse horror narratives, comparing the underlying narrative patterns and most prominent horror constituents that can be discerned in individual narratives belonging to given sub genres, there is still a plethora of other factors that render Japanese and American narratives worth juxtaposing. They were not elaborated upon in this book, but some of them, such as the pace of the narrative, the delivery of horror and the underlying themes of horror fiction, are worth mentioning in the context of the discussion.

The Experienced and the Perceivable

One of the many important differences between Japanese horror fiction and American horror fiction lies in the pace of the story. The characteristic feature of Japanese horror fiction is the steady pace at which the plot unravels. The contemporary American style of narrating in horror fiction tends to speed up, then slow down at moments only to speed up again; the horror element may even temporarily disappear, allowing the characters to "recover" and try to convince themselves that nothing extraordinary is happening, which can be observed in *Stir of Echoes* or *Mist*. The terror in Japanese horror narratives, on the other hand, unravels rather steadily, despite the fact that it does not delay the introduction of the horror element. The pace is slow—which is not to say uneventful; the focus is on emotional impact rather than dynamic action, which is apparent in such narratives as *Kuroneko*, *Strangers* or *Silent Hill 2*.

An additional characteristic of all narratives, which sheds even more light on the matter of the dissimilar nature of Japanese and American horror narratives, is the manner of storytelling and the delivery of horror elements. Whereas American horror fiction relies strongly on the element of surprise and detailed, imaginative descriptions/depictions of the monster, meant to instill shock and awe in the audience, the Japanese narrative opts for gradual build-up of the readers' awareness of the horror element, with emphasis on the subjective awareness of the characters. As Izumi Kyōka, a famous author of *gensō bungaku* (fantastic literature), stated, to convey that which is mysterious (*fushigi*) in a monster, it is crucial not to write in a mysterious (*fushigi*-like) fashion; fantastical discourse leads to text that is "exorbitant" and offers less ghostliness (*sugomi*) than simple recounting of the words or actions of the fantastic being itself (Kyōka in Figal 1999: 170). Accordingly, the monster in Japanese horror narratives tends to be de-mystified by the plain manner in which it is usually introduced and addressed in the story, as can be seen in *A Short Night, A Quiet Obsession, Ring,* or *Strangers*. Japanese horror fiction does not shy away from naming the uncanny or showing it clearly.

In addition, in comparison to American horror narratives, which offer detailed descriptions or images of the object of horror, such the horrific appearance of the monster in *Bram Stoker's Dracula* or *The Howling,* or its horrific nature, as in *Pet Sematary* or *The Exorcist,* and use the character's reaction only to complement that image, Japanese horror fiction places far more emphasis on the character's reaction to horror stimuli. In literature, extensive passages tend to be devoted to description of the character's state of mind, such as Yoshimi's doubts in *Floating Water* or Harada's musings in *Strangers*. In film, this effect is achieved by long camera shots following the characters' expressions as they are confronted with the source of fear, which can be observed in many scenes in *Ringu*, *Shikoku* or *Dark Water*, and in games by captions relaying the characters' thoughts (as used extensively in the *Silent Hill* series). This tendency of Japanese narratives to be oriented towards the subjective experience of the characters instead of an objective representation of the events mirrors a very significant trait of Japanese culture, i.e., the focus on *koto* (which can be in simplified as "the experience" in this context) (Lebra 2004: 34).

Japanese cultural logic distinguishes two categories of perception of reality, *koto* and *mono*, which might be simplistically equated to "the experience" and "the thing" (Lebra 2004: 34). The Western culture and civilization are, according to Lebra, *mono*-oriented; Western epistemology and ontology, as well as philosophical discourse, are based on opposition logic, which is, in turn, based on perceiving reality as being composed of elements that can be clearly identifiable and objectified (Lebra 2004: 34). In comparison to object-biased discourse, which conceptualizes items and subjects rather than experiences and phenomena, event-biased discourse places the emphasis on the event, on that which is happening, on the context of a given situation—on that which can be felt, especially over a period of time, but not necessarily perceived (Lebra 2004: 34). *Koto* are always subjective, tied up in personal contexts and, as opposed to the *mono*-phenomena, which are objective, *koto*-phenomena exist only if experienced; naturally, therefore, they require the participation of the subject perceiving them (Lebra 2004: 34; Raud in Lebra 2004: 34). Japanese horror narratives indeed tend to focus on the experience rather than the object—that is, on the terror experienced by the characters rather than on the creature evoking the terror.

Remakes: Re-imagining the Alien

Another point worth raising while discussing the differences between American and Japanese horror narratives is the phenomenon of remakes. Daniel Herbert points to the fact that the contemporary cultural dialogue between Hollywood and East Asian cinema is a cultural manifestation of new social relations (Herbert in Lukas and Marmysz 2010: 154). Like any cultural process, this dialogue both reflects social reality and exerts real force upon the construction of that reality; the remakes delineate a "transnational space of flows between 'East' and 'West'" and redirect and remake these flows (Herbert in Lukas and Marmysz 2010: 154).

Although only a couple of titles discussed in this book are remakes, the remakes themselves cast an even more interesting light on the matter or American and Japanese horror. Between the years 2002 and 2011, a number of Japanese horror films and games were remade: *Ring* (*Ringu*, 1998), *Silent Hill* (*Sairento Hiru*, 1999), *Ju-on: The Grudge* (*Ju-on*, 1999), *Pulse* (*Kairo*, 2001), *Dark Water* (*Honogurai mizu-no soko kara*, 2002) and *One Missed Call* (*Chakushin Ari*, 2003)—as well as a few South Korean, Thai and other East Asian horror films. The American remakes of Japanese horror films (or, for that matter, any Asian horror films) enjoyed both immense popularity and commercial success, and are far more numerous than Japanese remakes of Western horror films, which are virtually non-existent.

While discussing remakes, it is very important to keep in mind that since the film must earn its success, often-times its artistic, symbolic or psychological values are likely to be compromised by the commercial goals of its producers. Additionally, to function properly within the target cultural frame, the film must present to the audience a setting and a story that are comprehensible and possible to identify with. The majority of remakes seem to aim at replicating the atmosphere of horror of the original film, but the changes to the characters and the plot, required to make the product more familiar, frequently undermine that goal. Those changes, apart from affecting the final outcome of the remaking process, also speak volumes about cultural differences.

One of the most striking differences between the original texts and the remade products are the characters of the villains. For instance, *The Ring* completely dehumanized its main source of horror, Samara; in contrast to Sadako, who had a legitimate reason to bear a grudge against society, Samara is portrayed as inherently evil, not related to her parents at all and even possibly not human, making it much more difficult for the audience to understand her or feel sympathy for her. Similarly, in the film remake of *Silent Hill*, Dahlia is still Alessa's mother, but it is not she who hurts Alessa, but Alessa's aunt, Christabella. This removes the element of a mother hurting her own child, which is possibly uncomfortable for the American audience. In the same way, the 2006 *Silent Hill* removes other morally ambiguous or morally complex concepts, such as the alien god or the dissonance between Dahlia's cruel methods and her goal of bringing paradise to Earth. Most importantly, the ugliness and ferocity of the nightmare are no longer the product of suffering and delusion, but of demonic power. The Otherworld born of Alessa's pain and God's power, which the players explore in the original game, is replaced in the film by a hellish dimension brought into existence by the Reaper, who represents evil and darkness. Such changes speak volumes of the way in which both cultures perceive the balance of good and evil—which in American narratives is more often than not clear cut, and in Japanese narratives, frequently undermined and subverted.[1]

The "positive" characters depicted in the remakes are also usually quite different. The protagonists tend to be more aggressive and less emotionally vulnerable; in *The Ring*, Rachel seems much more impatient and aggressive than Reiko; she never stays in one place, and she behaves more assertively and yet seems emotionally detached from what is happening. In general, female protagonists, such as Karen in *The Grudge* (remake of *Ju-on: The Grudge*) or Dahlia in *Dark Water* (remake of *Dark Water*) are more aggressive than the characters they are based on. They also tend to be more dismissive of the curse, like Bethany in *One Missed Call* (remake of *One Missed Call*) or Mattie from *Pulse* (remake of *Pulse*), presenting an ontological resistance towards the supernatural, characteristic of American narratives.[2]

The Real Beneath the Unreal

Horror fiction processes the fear of those who create it and those who are meant to receive it. While the expression of that fear tends to vary, the sources of social fears are less diverse than the shapes in which they are articulated. Horror, as Grixti points out, reflects social unease; the assumptions and concerns underlying the texts of horror fiction are aligned with "some of the theories, beliefs, and anxieties which have dominated our century's attempts to understand itself, and with some of the images which contemporary society has found fit to express its conception of itself and of its habitat" (Grixti 1989: 3). Horror presents the space within which objects of social anxiety may be presented, objects such as violence (Grixti 1989: 23) or a stigmatized sector of the population (Grixti 1989: 25). In other words, beneath the "unreal" fears depicted in horror fiction, there are real anxieties and tensions. Regardless of the country it originates from, horror fiction speaks of fear in general. Being rooted in everyday reality of those who create it and those who receive it, horror fiction often-times puts a supernatural costume on fears related to the natural, the rational and the commonplace.

A great deal of horror narratives naturally revolve around fears concerning death; in American society, death is a mystery, surrounded by many taboos; and it is represented as such in many horror texts, such as *Pet Sematary*—specifically Louis' memories of understanding the concept of death for the first time or Rachel's hysteria over Ellie's questions about her cat dying. The fear of dying in itself is more common, and, therefore, the reactions of the characters related to this fear are depicted similarly in all narratives, American and Japanese alike, as can be seen, for example, in the behavior of the protagonists of *The Howling, The Mist, One Missed Call* or *Ring*. Additionally, fear of death encompasses many focused types of fear directed toward others. Such fears might be related to parental responsibility, as seen in Reiko's fear for Yōichi in *Ring*, David's behavior concerning Billy in *The Mist* or Harry's search for Cheryl in *Silent Hill*, or to losing one's significant other, like Louis' loss of Rachel in *Pet Sematary* or James' loss of Mary in *Silent Hill 2*.

Another anxiety horror texts frequently touch upon are fears related to sexuality; many monsters are in fact obviously sexual in nature—many of them visually point to sex, sexual organs or sexual activities. However, the real fear underlying the appearance of a monster with strong sexual connotations is the fear of sexuality lying deep within the subject, threatening to surface. Considering the Puritan roots of American society, horror seems like a natural and rich environment for that which tends to be repressed in American culture. Untamed and threatening sexuality can be observed in many horror texts, either merely inappropriate, as in *Bram Stoker's Dracula*, where Lucy becomes sexually aggressive and lewd, or downright vulgar, as in the behavior of the possessed Regan in *The Exorcist*. Japanese monsters and storylines, on the other hand, frequently include openly sexual elements, such as the monsters in *Silent Hill 2*, Harada's relationship with the ghost of Kei in *Strangers* (and the story it alludes to, *The Peony Lantern*), the way Shige seduces the samurai before biting their throats in *Kuroneko* or one of the pivotal points of *Tomie*, where the obsession regarding Tomie is clearly sexual. In Japanese horror texts, however, the sexual element is not meant to amplify the horror, but merely to provide an additional dimension to the narrative.

One more prominent anxiety expressed in horror fiction is the fear of violence and rejection, in the broad sense of the term. Due to its nature, it is only natural that horror fiction explores themes of violence, regardless of whether it comes from the Other, as it can be conventionally seen in monster narratives (including vampire narratives and werewolf narratives), such as *Cycle of the Werewolf*, or *Kuroneko*, or violence from other human beings, as it is depicted in *The Shining*, where Wendy constantly fears that Jack may hurt Danny, or in *Silent Hill*, where Alessa is immolated by her mother. Horror does not shy away from uncomfortable themes of abuse—violence directed towards loved ones and violence from the hand of the loved ones, like Kayako being brutally murdered by her husband in *Ju-on: The Grudge* or Yumi being abused by her mother in *One Missed Call*. Closely related to the fear of violence is the fear of rejection and ostracism, as presented in *The Sixth Sense*, where Cole is alienated and bullied by other kids. Nevertheless, this element is more frequent in Japanese horror fiction—e.g., in *Kakashi*, where Kaoru is ostracized by the villagers, or in the way Sadako and Kei were rejected by society before their deaths in *Ring* and *Strangers*.

Cultural Horror

While discussing the functions and significance of horror fiction in his book *Terrors of Uncertainty*, Joseph Grixti quotes an excerpt from Stephen King's famous non-academic book on horror, *Danse Macabre*, which states that fiction tells us truths about ourselves by means of telling us lies about people who do not exist (King as quoted in Grixti 1989: 5). To agree with such a statement, Grixti elaborates, is to "embrace an assumed set of shared values and ideas about what constitutes the norm and about which 'truths' will apply within the convention of that norm" (Grixti 1989: 5–6). Texts of horror fiction, he argues, are therefore commentaries; they explore and evaluate, and even influence to an extent, "a set of cultural and cognitive experiences" (Grixti 1989: 6). The texts of horror fiction are—just like texts of other fiction—commentaries of a certain kind; they explore and evaluate, as well as influence, cultural and cognitive experiences of the audience (Grixti 1989: 6). Texts of fiction are made up of coded meanings, and the appropriation and decoding of those meanings depends on the way in which a given culture sees reality (Grixti 1989: 6). Horror personifies fears and anxieties, and it makes them explicit; it expresses that which sometimes cannot be said directly and allows it to take shape. The shapes of our fears and anxieties and the manner in which those shapes are interpreted depend on the cultural frame the authors and audience belong to, and are influenced by the cultural context, by the society in which people live (Grixti 1989: 15).

In scaring its audience, horror fiction performs a social function; it offers concrete shapes to repressed or sometimes unspecified fears. Moreover, it becomes a mirror reflecting an image of a given culture. A distorting mirror it may be, but still a mirror. As Cowan notes, "what scares us reveals important aspects of who we are, both as individuals and as a society" (Cowan 2008: 10). Different images we can see in horror texts, different narrative patterns of horror fiction articulate various differences between cultures.

It can be argued that in a global sense, Japanese horror fiction and American horror fiction are not that different. Both aim at evoking an emotional response that in its very nature is not only culturally but also biologically universal. However, the ways in which those fears find expression in both cultures differ fundamentally. American and Japanese narratives feature distinct forms of horror; the shape and the nature of the threat, the reactions of the characters and the overall logic of the narrative are all determined by the cultural contexts. For this reason, from the academic point of view, the differences are important and more interesting than the similarities, because acknowledging and striving to understand the differences allows us to gain insight into the world of another culture.

Notes

Preface

1. Although a video game may allow for more than one ending, the number of possible endings is limited, usually to a small number like three or four, which resembles a work of literature or a film with an open ending or DVD edition of a film with alternative endings included.

Introduction

1. In case of the Euroamerican reception of Japanese text, there are two notions worth mentioning. One of them is "Japaneseness"—a notion promoted, as Picard points out, primarily in the West, which denotes some sort of elusive quality characterizing "truly" Japanese products, such as films, video games or literature (Picard in Perron 2009: 101). Since at the very core of "Japaneseness" lies the conviction that Japanese culture and Japanese cultural products are original and unique, the concept is marked by profound Orientalist traits (Picard in Perron 2009: 101). The crucial "specificity" that naturally accompanies "Japaneseness" (Picard in Perron 2009: 101) is nothing more than exoticism in a new costume. Another important concept is Japanism. Brian Moeran identifies Japanism as "a way of coming to terms with Japan that is based on Japan's place in Western European and American experience. Japanism is a mode of discourse, a body of knowledge, a political vision of reality that represents an integral part of Western *material* civilisation both culturally and ideologically, with supporting institutions, vocabulary, scholarship, imagery and doctrines" (Moeran in Ben-Ari et al. 1994: 1). Most importantly, Moeran stresses that "in talking about Japanism in this century, we are referring to a *Western* academic tradition, a style of thought, and a corporate institution designed to dominate, restructure and thus gain authority over Japan" (Moeran in Ben-Ari et al. 1994: 1 2).

2. Examples include *Forest of Hands and Teeth*, a young adult horror novel by Carrie Ryan, or *Blood: The Last Vampire*, a novel belonging to the same sub-genre by Mamoru Oshii, a children's horror series *Goosebumps* (books and TV series) created by R. L. Stine or the Japanese anime TV series *Gakkō no Kaidan* [*School Ghost Stories*], aired by Fuji TV.

3. Japanese horror fiction rarely operates within the already mentioned Euroamerican opposition of natural/supernatural, but instead portrays the world as inclusively strange. This is especially noticeable in horror anthologies and short stories; such forms of fiction rarely strive for a comprehensible, coherent storyline that would offer an explanation of the story, relying instead on the atmosphere of fear mixed with insoluble mystery. Examples of this include *Dark Tales of Japan* [*Nihon no kowaiya*] (2004) or the series *Tales of Terror from Tokyo* [*Kaidan shinmimibukuro*] (2003–05) or short stories such as Hyakken Uchida's *Fireworks* [*Hanabi*] or *Reunion* [*Daisukina ane*] by Takahashi Katsuhiko.

Chapter 1

1. Actually, the narratives that I refer to as "non-layered" are also layered in a manner of speaking; however, they only make use of two layers. An example of this are zombie narratives, where the only available layers are the introductory layer and the layer of the story proper, i.e., the moment when the characters believe they are being attacked by humans whose odd behavior and/or appearance can be explained rationally, and the moment when they already understand that they are facing an inexplicable, irrational threat. There are no further plot twists or sudden changes. When I write "multi-layered," I refer to narratives with more than one transition between layers, such as *The Others*, *Silent Hill 1* or *Rosemary's Baby*.

2. One of the traditional elements of any ghost story is the ghost's inability to affect the nature of the person it is haunting. As opposed to the vampire, which may change its prey into its minion (or, in the conventional narratives, may even doom its victim's soul to eternal damnation), or the werewolf, which can transform the victim into a werewolf as well, the ghost can only torment and kill the haunted person. It cannot, however, change or influence the ontological status of the human being it is haunting.

3. This particular figure is common to, but by no means restricted to, American fiction. Apart from the other title discussed here, *The Others* (2001), the "unaware" ghost featured in American titles such as *The Messengers* (2007) can also be found in horror cinema of other countries: Spain (*KM 31: Kilometre 31*, 2006), Philippines (*The Echo*, 2004) or Great Britain (*Reeds*, 2010).

4. Despite the fact that *The Others* was a joint production of the U.S., Spain, Italy and France, the film was produced and distributed by an American film company, Dimension Films, and conforms to the American standards of aesthetics and storytelling.

5. An interesting aspect of this moment is that in *A Quiet Obsession* technology (the present) surrenders before the ghost (the past), whereas in modern horror narratives it usually happens the other way round, e.g., in *Ring* the technology (tapes, TV sets) serves the ghost's purpose.

6. In Europe *Project Zero* was marketed under the name *Fatal Frame*. Because papers cited in the text refer to the game as *Fatal Frame*, for the sake of clarity I shall use the same title.

7. See Warner 2006: 16; Bernardin and Tonkovich 2003: 190; and Robinson 2009: 152. This motif is featured in *Don't Look Up* (*Joyūrei*) (1996), where the actress playing the lead role in the movie being filmed mentions her mother's fear of her soul being sucked in by the camera.

8. In fact, Eric's ontological status is not clear. He does not seem to be a ghost, since he is at all times tangible and can be injured. He is not an undead either, as he does not have any traits characteristic to any of the undead, such as decomposition or coldness and pallor.

9. *Banchō Sarayashiki* is a story of a maid, Okiku, slain by a samurai over a broken expensive plate. Her ghost rose every night from the well where her body had been dumped and counted from one to nine (ten being the number of the broken plate) and then broke into a terrible wail, eventually driving the samurai insane.

10. The ghost of Otsuyu, accompanied by the ghost of her maid carrying a peony lantern, visits her lover, Saburo, every night and has sex with him. Once it is discovered she is a ghost, protective *fuda* are placed in Saburo's house to guard it against the spirits. Saburo pines for Otsuyu and his health deteriorates. His servants, afraid that he will die from sadness, remove the protective *fuda*, and Otsuyu can enter. In the morning, the servants find Saburo dead, with a blissful expression on his face, next to Otsuyu's skeleton. See Araki 1998.

11. It is interesting to note that although Japanese ghosts usually cannot be stopped or driven away, they can be sometimes kept at bay by protective *fuda*, just like in *Botan Dōrō*.

12. *The Ring Virus* is actually the most accurate film adaptation of the book, as it includes the original contents of the tape, the fact that "Sadako" had been born with male pseudohermaphroditism and the scene

in the small pox sanatorium. The reason *The Ring Virus* is listed here is the fact that despite the extent of accuracy, Kim Dong-bin still included in his film the scene where the ghost crawls out of the TV. Additionally, it too has a female single-mother protagonist.

13. There are more traditional elements in that scene than Sadako's hair and dress. For example, Sadako emerges from the well in which she died. (Okiku, the ghost of one of the most famous Japanese ghost stories, was also thrown into a well from which she arose to torment her victim). She is also mostly filmed from the waist up, which creates the impression that she has no feet as she moves towards Ryūji (in comparison, there is more than one clear shot of Samara's feet in the same scene in *The Ring*).

14. The majority of conventional vengeful ghosts interact verbally with their victims. An example of this might be the renowned counting of plates of Okiku ["*o-sara ga ichi-mai, nimai...*"] or Oiwa's accusation, "You're so cruel, Lord Iemon" ["*urameshii, Iemon-dono*"]. However, modern ghosts in Japanese novels, cinema and video games also tend to use words that shed light on their actions, although silent ghosts are not unheard of (i.e. Kiyoshi Kurosawa's *Séance* [2000]).

15. In the book, the original tape began with words "WATCH UNTIL THE END. YOU WILL BE EATEN BY THE LOST (*mōja*, lit. "the dead")" and ended with instructions to copy the tape and show it to someone else within seven days (Suzuki 2007: 76).

16. In this story the ghost of a deceased wife of a samurai takes revenge on her husband, who broke his promise to her never to remarry, by literally tearing off the head of his new bride. See Hearn in Joshi 2002, 74–80.

Chapter Two

1. Scott Poole describes the vampires in *Twilight* as having their "subversive power diffused." Poole points out that "Meyer's vampires are literally defanged, their immemorial associations with sex and excess fully domesticated" (Poole 2011: 214).

2. *Vagina dentata*, "the saw toothed orifice that waits to mutilate the male," is a very relevant image, due to significant sexual tension between Charley and Amy, who was Charley's girlfriend (Gilmore 2001: 41).

3. E.g. they must suck blood of all samurai they encounter. If they do not, they will cease to exist. By comparison, the Euroamerican vampire is defined by prohibitions; it cannot go into the sun, and it cannot face the cross, etc.

4. An exception from this general rule is the Dracula portrayed in the previously discussed *Bram Stoker's Dracula*.

5. In subtitles: "Dracula." In the original Japanese dialogue the word "*kyūketsuki*" is used.

6. It is difficult to judge how much the human personality of "Sharon" corresponds to the vampire's real personality or whether it is the only identity it can assume. Since the Chiroptera are capable of blending in with humans, they must comprehend things such as abstract concepts, social reality and technology. When they are shown in their true form, however, they seem to be merely animals. Nothing about their behavior, origin or thinking patterns is revealed.

7. Foster points out after Yanagita and Komatsu that *yōkai* are just *kami* that are not worshipped; that is, they have the same ontological status and powers as deities (Foster 2009: 15).

8. Actually, there are two conflicting theories explaining the appearance of the monsters in the story. One of them are the fanatic ravings of Mrs. Carmody, an amateur preacher, and the other one are constant allusions to a military scientific project, referred to as the "Arrowhead Project." Neither of those is explicitly confirmed, however, and the monsters seem to fit neither of them as well.

9. Angela's Otherworld seems to be more developed than Eddie's, and it includes many elements pointing to the sexual abuse she suffered, such as suggestively shaped reliefs made out of skin and pistons thrusting back and forth in the walls. A significant monster haunting Angela is Abstract Daddy, a creature resembling a bed with two figures, one bigger and stronger and one smaller and

weaker, struggling under putrid, fleshy covers. The monster moves on all fours, and attacks by lunging with its bed-like form onto James when he tries to protect Angela.

10. The character of Hisako Yao is, for instance, one of many references to actual Japanese folklore and culture in *Siren*. Originally one of the villagers who have eaten the god's flesh, she was the one Datatsushi caught sight of and cursed with an immortal life. This makes Hisako reminiscent of a folk character called Yao Bikuni (eight-hundred-[year-old] Buddhist nun), who lived to eight hundred years after having eaten the flesh of a mermaid (Stone and Walter 2008: 182). Both characters also share the name Yao, although different *kanji* is used. Akira Shimura even refers to Hisako as Yao Bikuni at one point, calling her a monster who has not aged. Another reference to Japanese folklore is the *tsuchinoko* Kyoya and Miyako encounter in an abandoned house; *tsuchinoko* is an actual legendary creature in Japan whose existence has not been scientifically proven (Foster 2009: 1). In the game the player can find a poster offering a reward for catching a *tsuchinoko* alive.

11. Datatsushi is a fictitious being, but the game contains references genuine Shintō practices. For example, there is a spring named "Mizuhiruko" in the village, near the shrine devoted to a sea and fishermen deity, Hiruko (Bremen and Martinez 1995: 70). Significantly enough, the shrine devoted to Hiruko is deserted, whereas the cult of Datatsushi thrives.

Chapter Three

1. *Killing Ariel* is interesting because although it does draw from the folklore, introducing such concepts as Incubus and Succubus, it merges the two into one entity capable of switching sex as it pleases.

2. Possession as a horror device is in and of itself popular in American horror fiction and not limited to demons. Human being can be possessed by spirits of other human beings (e.g. *Gothika*), by old gods and deities (e.g. *Pet Sematary*) or by alien consciousness (e.g. Brian Keene's *The Rising*).

3. In the case cited in Chamberlain, the fox spirit was actually eager to leave the possessed girl after some time, but demanded offering in return. Once the offerings were placed in the requested place, the fox left the girl. See Chamberlain 2007: 123.

4. *O-harae* or *o-harai* is the general term for rituals of purification in Shintō. The purpose is the purification of pollution or sins (*tsumi*) and uncleanness (*kegare*). *Harae* is often referred to as the purification, but is also known as an exorcism meant to restore the spirit of the object of purification to its original pristine state. (Varley, H. 2000: 9).

5. See Haga, *Japanese Folk Festivals Illustrated*. It is, however, important to note that in both the Japanese tag and hide and seek it is the first person to be caught, not last, that becomes the *oni* (Haga 1970: 187).

6. All the characters discussed in the first chapter, as well as in chapter 5, follow this pattern (Robert Thorn, Katherine Winter, Chris McNeil, Katie Featherstone). Further examples include Rick (*Killing Ariel*, 2008), Joseph Crone (*III-11-1*, 2011), Peter Kelson (*Lost Souls*, 2000), Frankie Paige (*Stigmata*, 1999), Christine York (*End of Days*, 1999) or Samantha Howard (*Blessed*, 2004).

7. As Cowan explains, "In ancient Hebrew tradition, a Nazirite is someone consecrated to God through a series of ritual actions and prohibitions.... In the cinema horror inversion of naziresis, a variety of ritual preparations seek to ensure the birth of a satanic saviour who will deliver the world from the power of God" (Cowan 2008: 188).

8. Again, it is worth noting that as a small child, Damien still prevails; despite the fact that, as Hutchings points out, Damien is "fathered by the Devil and born of a jackal" and that he is therefore "intrinsically and irredeemably evil" (Hutchings 2008: 236), no murder of a child occurs on screen.

9. The aesthetic and spiritual aspects of the cult take inspiration and draw elements from existing religions: "The religion of Silent Hill refers to elements of various religions, including the early Christianity, Japanese folktales and Aztec rituals and ceremonies. The native beliefs of American

people revolve around animals and spirits that dwell in places, and the people who borrow their power and thus become stronger" (Konami 2003: 257).

10. Incubus shares the name with a demon seducing humans in their sleep, but nothing more. Visually it resembles Baphomet, an imagined deity symbolizing balance (Yust 1968).

11. *Kakashi*, loosely translated as scarecrow or figure head, can refer either to a human-shaped dummy set in the field, which corresponds to a Western scarecrow, or to animal meat or hair burned in order to scare wild animals away. The opening sequence refers to both types of *kakashi*, but for the sake of clarity the word "scarecrow" will be used, as the human-shaped scarecrows are the main focus of the film.

Conclusion

1. For instance, as Tania Krzywinska points out in *Hands-on Horror*, the whole story of *Silent Hill 2* attempts to "disrupt the conventional good/evil paradigm" (Krzywinska 2002: 222); this is achieved by questioning the assumed "good" status (moral goodness) of the character James (Krzywinska 2002: 222).

2. Comparisons between Japanese texts and their American remakes frequently reveal numerous fascinating details concerning Japanese reality and ways in which it is adapted or cannot be adapted into American texts. For instance, in the original *Dark Water*, Yoshimi, about to run out of the flat in search of her daughter, pauses briefly to put on her shoes. This act, which seems like a waste of time in such a dramatic moment, might appear absurd or unconvincing to a Western viewer. For the Japanese audience, this cultural reflex would be only natural, since preserving the spiritual purity of the household by protecting it from the outside pollution belongs to the same realm of reality as the presence of vengeful spirits; as an act, putting on shoes to protect the inside from the pollution from the outside is merely a reflex that does not require conscious decision-making.

Bibliography

Primary Sources

Blatty, William. 1971. *The Exorcist*. New York: Harper & Row.
Benneville, James. 2009. *Yotsuya Kwaidan, or, Oiwa Inari*. Originally published 1917 by J.B. Lippincott.
Brandner, Gary. 1985. *The Howling*. London: Arrow Books.
Freeman Mitford, Algernon Bertram. 1966. *The Vampire Cat of Nabeshima*. In *Tales of Old Japan*. Rutland, VT: C. E. Tuttle.
Hearn, Lafcadio. 1901. "On a Promise Broken." In Joshi, S.T., ed. 2002. *Great Tales of Terror*. Mineola, N.Y: Dover. 74–80.
Hearn, Lafcadio. 1904. *Kwaidan*. Boston: Houghton Mifflin.
Hearn, Lafacadio. 1904. "Of a Mirror and a Bell." In *Kwaidan*.
Hearn, Lafacadio. 1904. "Diplomacy." In *Kwaidan*. Boston: Houghton Mifflin.
Hirano, Kōta. 2003. *Hellsing*. Milwaukie, OR: Dark Horse Manga.
Itō, Junji. 2001. *Tomie 2: Graphic Novel*. Fremont, CA: Comics One.
Jackson, Shirley. 1999. *The Haunting of Hill House*. New York: Penguin.
Kaji, Kengo, and Kenji Okamura. 1997. *Lycanthrope Leo*. San Francisco: Viz.
Kikuchi, Hideyuki. 2006. *The Stuff of Dreams*. Milwaukie, OR: DH Press.
Kikuchi, Hideyuki. 2009. *Wicked City*. New York: Tor.
Kikuchi, Hideyuki. 2011. *Demon City Shinjuku*. Carson, CA: DMP.
King, Stephen. 1985. *Cycle of the Werewolf*. New York: Penguin.
King, Stephen. 1989. *Pet Sematary*. London: Hodder and Stoughton.
King, Stephen. 1990. *It*. New York: Signet.
King, Stephen. 1990. *Langoliers*. In *Four Past Midnight*. New York: Viking, 1990.
King, Stephen. 1991. *'Salem's Lot*. New York: Plume.
King, Stephen. 1994. *The Shining*. London: Chancellor Press.
King, Stephen. 2001. *The Mist*. London: Little, Brown.
Koontz. Dean R. 1996. *Tick Tock*. London: Headline Feature.
Kyōka, Izumi. 2005. "A Quiet Obsession." In *In Light of Shadows: More Gothic Tales by Izumi Kyōka*. Honolulu University of Hawaii Press.
LeFanu, Sheridan. 2001. *Carmilla*. Doylestown, PA: Wildside Press.
Levin, Ira. 2003. *Rosemary's Baby*. New York: New American Library.
Lovecraft, H.P. 2008. *The Outsider*. London: Penguin.
Matheson, Richard. 1999. *A Stir of Echoes*. New York: Tom Doherty.
Mitford, A.B. 1966. *Tales of Old Japan*. Rutland, VT: C. E. Tuttle.
Nagai, Gō. 1995. *Devilman*. Los Angeles: Verotic.
Nagai, Gō. 1997. *Devilman Lady*. Tokyo: Kodansha.
Niles, Steve, and Ben Templesmith. 2003. *30 Days of Night*. San Diego: Idea & Design Works, LLC.
Ōishi, Kei. 2003. *Ju On*. Milwaukie, OR: DH Press.
Otsuichi. 2010. *Summer, Fireworks, and My*

Corpse. San Francisco: Haikasoru VIZ Media.
Rice, Anne. 1977. *Interview with a Vampire*. London: Futura.
Straub, Peter. 1976. *Julia*. New York: Pocket Books.
Suzuki, Kōji. 2004. *Ring*. New York: Vertical.
Suzuki, Kōji. 2006. *Dark Water*. New York: Vertical.
Takahashi, Katsuhiko. 2010. "Reunion." In Higashi, Masao. 2010. *Kaiki: Uncanny Tales from Japan, Vol. 2, Country Delights*. Fukuoka: Kurodahan Press.
Takekawa, Sei. 1991. "On a Moonless Night." In Mitsios, Helen, and Jay McInerney. 2003. *New Japanese Voices*. New York: Grove/Atlantic.
Tōme, Kei. 2004. *Lament of the Lamb*. Los Angeles: Tokyopop.
Uchida, Hyakken. 2006. *A Short Night*. In *Realm of the Dead*. Normal, IL: Dalkey Archive Press.
Uchida, Hyakken. 2006. *Fireworks*. In *Realm of the Dead*. Normal, IL: Dalkey Archive Press.
Uchida, Hyakken. 2006. *Vortex*. In *Realm of the Dead*. Normal, IL: Dalkey Archive Press.
Ueda, Akinari. 2008. *Tales of Moonlight and Rain*. New York: Columbia University Press.
Umezu, Kazuo. 2007. *Reptilia*. San Diego: IDW.
Yamada, Taichi. 2003. *Strangers*. New York: Vertical.

Secondary Sources

Abbott, Stacy. 2006. "Embracing the Metropolis: Urban Vampires in American Cinema of the 1980s and 90s." In Day, Peter. 2006. *Vampires: Myths and Metaphors of Enduring Evil*. Amsterdam: Rodopi.
Abbott, Stacey. 2007. *Celluloid Vampires: Life After Death in the Modern World*. Austin: University of Texas Press.s
Aguirre, Manuel. 1990. *The Closed Space: Horror Literature and Western Symbolism*. Manchester: Manchester University Press.
Akita, Kimiko. 2006. "Orientalism and the Binary of Fact and Fiction in Memoirs of a Geisha." In *Global Media Journal* 5, issue 9. Retrieved 2006 from http://lass.calumet.purdue.edu/cca/gmj/fa06/gmj_fa06_akita.htm.
Ashcroft, Bill, Gareth Griffiths ,and Helen Tiffin. 2006. *The Post-Colonial Studies Reader*. London: Routledge.
Badley, Linda. 1996. *Writing Horror and the Body: The Fiction of Stephen King, Clive Barker, and Anne Rice*. Westport, CT: Greenwood Press.
Balmain, Colette. 2008. *Introduction to Japanese Horror Film*. Edinburgh: Edinburgh University Press.
Balmain, Colette, and Lois Drawmer. 2009. *Something Wicked This Way Comes: Essays on Evil and Human Wickedness*. Amsterdam: Rodopi.
Bargen. Doris. 1997. *A Woman's Weapon: Spirit Possession in the Tale of Genji*. Honolulu: University of Hawaii Press.
Bauman, Zygmunt. 2000. *Ponowoczesność jako źródło cierpień* [*Post-Modernity and Its Discontents*]. Warszawa: Wydawnictwo Sic!
Ben-Ari, Eyal, Brian Moeran, and James Valentine, eds. 1994. *Unwrapping Japan*. Honolulu: University of Hawaii Press.
Bernardin, Susan, and Nicole Tonkovich, 2003. *Trading Gazes: Euro-American Women Photographers and Native North Americans, 1880–1940*. New Brunswick, N.J: Rutgers University Press.
Bernstein, Andrew. 2006. *Modern Passings: Death Rites, Politics, and Social Change in Imperial Japan*. Honolulu: University of Hawaii Press.
Bestor, Victoria, Theodore Bestor, and Akiko Yamagata. 2011. *Routledge Handbook of Japanese Culture and Society*. Abingdon: Routledge.
Bishop, Kyle. 2010. *American Zombie Gothic: The Rise and Fall (and Rise) of the Walking Dead in Popular Culture*. Jefferson, N.C: McFarland.
Blanco, Maria, and Esther Peeren. 2010. *Popular Ghosts: The Haunted Spaces of Everyday Culture*. New York: Continuum.
Brazell, Karen. 1998. *Traditional Japanese Theater: An Anthology of Plays*. New York: Columbia University Press.

Bremen, Jan, and D.P. Martinez. 1995. *Ceremony and Ritual in Japan Religious Practices in an Industrialized Society*. London: Routledge.
Browning, John, and Caroline Picart. 2009. *Draculas, Vampires, and Other Undead Forms: Essays on Gender, Race, and Culture*. Lanham, MD: Scarecrow Press.
Brzostek. Dariusz. 2009. *Literatura i Nierozum. Antropologia Fantastyki Grozy [Literature and Non-reason]*. Torun: Wydawnictwo Naukowe UMK.
Bunson, Matthew. 2000. *The Vampire Encyclopedia*. New York: Gramercy Books.
Bush, Laurence. 2001. *Asian Horror Encyclopedia: Asian Horror Culture in Literature, Manga, and Folklore*. San Jose: Writers Club Press.
CAC Nielsen Cinema Audience Report. http://www.cinemaadcouncil.org/cac_research_nielsen.php. Accessed December 2012.
Cardin, Matt. 2007. "The Angel and the Demon." In Joshi, S.T., ed. 2007. *Icons of Horror and the Supernatural, Volume 1*. Westport, CT: Greenwood Press.
Carroll, Noel. 1990. *The Philosophy of Horror, Or Paradoxes of the Heart*. New York: Routledge.
Carter, Margaret. 2007. "The Vampire." In Joshi, S.T., ed. *Icons of Horror and the Supernatural, Volume 1*. Westport, CT: Greenwood Press.
Chamberlain, Basil. 2007. *Things Japanese: Being Notes on Various Subjects Connected with Japan*. Berkeley: Stone Bridge Press.
Chambers, Anthony. 2007. *Tales of Moonlight and Rain*. New York: Columbia University Press.
Cherry, Brigid. 2009. *Horror*. London: Routledge.
Choi, Jinhee, and Mitsuyo Wada-Marciano. 2009. *Horror to the Extreme: Changing Boundaries in Asian Cinema*. Hong Kong: Hong Kong University Press.
Crowley, Cheryl. 2007. *Haikai Poet Yosa Buson and the Bashō Revival*. Leiden: Brill.
Conrich, Ian. 2010. *Horror Zone: The Cultural Experience of Contemporary Horror Cinema*. London: I. B. Tauris.
Cowan, Douglas E. 2008. *Sacred Terror: Religion and Horror on the Silver Screen*. Waco: Baylor University Press.
Davis, Colin. 2010. "The Skeptical Ghost: Alejandro Amenabar's *The Others* and the *Return of the Dead*." In Peeren, Esther, and Maria del Pilar Blanco. 2010. *Popular Ghosts: The Haunted Spaces of Everyday Culture*. New York: Continuum.
Derry, Charles. 2009. *Dark Dreams 2.0: A Psychological History of the Modern Horror Film from the 1950s to the 21st Century*. Jefferson, NC: McFarland.
Dollimore, Jonathan. 1998. *Death. Desire, and Loss in Western Culture*. New York: Routledge.
Dundes, Alan. 2008. *Bloody Mary in the Mirror*. Jackson: University Press of Mississippi.
Dziemianowicz, Stefan. 2007. "The Werewolf." In Joshi, S.T., ed. 2007. *Icons of Horror and the Supernatural, Volume 1*. Westport, CT: Greenwood Press.
Ekman, Inger, and Petri Lankoski. 2009. "Hair-Raising Entertainment: Emotions, Sound, and Structure in Silent Hill 2 and Fatal Frame." In Perron, Bernard. 2009. *Horror Video Games: Essays on the Fusion of Fear and Play*. Jefferson, N.C.: McFarland. 181–199.
Ericson, Joan. 1997. *Be a Woman: Hayashi Fumiko and Modern Japanese Women's Literature*. Honolulu: University of Hawaii Press.
Figal, Gerald. 1999. *Civilization and Monsters: Spirits of Modernity in Meiji Japan*. Durham: Duke University Press.
Foster, Michael Dylan. 2003. "'Am I pretty?' The 'Kuchi-sake-onna' Legend as Seen in Women's Weekly Magazines." In *Nihon yōkaigaku taizen*. Ed. Kazuhiko, Komatsu. Tokyo: Shōgakkan.
Foster, Michael Dylan. 2009. *Pandemonium and Parade: Japanese Monsters and the Culture of Yōkai*. Berkeley: University of California Press.
Freeman-Mitford, A.B. 1966. *Tales of old Japan*. Rutland, VT: C. E.
Gemra, Anna. 2008. *Od gotycyzmu do horroru: Wilkołak, wampir i monstrum Frankensteina w wybranych utworach*. Wrocław: University of Wrocław Press.
Gilmore, David. 2001. *Misogyny: The Male*

Malady. Philadelphia: University of Pennsylvania Press.

Gilmore. David. 2003. *Monsters: Evil Beings, Mythical Beasts, and All Manner of Imaginary Terrors*. Philadelphia: University of Pennsylvania Press.

Giral, Anabel Altemir, and Ismael Ibanez Rosales. 2011. "Otherness in *The Others*: Haunting the Catholic Other, Humanizing the Self." In Hansen, Regina, ed. 2011. *Roman Catholicism in Fantastic Film: Essays on Belief, Spectacle, Ritual and Imagery*. Jefferson, N.C: McFarland.

Grixti, Joseph. 1989. *Terrors of Uncertainty: The Cultural Context of Horror Fiction*. New York: Routledge.

Haga, Hideo. 1970. *Japanese Folk Festivals Illustrated*. Tokyo: Miura Print.

Hall, Melissa. 2007. "The Ghost." In Joshi, S.T., ed. *Icons of Horror and the Supernatural, Volume 1*. Westport, CT: Greenwood Press.

Hand, Richard. 2005. "Aesthetics of Cruelty: Traditional Japanese Theatre and the Horror Film." In McRoy, Jay. 2005. *Japanese Horror Cinema*. Edinburgh: Edinburgh University Press.

Harper, Jim. 2009. *Flowers from Hell: The Modern Japanese Horror Film*. Hereford: Noir.

Has-Tokarz, Anita. 2010. *Horror w literaturze współczesnej i filmie*. Lublin: Maria Curie-Skłodowska University Press.

Hayao, Kawai. 1988. *Japanese Psyche: Major Motifs in the Fairy Tales of Japan*. Dallas: Spring Publications.

Hearn, Lafcadio. 2006. *Glimpses of an Unfamiliar Japan*. Teddington, Middlesex,: Echo Library.

Henshall, Kenneth. 1999. *Dimensions of Japanese Society: Gender, Margins and Mainstream*. New York: St. Martin's Press.

Herbert. Daniel. 2010. "Trading Spaces: Transnational Dislocations in *Insomnia/Insomnia* and *Ju-On/The Grudge*." In Lukas, Scott, and John Marmysz. 2010. *Fear, Cultural Anxiety, and Transformation: Horror, Science Fiction, and Fantasy Films Remade*. Lanham, MD: Lexington.

Hinohara, Shigeaki. 1994. "Facing Death the Japanese Way: Customs and Ethos." In Hoshino, Kazumasa. 1994. *Japanese and Western Bioethics Studies in Moral Diversity*. Dordrecht: Kluwer Academic. 155–160.

Holland-Toll, Linda J. 2001. *As American as Mom, Baseball, and Apple Pie: Constructing Community in Contemporary American Horror Fiction*. Bowling Green, OH: Popular Press.

Hutchings, Peter. 2008. *Historical dictionary of horror cinema*. Lanham, MD: Scarecrow Press.

Inouye, Charles. 1998. *The Similitude of Blossoms: A Critical Biography of Izumi Kyōka (1873–1939), Japanese Novelist and Playwright*. Cambridge: Harvard University Asia Center.

Inouye, Charles Shirō. 2005. "A Quiet Obsession." In *In Light of Shadows: More Gothic Tales from Izumi Kyōka*. Honolulu: University of Hawaii Press.

Ivy, Marylin. 1995. *Discourses of the Vanishing. Modernity, Phantasm, Japan*. Chicago: University of Chicago Press.

Iwasaka, Michiko, and Barre Toelken. 1994. *Ghosts and the Japanese: Cultural Experience in Japanese Death Legends*. Logan: Utah State University Press.

Jones, Stephen, and Kim Newman. 1998. *Horror: The 100 Best Books*. New York: Carroll & Graf.

Jones, Stephen, and Kim Newman. 2005. *Horror: Another 100 Best Books*. New York: Carroll & Graf.

Joshi, S.T. 2007. *Icons of Horror and the Supernatural: An Encyclopedia of Our Worst Nightmares*. Westport, CT: Greenwood Press.

Joshi, S.T. 2011. *Encyclopedia of the Vampire: The Living Dead in Myth, Legend, and Popular Culture*. Santa Barbara: Greenwood Press.

Joya, Mock. 1985. *Mock Joya's Things Japanese*. Tokyo: The Japan Times.

Kasulis, Thomas. 2004. *Shinto: The Way Home*. Honolulu: University of Hawaii Press.

Kelts, Roland. 2006. *Japanamerica: How Japanese Pop Culture has Invaded the U.S.* New York: Palgrave Macmillan.

King, Stephen. 1982. *Danse Macabre*. New York: Berkley.

King, Stephen, et al. 1989. *Bare Bones: Con-

versations in Terror with Stephen King. London: New English Library.
Kishimoto, Hideo. 1968. "Some Japanese Cultural Traits and Religions." In *The Japanese Mind: Essentials of Japanese Philosophy and Culture*. Honolulu: University Press of Hawaii.
Knee, Adam. "The Power of the Past in the Contemporary Thai Horror Film." In Schneider, Steven, and Tony Williams, eds. 2005. *Horror International*. Detroit: Wayne State University Press.
Konami. 2003. *Sairento hiru surī kōshiki kanzen kōryaku gaido/ Ushinawareta kioku: Sairento hiru kuronikuru* [Silent Hill 3 Official Strategy Guide / Lost Memories: Silent Hill Chronicle]. Tōkyo: Konami.
Kotański, Wiesław. 1968. "Posłowie" ["Afterword"]. In *Po deszczu przy księżycu*. Ossolineum. 252–286.
Kristeva, Julia. 1982. *Powers of Horrors—An Essay on Abjection*. New York: Columbia University Press.
Krzywinska, Tanya. 2002. "Hands on Horror." In Geoff King and Tanya Krzywinska, 2002. *ScreenPlay: Cinema/Videogames/Interfaces*. London: Wallflower.
Kurosawa, Kiyoshi. 1993. "What Is Horror Cinema?" In Kurosawa, Kiyoshi. 2001. *Eiga wa osoroshii* [Film Is Scary]. Tōkyo: Seidosha, 23–26. Translated by Richard Kendall. Retrieved 2010 from research.yale.edu/eastasianstudies/Kurosawa.pdf.
Lacefield, Kristen. 2010. *The Scary Screen*. Aldershot: Ashgate.
Lane, William. 1974. *The Gospel According to Mark: The English Text with Introduction, Exposition, and Notes*. Grand Rapids: Eerdmans.
Leiter, Samuel. 2002. *Kabuki Plays on Stage*. Honolulu: University of Hawaii Press.
Lewis, Paul. 2006. *Cracking Up: American Humor in a Time of Conflict*. Chicago: University of Chicago Press.
Lifton, Robert. 1996. *The Broken Connection: On Death and the Continuity of Life*. Washington. D.C.: American Psychiatric Press.
Lim, Bliss. 2009. *Translating Time: Cinema, the Fantastic, and Temporal Critique*. Durham: Duke University Press.
Link, Luther. 1995. *The Devil: A Mask Without a Face*. London: Reaktion.

Littleton, C. Scott. 2002. *Shinto: Origins, Rituals, Festivals, Spirits, Sacred Places*. Oxford: Oxford University Press.
Long, Susan Orpett. 2005. *Final Days: Japanese Culture and Choice at the End of Life*. Honolulu: University of Hawaii Press.
Magistrale, Tony. 2005. *Abject Terrors: Surveying the Modern and Postmodern Horror Film*. New York: Peter Lang.
Marak, Katarzyna. 2012. "Points of Contact: Cultural Contexts in Understanding Japanese Literature and Cinema." In Bohorodycz, Beata, Arkadiusz Jabłoński and Maciej Kanert, eds. 2012. *Silva Iaponicarum Special Edition: Japan: New Challenges in the 21st Century*. Poznań: Adam Mickiewicz University Press. 247–257.
Mariconda, Steven. 2007. "The Haunted House." In Joshi, S.T., ed. *Icons of Horror and the Supernatural, Volume 1*. Westport, CT: Greenwood Press.
Martinez. Dolores. 1998. *The Worlds of Japanese Popular Culture: Gender, Shifting Boundaries and Global Cultures*. Cambridge: Cambridge University Press.
McCrea, Christian. 2009. "Gaming's Hauntology: Dead Media in Dead Rising, Siren and Michigan: Report from Hell." In Perron, Bernard. 2009. *Horror Video Games: Essays on the Fusion of Fear and Play*. Jefferson, N.C.: McFarland.
McDonald, Keiko. 1994. *Japanese Classical Theater in Films*. Rutherford Cranbury, N.J: Fairleigh Dickinson University Press/Associated University Presses.
McRoy, Jay. 2005. *Japanese Horror Cinema*. Edinburgh: Edinburgh University Press.
McRoy, Jay. 2008. *Nightmare Japan Contemporary Japanese Horror Cinema*. Amsterdam: Rodopi.
Metcalf, Peter. and Richard Huntington. 1979. *Celebrations of Death: The Anthropology of Mortuary Ritual*. Cambridge: Cambridge University Press.
Miller, Laura. 2006. "Introduction." In Jackson, Shirley. 2006. *The Haunting of Hill House*. New York: Penguin.
Morgan, Jack. 2002. *The Biology of Horror: Gothic Literature and Film*. Carbondale: Southern Illinois University Press.
Moore, Charles. 1968. *The Japanese Mind: Essentials of Japanese Philosophy and Cul-*

ture. Honolulu: University Press of Hawaii.
Mueller, Laura. 2007. *Competition and Collaboration: Japanese Prints of the Utagawa School*. Leiden: Hotei.
Muir, John. 2007. *Horror Films of the 1980s*. Jefferson, N.C: McFarland.
Murakami, Hyōe, and Donald Richie. 1980. *A Hundred More Things Japanese*. Tokyo: Japan Culture Institute.
Nanboku, Tsuruya. 1998. *Yotsuya Ghost Stories*. In Brazell, Karen, and James T. Araki, eds. 1998. *Traditional Japanese Theater: An Anthology of Plays* New York: Columbia University Press.
Nitsche, Michael. 2009. "Complete Horror in Fatal Frame." In Perron, Bernard. 2009. *Horror Video Games: Essays on the Fusion of Fear and Play*. Jefferson, N.C.: McFarland. 200–219
Olivier, Bert. 2009. "Nature as 'Abject,' Critical Psychology, and 'Revolt': The Pertinence of Kristeva." In *Philosophy and Psychoanalytic Theory: Collected Essays*. New York: Peter Lang.
Oshima, Mark. In Brazell, Karen. 1998. *Traditional Japanese Theater: An Anthology of Plays*. New York: Columbia University Press.
Oshima, Mark. In Leiter, Samuel. 2002. *Kabuki Plays on Stage: Darkness and Desire, 1804–1864*, volume 3 of *Kabuki Plays on Stage*. Honolulu: University of Hawaii Press.
Paffenroth, Kim. 2006. *Gospel of the Living Dead: George Romero's Visions of Hell on Earth*. Waco: Baylor University Press.
Perron, Bernard. 2009. *Horror Video Games: Essays on the Fusion of Fear and Play*. Jefferson, N.C.: McFarland.
Perron, Bernard. 2011. *Silent Hill: The Terror Engine*. Ann Arbor: University of Michigan Press
Petoia, Erberto. 2004. *Wampiry i Wilkołaki*. Kraków: TaiWPN Universitas.
Phillips, Kendall. 2005. *Projected Fears: Horror Films and American Culture*. New York: Praeger.
Picard, Martin. 2009. "Transnationality and Intermediality in Japanese Survival Horror Video Games." In *Horror Video Games: Essays on the Fusion of Fear and Play*. Jefferson, N.C.: McFarland.
Picken, Stuart. 1994. *Essentials of Shinto: An Analytical Guide to Principal Teachings*. Westport, CT: Greenwood Press.
Pickering, W. 1984. *Durkheim's Sociology of Religion: Themes and Theories*. London: Routledge & Kegan Paul.
Plutschow, Herbert. 1990. *Chaos and Cosmos: Ritual in Early and Medieval Japanese Literature*. Leiden: E.J. Brill.
Plutschow, Herbert. 1996. *Matsuri: The Festivals of Japan*. London: Routledge.
Poole, W. Scott. 2011. *Monsters in America: Our Historical Obsessions with the Hideous and the Haunting*. Waco: Baylor University Press.
Pruett, Chris. 2010. "The Anthropology of Fear: Learning About Japan Through Horror Games," In *Loading...* 4, no. 6 (2010).
Pulliam, June. 2007. "The Zombie." In Joshi, S.T., ed. 2007. *Icons of Horror and the Supernatural, Volume 1*. Westport, CT: Greenwood Press.
Reader, Ian. 1991. *Religion in Contemporary Japan*. Honolulu: University of Hawaii Press.
Reider, Noriko. 2000. "The Appeal of Kaidan Tales of the Strange." *Asian Folklore Studies* 59, no. 2: 265–283.
Reider, Noriko. 2001. "The Emergence of Kaidan-shu: The Collection of Tales of the Strange and Mysterious in the Edo Period." *Asian Folklore Studies* 60, 265.
Reider, Noriko. 2010. *Japanese Demon Lore Oni, from Ancient Times to the Present*. Logan: Utah State University Press.
Reizler, Kurt. 1944. "The Social Psychology of Fear." *American Journal of Sociology* 49, no. 6.
Richards. David. 1994. *Masks of Difference: Cultural Representations in Literature, Anthropology, and Art*. Cambridge: Cambridge University Press.
Roberts, Jeremy. 2010. *Japanese Mythology A to Z*. New York: Chelsea House.
Robinson, Mark. 2009. *The Framed World: Tourism, Tourists and Photography*. Farnham, England: Ashgate.
Rosenberger, Nancy, ed. 1994. *Japanese Sense of Self*. Cambridge: Cambridge University Press.

Russell, Jeffrey. 1987a. *The Devil: Perceptions of Evil from Antiquity to Primitive Christianity*. Ithaca: Cornell University Press.

Russell, Jeffrey. 1987b. *Satan: The Early Christian Tradition*. Ithaca: Cornell University Press.

Said, Edward W. 1978. "Orientalism." in Ashcroft, Bill, Gareth Griffiths and Helen Tiffin. 1978. *The Post-colonial Studies Reader*. London: Routledge. 87–91.

Sakai, Naoki. 1991. *Translation and Subjectivity: On Japan and Cultural Nationalism*. Minneapolis: University of Minnesota Press.

Schneider, Jay. 2006. *Horror Film and Psychoanalysis: Freud's Worst Nightmare*. New York: Cambridge University Press.

Smith, Robert. 1974. *Ancestor Worship in Contemporary Japan*. Stanford: Stanford University Press.

Snodgrass, Mary. 2006. *Encyclopedia of Gothic Literature*. New York: Facts on File.

Stone, Jacqueline, and Mariko Walter. 2008. *Death and the Afterlife in Japanese Buddhism*. Honolulu: University of Hawaii Press.

Sugiyama Lebra, Takie. 1976. *Japanese Patterns of Behavior*. Honolulu: University of Hawaii Press.

Sugiyama Lebra, Takie. 2004. *The Japanese Self in Cultural Logic*. Honolulu: University of Hawaii Press.

Tatarczuk, Marcin. 2011. *Kaidan: Japońskie opowieści niesamowite epoki Edo*. Warszawa: TRIO.

Tucker, Elizabeth. 1998. "Ghost Stories." In Brunvand, Jan. *The Study of American Folklore*. New York: Norton.

Turner, Jonathan, and Jan Stets. 2005. *The Sociology of Emotions*. Cambridge: Cambridge University Press.

Wallen, Martin. 2006. *Fox*. London: Reaktion Books.

Walvoord, John. 1983. *The Bible Knowledge Commentary: An Exposition of the Scriptures*. Wheaton, IL: Victor Books.

Ward, Donald. 1998. "Superstition." In Brunvand, Jan. *The Study of American Folklore: An Introduction*. New York: Norton.

Warner, Marina. 2006. *Phantasmagoria: Spirit Visions, Metaphors, and Media into the Twenty-first Century*. Oxford: Oxford University Press.

Weise, Matthew, 2009. "The Rules of Horror: Procedural Adaptation in Clock Tower, Resident Evil, and Dead Rising." In Perron, Bernard. 2009. *Horror Video Games: Essays on the Fusion of Fear and Play*. Jefferson, N.C.: McFarland.

Werness, Hope. 2007. *The Continuum Encyclopedia of Animal Symbolism in Art*. London: Continuum.

Williams, Yoko. 2002. *Tsumi: Offence and Retribution in Early Japan*. New York: Routledge.

Wood, Robin. 1986. *Hollywood from Vietnam to Reagan*. New York: Columbia University Press.

Xu, Gary. "Remaking East Asia, Outsourcing Hollywood." In Hunt, Leon, and Leung Win-Fai. 2008. *East Asian Cinemas Exploring Transnational Connections on Film*. London: I. B. Tauris.

Yamakage, Motohisa. 2006. *The Essence of Shinto: Japan's Spiritual Heart*. Tokyo: Kodansha International.

Young, Robert. 2001. *Postcolonialism: A Historical Introduction*. Malden, MA: Blackwell.

Yu, Eric. 2010. "A Traditional Female Vengeful Ghost or a Machine in the Ghost? Narrative Dynamics and Horror Effects in *Ringu*." In Hessel, Stephen, and Michelle Huppert. 2010. *Fear Itself*. Amsterdam: Rodopi.

Yukawa, Hideki. 1967. "Modern Trends in Western Civilization and Cultural Peculiarities in Japan." In Moore, Charles A., ed. 1968. *The Japanese Mind: Essentials of Japanese Philosophy and Culture*. Honolulu: University Press of Hawaii.

Yust, Walter. 1968. *Encyclopedia Britannica; or, A Dictionary of Arts and Sciences, Compiled upon a New Plan*. Chicago: Encyclopedia Britannica.

Żeromska, Estera. 2003. *Maska na japońskiej scenie*. Warszawa: TRIO.

Żeromska, Estera. 2010. *Japoński Teatr Klasyczny: Korzenie i Metamorfozy*, vol 2. Warsaw: TRIO.

Other Works Discussed

Alone in the Dark. 1992. Infogames.
Ayakashi [*Kai ~ayakashi~*]. 2006. Toei Animation.
Beneath Still Waters. 2005. Directed by Brian Yuzna.
Blood: The Last Vampire. 2000. Directed by Hiroyuki Kitakubo.
Bram Stoker's Dracula. 1992. Directed by Francis Coppola.
The Burrowers. 2008. Directed by J.T. Petty.
Castlevania: Legacy of Darkness 1999. VGA. Published by Konami.
The Cat People. 1942. Directed by Jacques Tourneur.
Cloverfield. 2008. Directed by Matt Reeves.
Dark Tales of Japan [*Nihon no kowaiya*]. 2004. Directed by Yoshihiro Nakamura and Masayuki Ochiai.
Dark Water [*Honogurai mizu-no soko kara*]. 2002. Directed by Hideo Nakata.
Dark Water. 2005. Directed by Waler Salles.
Dawn of the Dead. 1978. Directed by George A. Romero.
Daybreakers. 2009. Directed by Michael and Peter Spierig.
Deadgirl. 2008. Directed by Marcel Sarmiento.
Diary of the Dead. 2007. Directed by George A. Romero.
Doom. 2005. Directed by Andrzej Bartkowiak.
Dracula. 1931. Directed by Ted Browning.
Drag Me to Hell. 2009. Directed by Sam Raimi.
The Echo [*Sigaw*]. 2004. Directed by Yam Laranas.
The Exorcism of Emily Rose. 2005. Directed by Scott Derrickson.
The Exorcist. 1973. Directed by William Friedkin.
Fatal Frame [*Rei ~ zero*]. 2001. VGA. Published by Tecmo.
The Fly. 1986. Directed by David Cronenberg.
The Fog. 1980. Directed by John Carpenter.
Forbidden Siren [*SAIREN*]. 2003. VGA. Published by Sony Computer Entertainment, Inc.
Forget Me Not. 2009. Directed by Tyler Oliver.
Fright Night. 1985. Directed by Tom Holland.
Fright Night. 2011. Directed by Craig Gillespie.
Ghost Cat of Otama Pond [*Kaibyō Otama-gaike*]. 1960. Directed by Nobuo Nakagawa.
Ghost Ship. 2002. Directed by Steve Beck
Ghost Stories of Wanderer at Honjo [*Kaidan Honjo Nanafushigi*]. 1957. Directed by Gorō Kadono.
Gothika. 2003. Directed by Mathieu Kassovitz.
The Grudge. 2004. Directed by Takashi Shimizu.
The Hunger. 1983. Directed by Tony Scott.
Hyenas. 2011. Directed by Eric Weston.
Insidious. 2010. Directed by James Wan.
Ju-On: Black Ghost. 2009. Directed by Mari Asato.
Ju-on: The Grudge. 2003. Directed by Takashi Shimizu (theatrically released version).
Junk. 2000. Directed by Atsushi Muroga.
Kaidan. 2007. Directed by Hideo Nakata.
KakuRenBo. 2005. Directed by Shuhei Morita.
Kikōshi Enma. 2006–2007. Directed by Mamoru Kanbe.
Killing Ariel. 2006. Directed by Fred Calvert.
KM 31: Kilometre 31. 2006. Directed by Rigoberto Castañeda.
Kokkurisan: Gekijōban. 2011. Directed by Nahae Jiro.
Kuroneko [*Yabu no naka no kuroneko*]. 1968. Kaneda Shindo.
Lake of Dracula. 1971. Directed by Michio Yamamoto.
The Land of the Dead. 2005. Directed by George A. Romero.
The Last Exorcism. 2012. Directed by Daniel Stamm.
The Messengers. 2007. Directed by Oxide and Danny Pang.
Mimic. 1996. Directed by Guillermo del Toro.
Minotaur. 2006. Directed by Jonathan English.
Night of the Living Dead. 1964. Directed by George Romero.
Nightmare Detective 2 [*Akumu Tantei 2*]. 2008. Directed by Shinya Tsukamoto.

Nosferatu: The Symphony of Horror. 1922. Directed by Friedrich Murnau.
The Omen. 1976. Directed by Richard Donner.
100 Tales of Horror [*Kaidan Hyaku Shosetsu*]. 2002. FUJI TV.
One Missed Call [*Chakushin Ari*]. 2004. Directed by Takashi Miike.
One Missed Call. 2008. Directed by Eric Valette.
Onibaba. 1964. Directed by Kaneto Shindō.
Onmyōji. 2001. Directed by Yōjirō Takita.
The Others. 2001. Directed by Alejandro Amenábar.
Paranormal Activity. 2007. Directed by Shinichi Nagasaki.
Paranormal Activity: Tokyo Night. 2010. Directed by Toshikazu Nagae.
The Priest. 2011. Directed by Scott Charles Stewart.
Pulse [*Kairo*]. 2001. Directed by Kiyoshi Kurosawa.
Re-Animator. 1985. Directed by Stuart Gordon.
Reeds. 2010. Directed by Nick Cohen.
Resident Evil. 2001. Directed by Paul W. Anderson.
Resident Evil [*BAIOHAZĀDO*]. 1996. VGA. Published by Capcom.
Retribution [*Sakebi*]. 2006. Directed by Kiyoshi Kurosawa.
Return to House on the Haunted Hill. 2007. Directed by Victor Garcia.
Ring [*Ringu*]. 1998. Directed by Hideo Nakata.
The Ring. 2002. Directed by Gore Verbinsky.
Ring 2. 1999. Directed by Hideo Nakata.
Ring 0: Birthday. 2000. Directed by Norio Tsuruta.
The Ring: Terror's Realm. 2000. VGA. Published by Infogrames.
The Ring Virus. 2000. Directed by Kim Dong-bin.
Session 9. 2001. Directed by Brad Anderson.
Shaun of the Dead. 2004. Directed by Egdar Wright.
Shikoku. 1999. Directed by Shunichi Nagasaki.
The Shining. 1980. Directed by Stanley Kubrick.
Shock Labirynth [*Senritsu Meikyū 3D*]. 2009. Directed by Takashi Shimizu.
Silent Hill [*SAIRENTO HIRU*], 1999, VGA. Published by Konami.
Silent Hill, 2006. Directed by Christophe Gans.
Silent Hill 2 [*SAIRENTO HIRU 2*]. 2001. VGA. Published by Konami.
Sinners of Hell [*Jigoku*].1960. Directed by Nobuo Nakagawa.
The Sixth Sense. 1999. Directed by M. Night Shyalaman.
Sleepwalkers. 1992. Directed by Mick Garris.
Spiral [*Rasen*]. 1998. Directed by Jōji Iida.
Supernatural 2006–. Created by Eric Kripke
The Swamp Thing. 1982. Directed by Wes Craven.
Tales of Terror from Tokyo [*Kaidan Shinmimibukuro*]. 2003–2005. Directed by Eiji Arakawa and Kei Horie.
Tales of Terror: Haunted Apartment [*Kaidan Shinmimibukuro: Yūrei manshon*]. 2005. Directed by Akio Yoshida.
Teeth. 2007. Directed by Mitchell Lichtenstein.
TekeTeke. 2009. Directed by Kōji Shiraishi.
True Blood. 2008–. Created by Allan Ball.
28 Days Later. 2002. Directed by Paul W. S. Anderson.
Underworld. 2003. Directed by Len Wiseman.
Wall Man. 2006. Directed by Wataru Hayakawa.
What Lies Beneath. 2000. Directed by Robert Zemeckis.
White Zombie. 1932. Directed by Victor Halperin.
Vampire: The Masquerade—Redemption. 2000. VGA. Published by Activision.
Vanished [*Oyayubi Sagashi*]. 2006. Directed by Naoto Kumazawa.

Index

abject 11–12
abuse 203–204
afterlife 17, 40
Alessa (*Silent Hill 1*) 191
Alien (film) 9, 10
Alone in the Dark (game) 2
The Amityville Horror (film) 53
Antichrist 88, 183, 184–185
Ayakashi (animation) 63, 101

BAIOHAZĀDO see *Resident Evil*
bakeneko 100–101, 103
Barlow (*'Salem's Lot*) 91
beauty 43, 123, 125, 129, 130–131, 191
birth 182, 184, 190
Blood: The Last Vampire (film) 108–111
body: female 136; dead 140, 141–142, 197; monstrous 129, 130; undead body see zombie; violation of 133
Bram Stoker's Dracula 88–90
Buddhism and its concepts 14, 159, 161, 169, 188
The Burrowers 125

Calling (game) 75
Carmilla (Sheridan LeFanu) 90
the Castevets (*Rosemary's Baby*) 178, 181
Castlevania: Legacy of Darkness (game) 85
The Cat People 112
censorship see MPAA ratings
Chakushin Ari [*One Missed Call*] (film) 32, 82, 201
child/children 31, 33, 37, 173, 178, 182, 183, 185, 186, 201
Chiroptera (*Blood: The Last Vampire*) 109–110, 111
Christianity and its concepts 87, 88, 143, 158, 160–161, 162, 164, 177, 183, 189, 193, 194–196
Cloverfield 9, 125

contingency logic 13
corpse see body
cross (Christian symbol) 87, 95, 168, 172, 184
The Crow (film) 60
cult 181, 190–191, 193
curse 50, 51–52, 72, 73–76, 78–80, 80–81, 107, 153–154
Cycle of the Werewolf (Stephen King) 116–119

Dahlia (*Silent Hill 1*) 190–191
Damien (*The Omen*) 184–186
Dark Water (film) 200, 201, 202
darkness 8, 20, 113, 116, 139, 189
Datatsushi (*Siren*) 153
Daybreakers 87
Deadgirl 149
death 14, 17, 41, 46, 50, 61, 73, 77, 83, 89, 135, 140–143, 151, 156–157, 195, 197–198, 202–203
demon 158–176, 189, 198; see also oni
Demon City Shinjuku (Hideyuki Kikuchi) 170
Demon King (*KakuRenBo*) 175
Devil 88–89, 158, 161, 182–183, 187, 198
Devilman (Nagai Gō){ pen}170
Devilman Lady (Nagai Gō) 170
dimensions of horror 19–20
Diplomacy (Lafcadio Hearn) 61
Doom (film) 144
Dracula 87, 88–90, 105
Dracula (film, 1931) 144
Drag Me to Hell (film) 160

end of days 178, 182, 186, 188
End of Days (film) 183
the Enlightenment 13
evil 23, 30, 32, 62, 159, 161, 165, 177, 188, 195–196, 198

221

exorcism/exorcist 161, 165, 168, 171, 165; see also *o-harai*
The Exorcism of Emily Rose (film) 160
The Exorcist (William Blatty) 161–165
The Exorcist (film) 9, 72, 74, 162

the fantastic 13
Fatal Frame (game) 44–50
fear 2, 8, 10–11, 17, 67, 77, 112, 114, 120, 122, 140, 142–143, 157, 158, 176, 181, 195, 202–205
Floating Water (Kōji Suzuki) 142
The Fly (film) 9, 125
The Fog (film, 1980) 56–59
folklore 7, 10–11, 19, 42, 87, 99, 100–101, 111, 112–113, 121, 128, 143, 154–155, 160, 174
Forbidden Siren (game) see *Siren*
Forget Me Not (film) 82
fox 69, 121–122, 122–124, 125, 161
Fright Night (film, 1985) 93–96
Fright Night (film, 2011) 95–96
funeral and funerary practices 41, 61, 141, 152
fushigi 199

ghost 17–82, 198
Ghost Cat of Otama Pond (film) 101
Ghost Ship (film) 68
Ghost Stories at Yotsuya (play) 62–67
Ghost Stories of Wanderer at Honjo (film) 122
God (Christianity) see gods
God (*Silent Hill 1*) 189–190, 191–192
gods 88, 91, 153–154, 162, 164, 177, 183, 187, 189–192, 195
Gothika 56
The Grudge (film) 202

hatred 32, 52, 53, 61, 81, 81
The Haunting of Hill House (Shirley Jackson) 21–30
Helen Driscoll (*A Stir of Echoes*) 54, 55
hell/hells 139, 158–159, 169
Hellsing (Kōta Hirano) 100
Hill House (*Haunting of Hill House*) 21–22, 23, 26–27
home 20, 61, 142
Honogurai mizu no soko kara [*Dark Water*] (film, 2002) 43, 201
The Howling (Gary Brandner) 113–116
The Hunger (film) 87
Hyenas (film) 112

Ijintachi to no natsu (novel) see *Strangers*
illusion 69, 70, 102, 122, 124
innen see karma
insanity 23, 25, 28, 45, 65, 129

Insidious (film) 160, 161
Interview with the Vampire (Anne Rice) 9
It (Stephen King) 125

Ju On (Ooishi Kei) 142
Ju-on: The Grudge (film) 50–52, 80–81
Julia (Peter Straub) 28–32
Junk (film) 151

kaidan 13, 18, 42, 48, 71, 140
Kairo [*Pulse*] (film) 201
KakuRenBo: Hide and Seek 173–176
karma 14, 188
Kayako (*Ju-on: The Grudge*) 52, 80–81
Kei (*Strangers*) 68, 70
Kikōshi Enma (animation) 170
Killing Ariel 160
King, Stephen 125
Kirie (*Fatal Frame*) 48–49
kitsune see fox
Kokkurisan: Gekijōban (film) 82
Koontz, Dean R. 124–126
koto see *mono* and *koto*
Kuon (game) 45
Kuroneko (film) 100–104
Kyōka, Izumi 199

Lake of Dracula (film) 104–108
Lament of the Lamb (Tōme Kei) 100
Langoliers (Stephen King) 125
The Last Exorcism 160
layers of horror 19–20
loneliness 29, 69, 78, 80, 116, 139, 151
Lost Souls (films) 183
love 21, 32, 49, 90
The Loveliest Dead (Ray Garton) 59–60
Lycanthrope Leo (Kengo Kaji and Kenji Okamura) 124

Mayu kakushi no rei see *A Quiet Obsession*
Mijikayo see *A Short Night*
Minotaur (film) 125
The Mist (Stephen King) 126–128
mono and *koto* 200
monster 83, 84, 125–126, 128, 157, 174–175, 197, 199
mother 31, 89, 185, 201
MPAA ratings 15
murder 51, 54, 58, 60, 72, 101, 121, 129–131, 137, 204

Night of the Living Dead 144–148
Nightmare Detective 2 128
Noroi no yakata: Chi wo suu me (film) see *Lake of Dracula*
Nosferatu: The Symphony of Horror 90

Of a Mirror and a Bell (Lafcadio Hearn) 60
o-harai 171
Oiwa (*Ghost Stories at Yotsuya*) 65–66
Okiku (*Banchō Sarayashiki*) 68
Olivia (*Julia*) 31, 32
The Omen 183–186
On a Moonless Night (Sei Takekawa) 131–133
On a Promise Broken (Lafcadio Hearn) 61
100 Tales of Horror (TV series) 2
One Missed Call (film, 2008) 201
oni 159, 169–170, 174, 176; *see also* demon
Onibaba (film) 161
Onmyoji (film) 170
onnen 48, 50, 53, 62, 73, 74–75
onryō 64, 66, 67, 70, 78
oppositional logic 13, 200; *see also* contingency logic
Other 11–12, 40, 86, 90, 112, 197
The Others (film) 36–40
Otherworld (*Silent Hill* franchise) 139
Otsuya (*A Quiet Obsession*) 43, 44
Otsuyu (*Botan Dōrō*) 68
The Outsider (H. P. Lovecraft) 141

Paranormal Activity 165–169
Paranormal Activity: Tokyo Night 170–173
Pet Sematary (Stephen King) 141, 156
possession 27–28, 65, 160–161, 168–169
pregnancy 133, 180, 184, 190
Project Zero (game) see *Fatal Frame*
Pyramid Head *see* Red Pyramid Thing

A Quiet Obsession (Izumi Kyōka) 41–44

Red Pyramid Thing (*Silent Hill 2*) 136–137
religion 158–159, 176–177, 198; beliefs 37–38, 158, 178; outlook and system 60, 141, 183, 188, 193; rituals and symbols 66, 70, 82, 87, 153, 154
Reptilia (Kazuo Umezu) 128
Resident Evil (film) 148
Resident Evil (game) 45, 150–152
responsibility 49, 50, 67, 74, 137, 198, 203
retribution 19, 50, 53, 54, 56, 58, 61–62, 67, 80, 82
Retribution (film) 77–80
Reverend Lowe (*Cycle of the Werewolf*) 118
Ring (film) 71–75
The Ring (film) 75–77
Ring (Kōji Suzuki) 71–72
The Ring: Terror's Realm (game) 71
The Ring Virus (film) 71
Ringu see *Ring*
ritual 47–48, 74, 102, 155, 171, 191, 195
Rosemary's Baby (Ira Levin) 177–183

sacrifice 48, 99, 190, 191, 192
Sadako (*Ring*, film) 74–75
Sadako (*Ring*, novel) 72, 75
the Saeki house (*Ju-on: The Grudge*) 50, 51–52, 80
Sakebi see *Retribution*
'Salem's Lot (Stephen King) 90–93
salt 171, 180
Samara (*The Ring*) 76, 201
Sayori (*Shikoku*) 155–156
Self 11–12, 112, 197
Session 9 (film) 161
sex and sexual characteristics 68, 85, 136, 162, 203
shapeshifters see *kitsune*; *tanuki*
shapeshifting see therianthropy
Shaun of the Dead (film) 144
shibito (*Siren*) 152, 154
Shikoku 154–156
The Shining (film) 68
The Shining (Stephen King) 203
Shintō 141–142, 188, 195
Shock Labirynth (film) 82
A Short Night (Hyakken Uchida) 122–124
Silent Hill (also *Silent Hill 1*, game) 188–192, 201
Silent Hill (film) 192–193, 201
Silent Hill 2 (game) 133–140
sin 177, 188
Sinners of Hell (film) 188
Siren (game) 152–154
The Sixth Sense (film) 32–36
Sleepwalkers (film) 99–100
Sleepy Hollow (film) 32
society 53, 62, 74, 76, 78, 202–203, 204
soul/spirit 27, 42, 44, 47, 60, 92, 96, 109, 121, 142, 158, 161, 164, 188, 190, 192, 195
A Stir of Echoes (Richard Matheson) 53–56
strange (concept) 13–14, 18, 140
Strangers (Taichi Yamada) 67–71
subject 12, 142, 156–157, 200
suicide 68
Summer, Fireworks, and my Corpse (Otsuichi) 142
the supernatural 2, 3, 11, 12–14, 20, 35
Supernatural (TV series) 2
Suzuki, Kōji 2, 71–72
The Swamp Thing (film) 125

Tales of Moonlight and Rain 13
Tales of Old Japan (Algernon Freeman Mitford) 101
Tales of Terror: Haunted Apartment 62
tanuki 121–122, 125
Teeth (film) 125
TekeTeke 128

therianthropy 111–112
30 days of night (Steve Niles and Ben Templesmith) 96–99
Tōkaidō Yotsuya Kaidan see *Ghost Stories at Yotsuya*
Tomie (Junji Itō) 129–131
Toshio 52
transformation 97, 111–112, 118, 120–121, 122, 123, 154, 176, 190, 192
True Blood 87
Tsuki no nai yoru ni see *On a Moonless Night*
28 Days Later 98

Ueda, Akinari 13, 104
the uncanny 20
undead body *see* zombie
unknown, fear of 34, 40, 112, 120, 126–128, 146, 173
urami 14, 48, 61, 62, 78–79, 102

vagina dentata 94
vampire 84–111, 197; *see also* bakeneko
The Vampire Cat of Nabeshima (Algernon Freeman Mitford) 101
Vampire: The Masquerades—Redemption (game) 85

Vanished (film) 82
vengeful spirit 61–62, 77; *see also* onryō
Vincente (*30 Days of Night*) 98
violence 97, 103, 110, 129, 135, 144, 202, 203–204
virginity 99, 162
The Vortex (Hyakken Uchida) 122

Wall Man (film) 128
water 41
werewolf 84–85, 111–125, 197
White Zombie 144
witches and witchcraft 161, 181
woman 42, 60, 71
The Woman in Red (*Retribution*) 78, 79

Yabu no naka no kuroneko (film) see *Kuroneko*
Yone (*Kuroneko*) 103–104
Yotsuya Kwaidan, or, Oiwa Inari (James Benneville) 63
yōkai 42, 101, 122
yūrei 41, 48

zombie 84, 140–157

www.ingramcontent.com/pod-product-compliance
Ingram Content Group UK Ltd.
Pitfield, Milton Keynes, MK11 3LW, UK
UKHW041951140426
5217IPUK00015B/743